Russia remains an enigma to many outside observers. This delightfully easy-to-read book helps lift the veil of mystery by covering the highlights of Russian history, culture, music, literature, and politics. Further insights are provided by the author's memories of his life in Moscow during the height of the Cold War and by his observations during his return visit to Russia in 2016. His critique of current western policy towards Russia challenges key assumptions underlying U.S. and European views, making this book especially worthy of attention by thoughtful readers.

J Stapleton Roy, Director, Asia Program, Woodrow Wilson International Centre for Scholars, Washington, and former U.S. ambassador to Singapore, China, and Indonesia.

Return to Moscow is a candid, perceptive and sometimes sentimental testimony of a foreigner who is attached to Russia and who is truly concerned about its present and its future. Tony Kevin has a unique opportunity to compare the Soviet Union's heyday of the late 1960s – early 1970s with the accomplishments and problems of Putin's Russia today. Readers should decide whether the precarious and painful transition can be regarded as a success story or a failure, but the author is definitely more optimistic about the country than many Russians themselves tend to be these days. The book is a must-read for those who are interested in a deeper understanding of the country, its values and Russian foreign policy motivations, than Western Kremlinology usually offers.

Dr Andrey Kortunov, Director-General, Russian International Affairs Council, Moscow.

A moving personal testimony about the Russian people and society, which reflects on developments from the late Soviet years to the transformed Russia of today. Written with insight and sympathy, this book provides a unique window into how Russia has changed. At the same time, it reveals the profound continuities of a people buffeted endlessly by history yet characterised by an enduring resilience and humanity. This book will be read with pleasure and profit by anyone interested in how people lived in the Brezhnev years, and how Russians live today and what they think of the world about them.

Richard Sakwa, Professor of Russian and European Politics, University of Kent, UK, and Associate Fellow of Chatham House, London

Part history, part political, part personal but never dull, Tony Kevin vividly illustrates many of the facets of the kaleidoscope that is Russia today. Every chapter is a self-sufficient essay. Together this easily-read account provides a host of telling insights, anecdotes and personal opinions that illuminate the enigma of Russia's place in a fast-changing world. Tony Kevin, a former diplomat, has lost none of his analytical skills at dissecting and reviewing this, the most complex of the major powers. He often provides opinions that challenge conventional wisdom in a persuasive manner.

Julian Oliver, Founding Secretary General, EurActiv, Brussels.

Return to Moscow offers some fascinating insights of life in the Soviet Union around its collapse in 1991. The author then returns 25 years later to find a very different country but one which still offers a mix of despair and optimism. Writing from the other end of the world can provide a different and sometimes refreshing perspective on Putin's Russia. But the author tends to turn a blind eye to the dark side of contemporary Russia – the kleptocracy of the elite, the omnipresent security services and the continuing human rights abuses. He can also be faulted by asserting that Russia's 'patient propaganda war' on the West is only a response to Western attacks on Putin. But leaving aside his political views there is much interesting information in this very readable book.

Fraser Cameron, Director of the EU-Russia Centre

RETURN TO MOSCOW

TONY KEVIN

UWA PUBLISHING

First published in 2017 by
UWA Publishing
Crawley, Western Australia 6009
www.uwap.uwa.edu.au

UWAP is an imprint of UWA Publishing
a division of The University of Western Australia

THE UNIVERSITY OF
WESTERN
AUSTRALIA

National Library of Australia
Cataloguing-in-Publication entry:
Kevin, Tony, 1943- author.
Return to Moscow / Tony Kevin.
ISBN: 9781742589299 (paperback)
Political science—Russia—History.
Nationalism—Russia—History.
Russia (Federation)—Foreign relations—1991-
Russia (Federation)—Politics and government—1991-
Soviet Union—Foreign relations.
Soviet Union—Politics and government.

Cover image by Shutterstock
Typeset in 11 point Bembo
Printed by Lightning Source

 uwapublishing

This book is dedicated to the unique resilience and courage of the Russian people, who have triumphed over unimaginable cruelties at the hands of both invaders and their own past rulers, to create a society that is today worthy of admiration; to the beauties of Russia's landscape, history and culture; and to the grace of Russia's women, who continue to inspire me, in life as in art.

Contents

PART THREE – ...AND BACK AGAIN

Prologue

On 25 December 1991 the Soviet Union ceased to exist.[1] The Red flag above the Kremlin was lowered for the last time, and the Russian tricolour, the flag of the former Tsarist Empire, raised in its place.[2] The last President of the Soviet Union, Mikhail Gorbachev, surrendered his presidential office suite in the Kremlin to Boris Yeltsin as the first president of the new nation-state of the Russian Federation.

I was forty-eight then. For two-thirds of my life, and three-quarters of my working life as an Australian diplomat from 1968–98, the Cold War had been the dominant geopolitical reality of my world. The Soviet Union was a determining, seemingly permanent feature in a bipolar world balance of power. It was the solid, grim, strategically powerful and nuclear-armed counter-pole, the competing social and economic value system, to its global rival the United States.

When I was born in 1943, the Soviet Union had already existed as a formidable world power for twenty-six years. It had fought off two massive German-led European invasions, and in between those wars endured the terrible dislocations of a brutal Red–White civil war, followed by Stalin's ruthless collectivisation, purges and mass Gulag (prison labour camp) system. Millions of lives had been lost or irreparably scarred. Yet the Soviet Union emerged from World War II (during which I was born in 1943) as a defiant and proud superpower, hardened by its people's incredible sufferings, and ready to assume the mantle of co-leadership of the world with the United States, as the two dominant veto-wielding Permanent Members of the newly created United Nations Security Council.

Hard on the heels of World War II came the Cold War. Scholars dispute who or what really started the bitter rivalry between these recent wartime allies against Hitler, exactly when it began, and whether it could have been avoided.[3] But its defining characteristics were already clear by 1947, and remained so for the next four decades:

- a seemingly endless competition between the capitalist market economy and the communist planned economy, and between their very different proselytising visions of the good society;
- a US–Soviet nuclear standoff under the strategic straitjacket of Mutual Assured Destruction; notwithstanding this enforced stalemate, the ever-present fear of nuclear war triggered by accident or rash decisions by careless leaders;
- a constant jockeying for tactical and propaganda advantage in brutal but carefully contained proxy wars in the Third World;
- a stable central frontline in Europe between the two systems that remained safely delineated by the Warsaw Pact's concrete walls, watchtowers and barbed-wire coils; and
- periodic eruptions of civil protest in the captive East European nations chafing at Soviet restrictions on their freedoms and national aspirations, quickly suppressed by overwhelming Soviet military power and iron resolve to crush them, and with the West each time reluctantly acquiescing in the *status quo ante*.

This was the Cold War world in which I grew up and worked as an Australian diplomat. It seemed permanent. And starting in the early 1970s, this bizarre system seemed to become gradually safer, anchored by prudent US–Soviet strategic arms-limitation agreements and fail-safe nuclear-launch safeguards negotiated by US President Richard Nixon and Secretary of State Henry Kissinger with Soviet President Leonid Brezhnev, and by steadily growing East–West trade and cultural exchanges. The central European theatre of the (North Atlantic Treaty Organisation) NATO/Warsaw Pact confrontation was stabilised under the shared vision of the Helsinki Final Act, negotiated over several years in the CSCE, the Conference on Security and Co-operation in Europe.[4]

Prestigious academic careers were built in the 1980s around the proposition that the Cold War had become a permanent feature of world politics. Because it was there, fixed and immovable, it was accepted as a fact of life by many reasonable people. In the conventional wisdom, nobody from either side was really trying anymore to end – much less to 'win' – the now familiar nuclear stalemate. We had learned to accommodate its reciprocal restraints indefinitely. The task was to live with the Cold War in the hope that with the passage of time the Soviet system might slowly heal its internal wounds and become more liberal – more like our system. The phrases 'convergence' and 'peaceful coexistence' were the reassuring mental props on both sides of the divide.

Only a few wild-eyed zealots and armchair strategists in the West – some with particular axes to grind – defied the consensus, arguing passionately that the Cold War still mattered, that it still had to be fought resolutely and could be won by the West.

We know now that the apparent East–West stability was a temporary illusion. The initial post–World War II Soviet military advantage, held by a disciplined fully mobilised nuclear-armed nation under Josef Stalin, whose iron will and cruelty had equalled that of Adolf Hitler, began to ebb away soon after Stalin's death in 1953. The Soviet Union slowly and in fits and starts began to liberalise and to improve living standards. Meanwhile, the West began steadily to outperform the Soviet Union by every economic and social indicator, except in the central nuclear balance of terror. This included science and technology, as well as information technology and conventional war-fighting technologies, in the growth of sophisticated consumption-based economies, and in the magnetic attractiveness of its liberal consumer values and lifestyles to young people living in the Soviet-ruled world. Each successive Soviet leader after Stalin was less ruthless than the one before, and Soviet society slowly became more humane. In their own ways, Khrushchev, Brezhnev, Andropov and Gorbachev were all reforming communists, all trying to save a ship that they must have known in their hearts was not keeping up with the West. With Stalin's Terror gone, the only parts of the collectivist production and distribution system that still worked reliably and loyally were the nuclear-deterrent system and the state security system, the KGB. Everything else was breaking down, only kept working by the spread of corruption and side deals that oiled the wheels of a seizing-up command economy.

We also know in retrospect, when the Kremlin files were opened to independent scholars after 1991, how serious were the mass challenges to Soviet communist hegemony from inside the Warsaw Pact: in East Germany (1953), in Hungary (1956), in Czechoslovakia (1968), and repeatedly in fervently patriotic and Catholic Poland (1970, 1976, 1980–81). We know that the mobilising power of civil society resistance organisations Solidarity in Poland (founded in 1980) and Charter 77 in Czechoslovakia (1976) in the end demoralised and overwhelmed the 'Brezhnev Doctrine', which had insisted that no Warsaw Pact member country could ever leave the pact or disturb local communist parties' monopoly on power. Sclerotic, increasingly cynical and corrupt Communist Party local elites in East European countries, that had been propped up for so long by the military power and iron will of Moscow, in the end simply lost faith in themselves and abandoned government. When Gorbachev took away the Warsaw Pact props in 1989, with the ironically labelled 'Sinatra Doctrine',[5] these regimes collapsed like shaky ninepins one after the other, East Germany being the toughest and last to fall. Vladimir Putin watched all this happen as a young KGB officer in East Germany.

We know better now from the released files how terrifyingly close the East–West systemic competition had come to nuclear war in the Cuban missile crisis in 1962, a turning point in the Cold War. Nikita Khrushchev – a rash and impetuous risk-taker – had secretly sent four nuclear-armed submarines to Cuban waters, where he planned to station them as a permanent direct nuclear-deterrent threat to major US cities – 'Now, let us see how you Americans like having your cities put under the same nuclear threat that you are putting our cities under'. The Soviet submarines' discovery, containment and tactical depth-charge bombardment by surrounding US naval forces precipitated the nearest approach to World War III – which would have meant the final destruction of Western civilisation – in the history of the Cold War. The missiles were very nearly launched under pressure of days of sustained close-range depth charging from US naval surface vessels. Just one Soviet senior officer, Vasily Arkhipov, stopped the Soviet missile launch that would have started the war.[6]

His two despairing colleagues were ready to fire: our world today exists only because the Soviet Navy nuclear-launch protocol required three, not two, individual key entries. The heroic Arkhipov's naval career ended in disgrace.

I was nineteen at the time, still at university. We had no idea then how serious was the risk of nuclear war that Khrushchev's and Kennedy's brinksmanship had provoked. But out of those few days of sheer kick-in-the-guts terror in both capitals came a better understanding at the top of the need to build more safety and predictability into the Cold War, if the world was going to survive its risks. There followed years of genuine mutual efforts by Brezhnev, Nixon and Kissinger to stabilise the Cold War: the Strategic Arms Limitation Talks (SALT) beginning in 1969 and culminating in the achievement of the Anti-Ballistic Missile Treaty and the first SALT agreement in 1972. These were my years as Third and later Second Secretary in the Australian Embassy in Moscow as the Cold War began to stabilise.

In 1973, pressed by West European peace activists and by Soviet counterparts like dissident nuclear scientist Andrei Sakharov, all in different ways striving for a safer world, the Conference on Security and Co-operation in Europe (CSCE) began in Helsinki. The outcome three years later was the Helsinki Final Act, an agreed framework of Accords in three 'baskets': political-military; economic and environmental; and mutual human rights observance and monitoring.[7]

Henceforth, under détente (literally, 'relaxation') the competition between the rival systems in Europe was guaranteed by treaty to be more peaceful. Although this doctrine of peaceful coexistence was scorned at the outset by some American cold warriors as soft-headed, we see in retrospect that these Helsinki Accords – especially their human rights third basket – opened the way to the eventual demise of the Soviet communist system. The Accords exposed, both in the East European Warsaw Pact nations and in the Soviet Union itself, morale-destroying fact-based comparisons with Western economic and social performance and respect for human rights. As truth and quality consumer goods trickled in under the high ramparts of the Soviet system, the system progressively lost faith in itself and in its will to maintain the exhausting eternal military and social competition with the West. By 1985, the year of Mikhail Gorbachev's ascent to power, Soviet communism was already moribund. Gorbachev kept the ship's momentum going, using his great willpower and political magnetism, for another five years. But finally it was too much even for him, and in 1991 Soviet communism staggered to an exhausted end.[8]

Gorbachev had tried vainly to rejuvenate a communist society that had already come to mistrust and despise itself. He looked idealistically for a return to what he believed to be communism's worthy central organising principle for society: from each according to his ability, to each according to his needs. He called for *glasnost* and *perestroika* (i.e., 'clear thinking', and 'rebuilding' of communist society). He encouraged pluralist decentralisation of power: the growth of autonomous regional democratic parliaments (councils) freed from the iron hand of single-party Communist Party control. He encouraged the East European Communist Party regimes to look for their own national solutions according to their citizens' wishes.

He expected, in return, honesty and decency from the communist managerial elites, for he still believed in an ideal communist society. But the more freedom and flexibility he encouraged, the more corruption and xenophobic revanchism he unleashed. His lofty communist-based ideals were consistently rejected, or abused to advance lesser individuals' personal ambitions and local or ethnic nationalist agendas. The lid was off, and the pot was boiling over.

It all came to a head in 1991. In August, after a botched attempted coup by hardline communist ministers against an exhausted and discredited Gorbachev, Boris Yeltsin, a strong, charismatic man from Yekaterinburg in Western Siberia who had lost faith in communism and was fiercely ambitious to lead a Russian national state free from energy-sapping entanglements with the Soviet Union and Communist Party, seized his opportunity as Chairman of the Russian Parliament, one of the pluralist bodies Gorbachev had set up, to take full political control of Russia. Gorbachev, still the president and leader of the Communist Party, was left sidelined as an impotent bystander. Yeltsin honoured his pledge to American President George H. W. Bush to protect Gorbachev – still greatly admired in the West – from physical harm. But by mid-1991, nobody in Russian Government or society took any more notice of Gorbachev: real power had passed to Yeltsin.

The outlying Soviet governments quickly scrambled to break free of Moscow's faltering control. The Baltic States (Estonia, Latvia and Lithuania) were the first to secede from the Soviet Union in August 1991. Ukraine, Byelorussia and the Caucasian and Asian republics followed, in a messy piecemeal process over the ensuing four months.[9]

During an at times sombre, at times drunkenly exuberant, secret meeting on 8 December 1991 at a state hunting lodge deep in the Belavezha Forest in Western Byelorussia, Yeltsin and his Ukrainian and Byelorussian counterparts agreed on an audacious endgame plan, the Belavezha Accords, to terminate the Soviet Union and replace it by a face-saving fig leaf – a 'Commonwealth of Independent States' (CIS). Control over the CIS nuclear deterrent was to remain under Russian authority and all nuclear weapons withdrawn to Russian territory. Over the next two weeks, Yeltsin secured the agreement of all the other Soviet republican political leaders to this plan. On 21 December, at a meeting in Alma Ata, the plan was formally agreed by all.

On 25 December 1991, as I celebrated my first Christmas as Australian Ambassador to Poland in Warsaw, Gorbachev finally ceded to the inevitable, resigning as president of the now defunct Soviet Union. Gorbachev went into reluctant retirement, with the parting gift of a well-funded research foundation. The 74-year project of Soviet communism had ended not with a bang but a whimper.

Yeltsin, brimming with charisma and self-confidence, was now president of a new sovereign state, the Russian Federation, with boundaries identical to the former Russian Soviet Federative Socialist Republic (RSFSR). This Federation inherited the lion's share of the former Soviet Union – 75 per cent of its territory, 51 per cent of its population and 90 per cent of its estimated petrochemical reserves.[10] It was a more cohesive state, of more predominantly Russian ethnicity (80 per cent) and with a stronger Russophone linguistic unity. It had cast away the fourteen less prosperous smaller neighbouring former Soviet republics (six in the west – Ukraine, Belarus and Moldova, and the three already seceded Baltic States, Estonia, Latvia and Lithuania) and eight in the south (Armenia, Azerbaijan, Georgia, Kazakhstan,

Kyrgyzstan, Tajikistan, Turkmenistan and Uzbekistan). It also lost 26 million Russians who had made new lives as settlers in adjoining Soviet republics – mostly Ukraine, Kazakhstan and the Baltic States – and who were now left to take their chances in these newly independent neighbouring national states. Yeltsin assumed these states would remain friendly, given their intensely shared Soviet history and multiple ties.

Importantly, Crimea, which Khrushchev in 1954 had arranged to be transferred from the Russian into the Ukrainian Soviet Socialist Republic, as a gesture of his special affection for Ukraine on the 300th anniversary of the Ukrainian Cossacks' first request in 1654 to join the Muscovy state (Ukrainian Cossack autonomy ended finally in 1775), stayed within the now independent Ukraine under the Belavezha Accords principle of no border adjustments. The hope was that these two former Soviet republics, so closely bound together by Slav blood and language and three centuries of common history, would continue to be particularly good neighbours. 'Eternally Together', the 1954 commemorative poster proclaimed.[11]

Though relatively smaller Muslim and Asian minority nationalities and national autonomous regions remained within the borders of the new Russian nation, Yeltsin saw Russians as back in charge of this now democratic Russia. This still huge and resource-rich nation could now begin building a glorious national future as a market economy based on Russian values. To Yeltsin and his supporters, Russia's future seemed full of promise.

Yet it was a broken, bankrupt state. Factories were closing down, their assets being commandeered in corrupt privatisation deals by ruthless former communist managers. The only growth industry was the thriving Russian mafia. As the old state-owned production and distribution system collapsed during Russia's terrifying transition to capitalism, there was less food in the shops, less money for schools and hospitals, fewer secure jobs. A new and prolonged 'time of troubles' (*smutnoe vremya*) began for Russia and the other post-Soviet republics. Russia went through a demoralising decade from 1991–2000 of continued economic and social decline, degradation of military morale and battle readiness, and theft of public assets on a grand scale under 'paper-coupon' privatisation.

This painful 'period of transition' was seen as unavoidable by Western free-market economic advisers, who in the Yeltsin period had great influence in Moscow. There was huge capital flight abroad (mainly to London) by the most nimble privatisation profiteers. The strong took what they wanted, and the weak suffered the neglect and abuse of a disintegrating social welfare system. Malnutrition, depression and runaway alcoholism took their toll on Russian society. The population fell into sharp decline as women stopped having babies. It seemed that fewer and fewer Russians believed their country had any future. It seemed a spent force in the world.

Did the Soviet Union 'lose' the Cold War against the United States? Many Russians did not and still do not see it that way – they had made their own social choice to abandon Soviet communism – but some triumphalist Americans certainly believed so, and were keen to press their moment of strategic global dominance. Wiser voices in both West and East – people like Kissinger, Gorbachev, former West German Chancellor Gerhard Schröder, scholars like George Kennan, Stephen Cohen and John Mearsheimer, and former US ambassador Jack Matlock – urged the United States and NATO to hold back, to leave Russia time and psychological space in which to rebuild a new sense of national cohesion and purpose under its own emerging system of governance.

Sadly, they were not heeded. Western entrepreneurs, idealistic social engineers and rent-seekers moved in large numbers into Moscow and Saint Petersburg (formerly Leningrad). Western banks, media corporations and prestigious non-governmental organisations set about the great project to Westernise Russian society, starting in these two metropolitan centres of power and culture. Their unspoken goal was a docile Russia – a 'regional power' rather than ever again a rival superpower, that accepted Western hegemony and tutelage, with NATO expanded to the borders of Russia as strategic insurance. The best of them saw themselves as trying to help achieve a 'Moscow spring', a completion of the unfinished democratic revolution begun under Gorbachev and Yeltsin in 1989–91. For the worst of them, it was a time to make lots of money out of Russian resources, to carve out vast new consumer markets for Western products and services, to milk Russia of its best young scientists and technologists, and to neutralise any possible future Russian military threat to the West.

In Moscow and Saint Petersburg, for elites with some financial security, the 1990s were a time of excitement, of democratic debate and cultural ferment. But for the unprotected poor and middle-income state-employed classes across the nation, these were terrifying years of struggle in a society cast adrift, in a ship with no motor and with the feckless alcoholic Yeltsin at the helm.

It was, in fact, another social revolution as far-reaching as the communist one in 1917–21, though for the most part a bloodless one. Communist elements trying to turn back the clock took to the gun twice, in 1991 and in 1993, but both times were defeated by Yeltsin and his allies – in 1993, with state-ordered army shelling of poorly armed civilian rebels in Moscow. There followed a new Constitution in December 1993, and a new presidential election in 1996. With the advantages of incumbency, patronage and money, Yeltsin won again, though not without real opposition from the Russian Communist Party with its impressive leader, Gennady Zyuganov. Privatisation continued. Yeltsin's popularity continued to slide.

NATO was determined to extend its security *glacis* eastwards. In 1999, Poland, Hungary and the Czech Republic joined NATO. In a decisive second wave in 2004, four years into the Putin presidency, Bulgaria, Estonia, Latvia, Lithuania, Romania, Slovakia and Slovenia joined NATO. Starting in 2003, an 'intensified dialogue' with a view to eventual NATO membership began with Ukraine and Georgia.

What did NATO strategists think they were doing here? Especially after 2004, Russians saw a NATO noose tightening around their own historic strategic *glacis* that had given the Russian heartland safe strategic depth against Napoleon's invasion in 1812, against the World War I invasion by Imperial Germany, and against the Nazi surprise attack in World War II, a *glacis* that no fewer than 23 million Soviet citizens had died trying first to defend and then to recapture during the Great Patriotic War of 1941–45. In just two disastrous years, 1989–91, Gorbachev and Yeltsin had fecklessly given it all away. Now, the Western adversary military alliance was at Russia's gates again, exercising NATO forces on Latvia's borders less than 700 kilometres west of Moscow.

There is good eyewitness evidence (see *NATO Expansion: Was there a Promise?* posted 3 April 2014 in www.jackmatlock.com) that at the December 1989 Bush–Gorbachev Summit in Malta, which marked the symbolic end of the Cold War, the two presidents agreed verbally that the USSR would not oppose German reunification as a full NATO member, in return for which the United States would not take advantage of political changes in Eastern Europe to expand NATO further eastwards. Gorbachev and former Soviet Foreign Minister Shevardnadze also attest to this. Former US Ambassador to Russia Jack Matlock comments:

> The Malta understanding was between President Bush and President Gorbachev. I am sure that if Bush had been re-elected and Gorbachev had remained as President of the USSR, there would have been no NATO expansion during their terms in office. There was no way either could commit successors, and when Gorbachev was deposed and the USSR broke up, their understandings became moot.

In Bill Clinton's second US presidential campaign in 1996, he committed to support NATO expansion to Poland, the Czech Republic and Hungary, thereby openly abandoning the unwritten 1989 understanding at Malta. Why wasn't it written down? Because, it has been surmised, neither Bush nor Gorbachev, both under political pressures at home, were willing at the time to publicly reveal such politically embarrassing concessions to the former enemy.

Now in 2003–04, seven more former Warsaw Pact members had joined NATO, and Ukraine and Georgia were keen to go the same way. The strategically vital Russia–Ukraine border was just 600 kilometres south of Moscow. What had all the sacrifices been for, many Russians now asked themselves?

So it must have seemed to the vigorous young nationalist new president, Vladimir Putin, with his harsh and deprived childhood in struggling postwar Leningrad and his subsequent successful KGB career, to whom a declining Yeltsin had bequeathed the keys of state power in 2000. Over the next few years, Putin pursued a strong vision and will to rebuild and reassert the power, wealth and national pride of the Russian state. He brought under control the Second Chechen War (1999–2009), a bitter Muslim nationalist insurgency in Chechnya in the Caucasus, and in 2007 did a deal with a local Chechen strongman Ramzan Kadyrov to govern the war-devastated republic in collaboration with Moscow thereafter. He firmly enlisted the Russian Orthodox Church as a key partner in rebuilding Russian patriotism and conservative social values (a process begun by Yeltsin). Emphatically no communist, but a man who openly mourned the breakup of the Soviet Union as a state,[12] Putin soon showed that he was ready to manipulate and use the young institutions of Russian parliamentary democracy to advance the Russian national project as he saw it.

Initially an admirer of American capitalism and American 'can-do' market values, Putin became increasingly mistrustful of what he saw as hostile American political agendas against his nation, their eastwards expansion of NATO, and their use of 'democracy-building' NGOs to advance Western influence over the internal affairs of Russia's near neighbours, in particular the Baltic States and Ukraine. He came to suspect similar American subversive ambitions in Russia itself. While accepting the logic of economic globalised capitalism, and ready for Russia to compete in that world, he rejected American claims to exceptionalism and political hegemony within the global system. He was not prepared to accept America as the global leader and rules-setter, with Russia as a respectful acolyte grateful for any crumbs from the NATO table. He mistrusted American presidents George W. Bush and Barack Obama. In particular he mistrusted Obama's Vice-President Joe Biden and Obama's first Secretary of State, Hillary Clinton, for their liberal-hawk American triumphalist views of the world and their coldness towards Russia. In a Russian newspaper interview in 2010, commenting on the failed Obama attempt in 2008 to 'reset' relations with Russia, Putin admitted to having been slow to understand what he now saw as a constant pattern of US duplicity towards Russia:

I was simply unable to comprehend its depth...But in reality it is all very simple...They told us one thing, and they do something completely different. They duped us, in the full sense of the word.[13]

The more Putin consolidated his own power as president after 2000, advancing his nation-rebuilding agenda, and strengthening a top-down economy of state-guided capitalism, the more disliked and feared he became in Washington and NATO European capitals, even as he was becoming more popular at home in Russia for his defence of Russian interests.

The West soon tested Russia's strength and will militarily, first in a proxy war in 2008 in Abkhazia, a Russian-protected minority separatist region within the (now firmly pro-Western) Georgian republic; and then in continuing armed conflict in Eastern Ukraine since early 2014. In these proxy wars, both started by Western-supported anti-Russian centralising post-Soviet regimes against pro-Russian separatist regions, Putin's local Russophile allies defended their vital political and territorial interests, with essential but initially covert Russian military support. The Crimean peninsula, with its largely Russian population and its historic Russian naval base of Sevastopol, chose by popular referendum to reunite with the Russian motherland in March 2014, in response to what Crimeans saw as a hostile anti-Russian coup d'état in Kiev.[14]

The breakaway Eastern Ukrainian Russian-speaking region, with its key industrial cities of Donetsk and Luhansk tragically destroyed and depopulated by ruthless heavy Ukrainian Army shelling, became a region of frozen conflict under the de facto protection of Russia. Up to a million Ukrainian civilian refugees fled this ethnic Russian area, more than half into adjoining Russia. There remain coldly determined pro-Russian local forces and undeclared Russian support forces.

As the Russian economy and national morale recovered, and as Putin re-drew Russia's strategic red lines in Abkhazia and Eastern Ukraine, Putin and those politically close to him became more and more the personalised objects of Western disdain and economic sanctions. Putin, both feared and mocked by the West, came to be seen as the ugly face of a new aggressive Russia. At the same time, his popularity grew within Russia to steady levels, around 80 per cent.

With communism gone, the West now needed to define a new credible Russian enemy. It obviously could not be the Russian people. A plausible new enemy was identified in Putin and his allegedly brutal and greedy 'cronies', the rich and said-to-be-corrupt oligarchs of Putin's Russia. Starting in around 2008, a broad media campaign took shape in the Anglophone countries of the West, and now has a vigorous life of its own. Its proponents asked, what were the keys to Putin's success in Russia? How could he be countered and stopped? Not since Britain's concentrated personal loathing of their great strategic enemy Napoleon in the Napoleonic Wars was so much animosity brought to bear on one leader. Propaganda and demeaning language against Putin became more systemic, sustained and near universal in Western foreign policy and media communities than had ever been directed against any Soviet communist leader at the height of the Cold War.

This hostile campaign evoked an effective defensive global media strategy by Russia. Russia's state-supported international English-speaking media became increasingly sophisticated and internet adept. A new kind of information Cold War took shape, with – paradoxically – Western media voices more and more speaking with one disciplined Soviet-style voice, and Russian counter voices fresher, more diverse and more agile.

My professional interest in Russia had diminished after I completed my post–Cold War ambassadorial posting in Warsaw in 1994. With the end of the Cold War, the world had quickly become a different kind of diplomatic space. The Third World was now the only real game in town. Humanitarian idealists like UN Secretary-General Kofi Annan and Australia's Foreign Minister Gareth Evans believed there was now a responsibility to use the West's unchallenged military and economic power to protect and promote human rights in troubled countries like the republics of the former Yugoslavia, Rwanda, Somalia, Eritrea, South Sudan, Southern Africa, the Middle East, Libya, Syria, Egypt, Afghanistan, Cambodia and Burma. There seemed no limits to this new American-led liberal interventionism, to its passionate desire to remove from power those whom it defined as bad leaders and to remake the world into a better place. Humanitarian activism under 'the duty to protect' doctrine was all the fashion. A generation of Cold War–trained foreign policy planners was shunted aside as old hat, replaced by a new generation of 'liberal hawks' – benevolent interventionists ready to use the West's armed muscle to advance their global agenda of good intentions.

National sovereignty, and the international security system based on the UN Charter and UN Security Council system of collective security decision-making under the restraining safeguard of Permanent Member veto rights, had also become outmoded concepts, to be set aside and shrugged off whenever they conflicted with the interests and views of the new global superpower and its readily marshalled 'coalitions of the willing'. In vain did a now much-weakened Moscow protest in the name of the UN Charter.

US exceptionalism and triumphalism were the sustaining beliefs of these new liberal hegemonists of the Western Alliance: in America, in Europe (especially Britain), and in their loyal outliers Canada and Australia. These Western liberal hawks were actually more threatening to world peace than their prudent and cautious late Cold War predecessors. In those early pre-Islamist fundamentalism years, all seemed possible. Democratic 'springs' and 'colour revolutions' were popping up everywhere. The do-gooders moved restlessly from country to country, from crisis to crisis, sowing the wind. I saw the heyday of this as Australian Ambassador to Poland (1991–94) and then to Cambodia (1994–97).

First, there was the Bill Clinton–Tony Blair axis of good intentions in 1993–2001, then the George Bush–Tony Blair axis to eliminate the evil of Saddam Hussein in Iraq in 2001–07. It all had tragic consequences. Afghanistan and the entire Middle East region are still paying the terrible human price for the Western alliance's blunders and lies in the service of good intentions.

Until I retired from Australia's diplomatic service in 1998, and even thereafter when I became an independent commentator, I spent little time thinking about the politics or foreign policy of Russia. It seemed sidelined: a shrunken, irrelevant part of the world, left behind by history. Russia looked on helplessly as its former Slav protégé Yugoslavia was dismembered by successive Western-supported partitions in the 1990s – a dismemberment precipitated by Yugoslav leader Slobodan Milosevic's own cruelty and incompetence. Moscow watched glumly as the whole Balkan region, with its large South Slav populations, slid out of its historic close sphere of affinity and influence into the orbit of its former Cold War adversaries. Hungary, the former Yugoslavia, Bulgaria, Romania, Moldova – all gone.

My main windows into Russia now were books and movies, particularly John Le Carré's perceptive oeuvre of late Cold War spy novels, and Martin Cruz Smith's political thrillers built around the corruption and perils of late Soviet communism and the Yeltsin years. I could barely recognise, let alone understand, this strange damaged country I was reading about. I came to think of Russia as a dark Hollywood disaster movie, with social disintegration, a hopeless corrupt drunk at the helm, ruthless mafia thugs, murderous Chechen terrorists, ultra-nationalists of neo-fascist ideology, renegade arms dealers, desperate women trying to get out, and caches of decaying, out-of-control nuclear weapons.

Two terrible incidents summed up the tragic incompetence of this new Russia for me. On 12 August 2000, just eight months into Putin's presidency, the *Kursk* nuclear submarine sank due to technical failures during exercises off the north coast of Russia, with loss of all 118 crew on board. The rescue response was late, inept and ineffective. Then in September 2004, the three-day siege of a school in Beslan, North Ossetia, occupied by Chechen terrorists ended in security forces losing patience and violently storming the building, resulting in the deaths of at least 330 hostages, including 186 children.

Nor did I recognise or understand at the time the subtle pressures inflicted by the West on Russia in these aimlessly drifting 'years of transition' first under Yeltsin, and then during the first years of Putin's presidency. I should have, because I actually had had first-hand working experience in the 1990s, as Australian ambassador both in Poland and then in Cambodia, of just how powerful and interventionist American liberal imperialism on the march could be. I somehow did not connect those dots with what was happening in Russia.

In Poland in 1991–94, the charming and personable American ambassador, my colleague Tom Simons, inherited the political vacuum left by the collapse of the Russian colonial satrapy there. He handled his power courteously, and the Poles welcomed the new American-led order intelligently and with their eyes wide open. For them, it was a relief after four crushing decades of Soviet hegemony, and their best strategic opportunity in centuries to advance Polish national interests. The economic transition from state to private ownership was traumatic enough in Poland, but the Solidarity trade union and the Catholic Church's strong social justice values protected Polish workers' interests from the worst excesses of free-enterprise privatisation. Poland came out of the transition an enthusiastic and increasingly dynamic new NATO and European Union (EU) member, ready to claw back strategic advantage from its former Russian overlord – especially in the renascent Baltic States and in the pluralistic, weakly governed key borderland nation of Ukraine, which had for many centuries been contested territory between Poland and Russia, and which now presented Poland with new opportunities for expanded influence.

In Cambodia in 1994–97, I took part in a quite different national trajectory. The Cambodian People's Party, the post-communist party shrewdly led by Hun Sen, declined to be shunted out of power by local protégés of US-funded human rights and democracy-building NGOs and the foreign policy arms of the Democratic and Republican parties. Hun Sen became a hated man in Western human rights circles. But he had the backing of a still strong neighbouring Vietnam and the tacit sympathy of China. Unusually, I found common ground with my realist-minded colleagues, the American, French and ASEAN ambassadors. We argued that Hun Sen's Cambodian People's Party, for all its faults of corruption and authoritarianism, would provide more security and stability for Cambodia's people after thirty years of dreadful genocidal Khmer Rouge rule and civil war than the offered leadership alternatives at that time. Our views prevailed. The liberal hawks were neutralised, and their hoped-for regime change in Cambodia did not happen. But for a few years it was a close-run thing. I did not think then that there might be any relevance from my experiences in the nineties in Poland and Cambodia to what was happening in Russia. In retrospect, however, I now see that there was.

My interest in Russia revived in the late 2000s as it gradually became an international player again under its tough and energetic new president, and as relations between the West and 'Putin's Russia' went into decline. I began once more to read media and journal articles, and to observe critically how Russia – still a nuclear-weapons state and major conventional military power – was increasingly now stereotyped by the West as the irresponsible rough beast of world politics. I saw how disdain for Russia had become habitual in Western foreign policy communities. Especially as Ukraine boiled over into lethal civil war after the Maidan Square uprising in Kiev in February 2014, which Russia condemned as an illegal coup d'état, I saw that important things were happening in this part of the world, changes that I needed to follow. Russia was back, and so was NATO's enmity to it. I began to think critically about what misperceptions and contradictions might be embedded in prevailing Western narratives about Putin and Putin's Russia.

And my curiosity about what was really happening in Russia began to grow. I had last visited the country when it was a broken-backed state in September 1990, fifteen months before Yeltsin's final self-inflicted dissolution of the Soviet Union – what had been happening since then?

What kind of a country is Russia now, twenty-five years – a full generation – after the demise of Soviet communism? Is Putin trying to bring back a new authoritarian state, under the cloak of Russia's revived Tsarist tricolour flag? Or is he simply the biggest crook of them all, protecting and presiding over a bunch of equally corrupt mafia 'cronies'? Or could he perhaps be a farsighted and resolute national statesman, a sort of modern Russian Bismarck, trying to hold Russia's ground in the ruthless new international power game, while at home steering a careful course between extremes of fascist-leaning ultra-nationalism and reckless naive liberalism?[15]

The 100th anniversary this year of the two 1917 Russian revolutions will inevitably be a time for serious stocktaking in Russia and abroad. How do Russians now see themselves and their national destiny in the world, after their past hundred years of systemic turmoil and misery, and their successful Soviet-led reindustrialisation after 1920 and victory in World War II? How do Russians envisage the future possibilities of their state and their national destiny, after four generations of war and trauma inflicted on the Russian people; after the international diaspora over many decades of some of their best and brightest people as refugees from communism and anti-Semitism; after all the personal tragedies of international political sympathisers who broke their hearts and sacrificed their lives and families in the cause of advancing Soviet communism – 'the God that failed'?[16] So many widows, orphans and traumatised families. So many lives lost or scarred around the world, in this tragic extended history of many years of worldwide military and ideological competition.

What is there of value in this new Russia, if so much past sacrifice is to have any meaning? What was it all for, if Putin's Russia is now to be cast again as the world's greatest villain and threat to peace? If the Western world is to be persuaded to fall back again into a new Cold War against Russia: no longer communist, but somehow again, or still, the eternal arch-enemy of Western democracy?

Is the Putin dispensation strong, or is it fragile? If it is fragile, how to explain his 80 per cent public approval ratings across Russia in reputable polling? His assured command over a talented and loyal corps of senior state administrators and advisers? His political longevity – seventeen years and still going strong?

So many huge questions about this country. And for me, one large personal question: why am I unable to get Russia out of my system, this strange country I have not set foot in since 1990? Why does this lovely and wounded land, its culture and language, its people, its music, art and literature, continue to draw me back and enthral me, to tug at my emotions and bring tears to my eyes?

So I decided to go back and have a look, while I am still physically mobile enough: not with any academic, professional, political or socio-economic research agenda, but as an intelligent observer with some relevant former diplomatic experience of living and working there forty-five years ago, and now on a private holiday adventure of my own.

When I applied in 2015 for my tourist visa to visit Russia for a month in 2016 (the maximum time allowed), the application form at the Russian Consulate in Canberra asked me: Have you ever been issued a Russian visa? I was about to answer yes, and look up the dates of my sojourn in 1969–71 and brief visits in 1985 and 1990, when I realised this was not the question. This was a new country now, going by the name of 'Russia', which I had never visited. I answered accordingly 'No', wondering if my literal truthfulness would be challenged. Two weeks later I got my visa – it must have been the right answer.

Russia has inherited so much from the Soviet Union – in territory, assets, state language, history, mixed cultures and ethnicities. Yet forty-five years is almost half a century, in any country let alone Russia. As L. P. Hartley observed in 1953, 'The past is a foreign country. They do things differently there'.[17]

All the more so in the case of Russia, risen phoenix-like from the ashes of the dying Soviet Union in 1991, which had itself risen phoenix-like from the ashes of the dying Tsarist Empire of all the Russias in 1917. More than any other nation, Russians have to ask themselves big existential questions about their recent history, not only about the two revolutions in 1917 that their great-grandparents lived through, and the Stalinist horrors their grandparents experienced, but now also about their parents' and their own struggles, privations and disappointments during late communism and the 1985–2000 de-communisation *smutnoye vremya* as well:

> Why did all this suffering keep happening in our Russian nation? Was it inevitable? *Why did we do all this to ourselves?* Weren't we making progress enough, the way we were before all these disruptive changes began in 1917? Weren't we happy enough as a people, the way we were? Why did we have to pull it all down and start again from zero, when other countries with comparable social and political problems did not undergo revolutions, but instead gradually introduced democracy? Who is to blame? Do we Russians suffer from a fatal tendency to reach out for reckless extreme solutions?[18]

Some luckier countries don't need to ask themselves such existential questions. Britain and most of its inheritor Anglophone dominions have enjoyed comfortable constitutional stability since the seventeenth century. The degree of peace and continuity in our political histories allows us to view them more lightly.

Russians cannot. There are huge shadows over recent generations of Russian lives. These are not only to be measured by the death tolls of wars and Stalinism. Russians must also confront a past marked by the forceful imposition, and later the rejection, of entirely new national value systems in the space of just four generations: from Tsarism to White Revolution to Leninism to Stalinism to Khrushchev-Brezhnevism to Gorbachevism to Yeltsinism to Putinism.

No wonder the Russians are world leaders in inventing political jokes. It may be the only way they can cope with all this disruptive political change.

I was lucky enough to experience a long moment of apparent stability in the Soviet Union, living in Moscow in 1969–71 as a young Australian diplomatic guest, at what seemed a plateau of Soviet power and self-confidence.

These were years when Russian dissidents like Alexander Solzhenitsyn and Andrei Sakharov (and a few years earlier, Boris Pasternak) had begun to look back reflectively at their cruel tumultuous past, to ask what could be salvaged from it, and even to take some comfort from the first signs of humanisation of social values taking place around them, despite the continuation of a stratified anti-democratic communist power structure and close KGB harassment. These great Russian dissidents were idealists who never gave up their faith in Russia's essential decency and honesty.

I went back again briefly in 1985 as part of an Australian delegation led by Minister John Button for the funeral of a forgettable leader, Konstantin Chernenko. At the funeral I saw signs of incipient social decay: a shabby capital, a proliferation of ageing bemedalled generals in greatcoats and grotesquely huge military caps, and the absence of anybody young or fresh-looking.

But the next leader, Mikhail Gorbachev, was a truly impressive new-generation Communist Party politician. He proceeded over the next five years to turn on its head the Cold War–dominated world that we had grown used to over the previous forty-odd years.

On my third visit for a three-day foreign policy conference in Vladivostok in 1990, I found a confused, demoralised, dysfunctional state in ruins. The Soviet Pacific Fleet was rusting away at moorings in the harbour. Children's playgrounds were deserted, haunted by homeless alcoholics and drug addicts. Broken glass and potholes were everywhere. Young, sad-eyed prostitutes desperately sought hard-currency clients, to help them build an emigration nest egg, or maybe even to love them and take them away. There was no aviation fuel at the airport to fly us foreign delegates back to Moscow: we were stranded for two days, waiting for new supplies to be commandeered from somewhere else and flown in, to enable us all to get home. It was such a sad and humiliating moment.

Now I am returning again twenty-six years later. What will I find this time?

PART ONE

THE WAY WE WERE...

Chapter 1

Going In

It was a happy pre-departure party in Canberra – my family, close friends, chilled vodka in iced shot glasses, trays laden with smoked salmon and sour cream on ryebread *zakuski,* and good conversation. I moved around talking to my guests, trying to ease their worries about the strange Russian midwinter holiday on which I was about to embark.

I assured them that I was not setting off for the land of Mordor, ruled over by Putin the Dark Lord with his all-seeing eye! I would not be blackmailed or compromised. I would not be arrested by secret police. I would not starve to death once I got outside the big cities into the said-to-be impoverished countryside.

I knew that such fears about Russia were very deep-rooted. Ryszard Kapuscinski commented at one point in his brilliant 1993 memoir *Imperium* about his travels in the Soviet Union in 1989–91 that, 'Russia fascinates the West, but also fills the West with fear'. This was as true of eighteenth- and nineteenth-century imperial Russia as it was of the Soviet Union, and it is still true now. Many Western diplomats and travellers in Russia have found that there is something different, and even scary, about the country. Few have found it a place in which they felt comfortable.

So what is this huge, strange, contradictory nation? Is it European? Is it Asian? Or is it something unique unto itself? Should we love it? Should we hate and fear it? Or maybe all of the above?

When Tsar Peter the Great in 1703 'broke a window through to Europe' on the desolate Baltic coast by building his new capital and naval base, Saint Petersburg, he launched a military challenge to the then dominant Baltic power of Sweden, and a bold claim for Russia to be accepted as a great European power.

In 1814, as Tsar Alexander I was triumphantly touring Paris and London with his army generals after the final defeat of Napoleon – a defeat in which Russian arms had played the leading role, after decades in which most of Europe had already accommodated to Napoleon's despotic New European Order – there was deep suspicion of the Russian Tsar. He was seen as an unpredictable man with absolute power over his huge army – and who seemed in no hurry to go home. Western leaders like Britain's Lord Castlereagh wondered if they might soon again be at war, this time against Russia.

Forty years later, in the Crimea, they were. In a major war fought in several theatres, Britain and France invaded Russia, in support of their ally Turkey. And sixty years later, during the Bolshevik Revolution, the Western powers invaded Russia again, from Murmansk in the north, trying to help the White cause in the Civil War.

We were uneasy allies in World War II, but we needed Russia as an ally then to defeat Hitler's Germany. The Soviet Union bore the brunt of the fighting, losing upwards of 23 million people over four years. Most of European Russia was ravaged as Nazi tanks rolled forward to the gates of Moscow, and were then at huge human and material cost pushed back all the way to Berlin.

Soon afterwards, we were again adversaries, in the forty-year Cold War. When Soviet communism collapsed in 1991, many on both sides hoped we might at last just be friends. Yet here we are now twenty-five years later, it seems enemies again. Russia seems just too big for the West to engage with in any comfortable way. Maybe we are doomed to be permanent adversaries, in the Great World Game of the Atlantic Alliance versus the Eurasian Heartland.

There is much to admire about Russia, a country that has great gifts to offer the world. The chains of communism were broken twenty-five years ago. Russia today is best described as a strong state capitalist economy.[1] Maybe it will become a more liberal economy, at the Russians' own chosen pace, or maybe it won't. Meanwhile, perhaps we need to begin to think about Russia with a little more respect? Perhaps we are now living in a self-reinforcing climate of ignorance and prejudice about Russia? Could our old conservatives like Henry Kissinger be more clear-eyed about Russia than liberals like Barack Obama or Hillary Clinton?

Of course it is a nation that still faces huge challenges. But is it really our place now to tell Russians how to run their country, to 'mark their report card'? Maybe we in the West have fallen into the habit of thinking about Russia in condescending, derogatory ways? Even serious Western discussion of policy towards Russia is now too often framed in disparaging language. I expressed the hope that my trip and the planned book to come out of it might make a little dent in this hard shell of prejudice.

My friends were impressed that I had managed to plan my whole itinerary within Russia online, without using tour companies or intermediaries. I had wanted to test whether such systems for independent travellers worked nowadays in Russia.

I was happy that my old friends Grahame Bates from Canberra and Julian Oliver from Brussels would accompany me for parts of my four weeks in Russia, providing welcome company and alternative perspectives.

I had designed an itinerary to take me beyond the familiar and comfortable Moscow–Saint Petersburg tourist axis, to visit two fascinating large cities that had been strictly off limits to Westerners in Soviet Russia: Gorky, now back to its old medieval name of Nizhny Novgorod, and Sverdlovsk, now back to its Tsarist name of Yekaterinburg. I had read in guidebooks that both cities (the fourth and fifth largest in Russia) were now beautiful, thriving centres. Nizhny Novgorod on the Volga River had been a key imperial fortress city in Moscow's seventeenth-century eastwards expansion into Tatar lands. Yekaterinburg was actually in Siberia, on the far side of the Urals: it would be much colder there than in Moscow. I would have to fly four hours to Yekaterinburg, and go by fast three-hour train to Nizhny. Grahame and I were to go to Suzdal, the famous monastery town near Moscow, and Julian and I to Yasnaya Polyana, Tolstoy's country estate where he wrote *War and Peace* and *Anna Karenina*. I was going to visit Peredelkino, where Pasternak lived in a

state writers' colony while he wrote *Doctor Zhivago*. How amazing it
would be to experience such places, and in midwinter, Russia's most
characteristic and evocative season!

I promised I would try to bring some of this varied experience
back home in my planned book *Return to Moscow* (*Vosvrasheniye v
Moskvy*). We drank toasts to my Russian journey: that it might be
healthy, safe, enjoyable, and I dared to hope even a little bit useful,
in the good cause of building a better understanding between our
Western world, and the great nation that I also admired – Russia.

Two days later, I caught a morning bus from Canberra to Sydney
International Airport and was soon aboard my plane. I flew to
Singapore and then non-stop to Helsinki. After a 28-hour hotel
stopover there to get over the worst of jetlag and acclimatise to the
cold, I stepped up from a Helsinki Central Station platform onto a
high Russian train – the Tolstoy Express – and over the threshold into
Russia. Russian trains have always been spacious: wide enough for
long berths for tall passengers. Night was falling. I looked forward to
a good journey into nostalgia: red velvet padded seats in a welcoming
dining car, convivial companions, ice-cold vodka in cutglass
decanters, opportunities to practise my Russian, perhaps a charming
Russian *dyevushka* or two to chat with...and on to Moscow in time
for breakfast. I was, in other words, expecting a journey in the great
tradition of Russian long-distance train travel: a time when Russians
traditionally relax, talk to strangers as if they were old friends, share a
glass or two of wine or something stronger...

Alas, it was not to be. This Tolstoy Express was clearly not one
of Russia's crack long-distance trains, contrary to the online sales
hype. It was a base-grade international train for people with more
time than money: any sensible Russian would more efficiently fly
the short air route from Helsinki to Moscow. My compartment
looked drab and worn. Although I had paid for a first-class two-
berth compartment, nobody had bothered to remove the empty
second-class upper bunks which thudded painfully into my head
whenever I stood up. The train was far from full with many empty
compartments, but I still had to share mine with a dull, asthmatically

wheezing and later heavily snoring Finn, who spoke no word of English or Russian.

When I went to the dining car things were no better – a few old lino-covered tables, and an apathetic staff more interested in gossiping among themselves and watching sport on television than serving customers. Obviously for good reason, I was their only customer. I had a warmed-over *solyanka* sour meat soup, black bread and a small flask of warmish vodka, and then retired disconsolately to bed for a fairly sleepless night, in some trepidation of what further disappointments and discomforts might await me in Moscow.

During the long night, I was awakened when we stopped at the border station in Vyborg (a Finnish and then Russian station) to undergo customs checking and present my travel documents. The Russian border guards were young, polite, smartly uniformed and female. It brightened an otherwise dreary night.

I arrived at Leningradsky Voksal in Moscow at around 8.00 am, in light snow. I walked down the platform into the terminal and found a telephone franchise store where I bought Russian SIM cards for my mobile phone and iPad. I bought time on the phone and sent a quick SMS to my family to say I had made it to Moscow. I also bought 1000 rubles' worth of iPad data for local 3G use, which I actually never exhausted, as most of the time I was able to access free wi-fi networks in cafes, my hostel room, or hotels outside Moscow.

I went out into the street in search of the local metro station. After a short walk through the snow, I entered Komsomolskaya Metro through heavy swinging doors. I bought a twenty-ride ticket and now faced several staircases and escalators down to my platform, with no ramps or lifts. A young man saw my plight and kindly helped with my two suitcases on the stairs: I must have looked very tired. I always found great courtesy and good manners on the metro, though the platforms and passages are not disabled-friendly. On crowded trains with all seats taken, older travellers, pregnant women or women with babies were invariably offered seats.

Six stops later I got off the train at Park Kultury, the nearest stop to my booked hostel. A local taxi, and ten minutes later I was unpacking in my tiny but cosy private room at Moscow Home Hostel, my temporary home for the next three weeks. How good it felt after the marathon four-day journey from Australia.

I lay back on my bed for a few hours' rest, idly thinking how utterly different it all felt from my first arrival in Moscow forty-seven long years ago. Memories rushed back of not one but the two past 'foreign countries' where I had lived from 1969 to 1971: my own Western world, so different then from our world of today; and the even more striking foreignness of the Soviet capital.

Few of us saw at the time that we were actually on the eve of real change in Russia, that would over the next two decades acquire unstoppable momentum. I could see no sign of change during my two years living there. Leonid Brezhnev, who was firmly at the helm of the party and state during my posting, had just one year before my arrival ruthlessly ordered the Red Army to suppress the Prague Spring – Alexander Dubcek's brave, futile effort to move Czechoslovakia forward to a new 'socialism with a human face'. It looked as if the old Soviet order was back in place, harsher and more determined than ever.

What dominated our impressions and imaginations as Western diplomats in Moscow were not so much our similarities with Russians, as fellow human beings who happened to live on opposite sides of the 'Iron Curtain' (a commonly used phrase in those days), but our world's profound political, economic and social differences from theirs. For it was truly a bipolar world. We used the word 'bipolar' as shorthand for the deadly competition of the two rival systems.

The West really feared Soviet Russia, and Soviet Russia really feared the West. We inhabited two utterly discordant political, economic and cultural spaces, with contradictory ideas and natures, in ways difficult to imagine today.

For today, despite real and sharp global political tensions and rivalries between Russia and the US-led NATO, or between the United States and China, all major world powers operate within the one shared global social and cultural space, united by a range of common information technologies and political, economic and social protocols and lifestyles. It was not so then.

My Moscow posting gave me, at a young impressionable age, the unusual privilege of truly living with one foot on each side of the Iron Curtain. As a diplomat, I was able to come and go freely enough between these two worlds still in silent deadly confrontation. There was also a Third World or 'non-aligned world', denoting the rest of the globe beyond the Western alliance and Warsaw Pact blocs: a lethal playground for the brutal but carefully contained flesh-and-blood battles of the Cold War. These wars on the world's periphery caused immense misery and dislocation to their affected populations, in almost every continent, but hardly discommoded the rival superpowers: the only exceptions being the US war in Vietnam, and the Soviet war in Afghanistan, both of which had large consequences at home. Except as a theatre of displaced East–West conflict, the Third World barely existed as an actor in world politics. Talented non-aligned leaders came and went, trying to carve out a more secure and respected place for themselves and their nations, but the endless US–Soviet rivalry was always the main game that chose the battlefields, and that defined Third World nations' possibilities for progress.

It was natural in those years to ignore or demonise the rival world, and most people in my Western world did. A friend of mine has nicely described how most of us saw life on the other side of the Iron Curtain: 'Half the world was shut away, and we were silenced into a complacent belligerence against that which we did not know'.[2]

But the same applied to the other side, too. Soviet regimes fed their people a constant diet of standardised false propaganda about how badly off ordinary people were in the West by comparison with Soviet citizens. To read these accounts, we were still mired in Dickensian squalor at the bottom, with obscene extremes of wealth at the top. Even top party apparatchiks were deceived by the pervasiveness of their own anti-Western propaganda. There is a well-sourced account of Gorbachev as a Minister for Agriculture in the early 1980s visiting a family-owned wheat farm in Canada, and psychologically overwhelmed on seeing how just one well-capitalised and well-mechanised family farm was able to grow wheat more efficiently than a collective farm of the same size on similar-quality land of similar climate in Russia with hundreds of workers. Yeltsin wept for shame and grief after he toured a typical American suburban shopping mall in the early 1990s, and saw the routine affluence enjoyed by working-class Americans around him: nothing in Soviet propaganda had prepared him for this.

In the Soviet world, a few focal points of reasoned, patriotic dissent had developed in the post-Stalin years, as the paralysing fear of the Gulag penal system began to fade into memory. In Russia itself, human rights dissidents like ex-prisoner Alexander Solzhenitsyn and the former nuclear physicist Andrei Sakharov, dissident creative artists and poets like Josef Brodsky and Yevgeny Yevtushenko, were writing and performing *samizdat* (self-published, unapproved work). Soviet Jewish 'refuseniks' were beginning to press for free emigration. In the politically restless and culturally advanced East European nations, there were dissident writers like Gunter Grass in East Germany, Milan Kundera and Vaclav Havel in Czechoslovakia, Czeslaw Milosz and Adam Michnik in Poland.

In the West, there were still a few diehard bands of pro-Soviet communists and fellow travellers. But also, a few brave literary people, often resolutely pacifist and apolitical, who strove to build bridges of cultural exchange and human affinity, determined to ignore East–West ideological tensions and differences. These were tiny minorities, largely unremembered now outside security-agency files. Most people passively accepted the status quo of the Cold War, and got on with everyday life in their own respective worlds.

For the military forces and the intelligence agencies, the Cold War was their central professional reality. The militaries had to be ready for the Cold War to turn hot at any moment: to plan for a conventional war in Europe (always, of course, assumed to have been started by the other side), to plan even for nuclear war at various levels of targeting horror. And meanwhile, to provide discreet or declared military training and weapons assistance to proxy allies in Third World wars and guerrilla uprisings. The Cold War kept both sides' military establishments busy and well funded. Each had an interest in talking up their opponent's potential, which of course was very real.

As it was with the spies. The tasks of the intelligence agencies of both sides were to collect information that could not be obtained through public channels; to seek to turn vulnerable people from the opposition to their own side; and to try to prevent the other side turning any of its vulnerable people to them. It was a world well portrayed by John Le Carré in his remarkable sequence of spy novels, which accurately reflect the changing moods of the Cold War over the years.[3]

This was a struggle dimly reflected in Australia by a succession of local Soviet spying scandals – the Petrov, Skripov and Combe–Ivanov 'affairs' – that though of negligible global importance, kept the Australian Security and Intelligence Organisation (ASIO) on its toes, and had real impacts on Australian domestic politics and foreign policy.

We diplomats – on both sides – had a peculiarly ambiguous mandate. We were not soldiers or spies, but we were not merely official post-boxes and visit facilitators either. Our task was to try to understand the adversary world, to connect with it professionally as diplomats, to learn as best as we could how it worked and where we thought it might be going, to engage with it in mutually advantageous political and trade dialogues as policy allowed, but not to succumb to its attractions whatever they might be. We had to become close, but not too close. We could not do our jobs by skulking fearfully in our embassies: we had to try to get out and engage with the rival world. The art was in finding safe and productive modes of engagement. It was a delicate balance. I am not sure in retrospect that my embassy did it very well – I think we suffered from an excess of caution – but that was the Cold War game we Australian diplomats tried to play.

Above all, the other world was always our potential 'hot' enemy. At the same time as we were trying to connect with them as diplomats, our allies' military forces and spies were drawing up priority lists of which of their cities to nuke first, when or if the Cold War went hot. No doubt the Soviet militaries were drawing up similar lists of our cities. It was a chilling thought, which never really went away.

Alone in my Moscow hostel room, I was thinking, why did I love the place so much? This strange, lovely, wounded land, whose culture and language, music, art and literature still meant so much to me. I could not answer that question then, and I cannot fully answer it even now.

My affection for Russia cannot be explained by either ethnic or ideological–political ties. My Central European Jewish part-heritage was in no way linked to Russian or Russian Jewish roots. My maternal grandparents, the Schicks and the Kellers, were fully assimilated middle-class German-speaking Viennese and Bohemian-Slovakian Jews. My other half, the Kevins, were middle-class professional Catholic Irish-origin Australians, with roots in Ulster's County Armagh. I had never been in the slightest attracted to communism as an ideology: my family's political leanings on both sides were firmly moderate Labor or social democrat.

Robert Dessaix's excellent travel memoir *Twilight of Love: Travels with Turgenev* (Scribner UK, 2005) put his finger on some important affinities between white Australians and Russians. We are both people on the periphery of Europe, outsiders who never quite made the European civilisational grade. Both of our peoples have smarted under European disdain: the arrogance towards outliers of those enjoying present or past metropolitan power, and the sense of defiance mixed with inferiority such arrogance generates in the recipients. Yet Australians and Russians are both proud of the scale and breadth of our nations, of our large and boundless plains and steppes, of our emptiness. We have both had to settle harsh inhospitable lands, and to seek reconciliation with indigenous inhabitants. We have both resorted to convict labour as a development strategy.

I thought also about the kinds of Westerners who have historically been drawn to Russia: people who felt like outsiders in their own countries. Scots like the diplomat Robert Bruce Lockhart, Irish like George Bernard Shaw, radicals like H. G. Wells, people of ambivalent sexuality like the Cambridge circle of secret communist traitors. Something about Russia draws people who feel they do not quite fit in to their own societies, for whatever reason. Maybe it is the affinity between underdogs, between misfits? Le Carré's 1989 novel *The Russia House* captures this mood well in his portrayal of its hero Barley Blair, the failed London publisher undergoing a prolonged mid-life crisis, and recruited by Western intelligence to spy on Moscow when a chance opportunity falls their way. Blair is asked why he goes to Russia so often. He replies, 'Because I like them: more than I like you Americans'.

Journalist and essayist Ryszard Kapuscinski in *Imperium* (New York, 1994) beautifully expresses his mixed love–hate feelings as a Pole for Russia. He recalls his painful memories of the cruel forcible deportation to Siberia he experienced as a small child from his Polish village near Pinsk, as it was being ethnically cleansed and repopulated by Russians after 1945. And yet his love and respect for Russia come through in *Imperium*, too, and his human sympathy at the miseries the great Soviet nation was going through as it tore itself apart in 1989–91.

It has been hard for writers, even those as fluent and insightful as Dessaix and Le Carré and Kapuscinski, to articulate more precisely their love for Russia. Much less can I. Le Carré says gracefully, in his Foreword to *The Russia House*:

> Nobody who visits the Soviet Union in these extraordinary years, and is privileged to conduct the conversations that were granted me, can come away without an enduring love for its people and a sense of awe at the scale of the problems that face them. I hope that my Soviet friends will find reflected in this fable a little of the warmth that I felt in their company, and of the hopes we shared for a saner and more companionable future.

I admire Russia's steady seriousness of purpose. This is a country ready to confront big questions. It is not a trivial or superficial or small-minded country. The Russian language itself is a wonderful instrument, a most beautiful and subtle language with the finest gradations of meaning, in expressing verbs of emotion especially. And the music, the art, the literature – how could one not love this country, the more one comes to know it?

Most of the Western writers who have lived and worked in Russia are rather silent about what originally drew them to this country. They have deliberately sheltered behind their neutral professional detachment, limiting their writing palettes to discussions of politics, economics, diplomacy and so on. Yet they all must have initially volunteered or at least consented to their assignments here, sometimes extended by choice over many years.

Robert Bruce Lockhart never really tells us why he, a young ambitious Scots-origin British commercial consul in Moscow, disdained by the Etonian diplomats of the British Embassy to the Tsar's Court in Saint Petersburg, came to love Russia so much during the turmoil of the 1917 Revolutions and Civil War, why he fell in love with the alluring and enigmatic Russian countess Moura Budberg, possibly a Soviet double agent, risking his career, marriage and national reputation for her.[4] We have to read between the lines of his *Memoirs of a British Agent* (1932) to guess at what drew him to Russia and its people so strongly.

American journalist Anne Garrels recently wrote affectionately with scrupulous professionalism about a typical Middle Russia industrial city in the South Urals, Chelyabinsk, that she visited regularly and came to know well over a twenty-year period. Her 2016 book *Putin Country – A Journey into the Real Russia* comes closest of any modern non-fiction writer I have encountered in reporting how Russians now feel about their country and its again troubled relations with the West. Here she reports the complex views of a magazine editor friend, an affluent stylish middle-class woman whom she calls 'Irina' (pp. 26–7):

She believes Russia has been and can again be an example for the world and that Western criticism merely reflects a desire to see Russia back on its knees. Despite all its current problems, she anticipates that Russia, with its natural resources, huge expanses, and talent, will once again be a country to be fully reckoned with.

To speak with her is to encounter a fierce defensiveness and many contradictions, but that is the point. Russians are trying to figure out who they are and where they fit into the world. Their embrace of much of Western culture and the selective denial of what doesn't fit into the official 'Russian' model seldom makes sense...

She represents many I have met in Chelyabinsk. They are sick of beating up on themselves. They are sick of their country being seen as nothing more than a mafia-ridden kleptocracy – even though they are the first to complain about corruption. They are sick of the West's beating up on them for their sins, especially now that they are more aware of Western sins.

Another example, on p. 225, describes 'Olga', a lawyer in Chelyabinsk, who rejects the idea that she is a mere 'zombie' mesmerised by state TV. She is fluent in English. She reads a wide range of internet posts. She opposes Putin's refusal to acknowledge there are Russian troops fighting in Ukraine, but she does not oppose Russian intervention there. While she is paying a stiff price for sanctions, she anticipates Russia will be stronger in the end. 'Russia is trying to raise its domestic production, and this is going to be a long process, but everyone understands this, and we are prepared to wait.'

Finally, 'Tamara' (p. 186) asserts that there was a prolonged attempt by the West, through Boris Yeltsin's Western advisers, to undermine and steal from Russia: 'All those financial manipulations, the rush to privatise, these ideas didn't come from here, they came from you, from the West, but the West didn't have to live with the results.'

Most Western political journalists don't go to these emotional places in Russian minds. They take refuge in their professional 'objectivity' and in their well-drilled acceptance of the current orthodoxies of received wisdom in the West about Putin's Russia. Sometimes they adopt the easy but intellectually dishonest cop-out – to profess to 'love' the Russian people, but to hate and despise their allegedly corrupt and evil current rulers.

Today, there is a well-founded career interest by Le Carré's 'grey men' in Western politics and journalism to return to the Cold War, even if there is no real reason to do so – except our own nightmares.

I did not want to write yet another book about Russian politics or economics or the new Cold War. I hoped I could report honestly on how it felt now for me to be back in Russia. Had it become a country in which I could now feel safe and 'at home'? Could I do what I had been unable to do as a young Cold War diplomat: simply enjoy the pleasure of being here again, living and moving freely among Russian people? And how well or badly would I be able to convey such complex truths in my book after I returned home, after just four weeks here? Could I drill down below superficial impressions, to say anything worthwhile to my Western readers?

I knew that I would not attempt an academic analysis or 'balanced adjudication' of Putin's Russia. There are political historians like Andrei P. Tsygankov, Stephen Cohen and Richard Sakwa, far better qualified than me to do this. My goal was far more modest: to try to convey a little of how Russians now see the world and their place in it, and to what extent Putin might be legitimately channelling and expressing those feelings. And I planned to do this impressionistically, by just going with the flow of Russian life and seeing what insights or ideas I might pick up on the way.

Finally, I knew that I would have to dip back into Russian history, even as far back as the Varangians, Kiev Rus', and the early Muscovy state. For two reasons: firstly, because Putin's Russia is determined to reclaim this history with pride and celebration as its own national heritage, and not to diminish and distort its importance as merely a prelude to the seventy-year communist experiment. And secondly, because the West's fear and disdain of Russia certainly predates communism. We need to be reminded of the long, often troubled history of Russia's relations with the West, why there have so often been deep mutual misunderstandings and outbreaks of war. We need better to understand how educated Russians feel about their own history.[5]

Chapter 2

Moscow 1969–71

Moscow in October 1969 seemed cold, grim and utterly alien. From the moment of arrival with my young wife, Valerie (I was twenty-five, she a little younger) after our long and exhausting flight from Australia, everything looked grey and strange. On our drive into the city from Sheremetyevo International Airport, there was no bright street advertising or neon lights: just a succession of overpoweringly huge red-painted billboards mounted on the roofs of serried ranks of uniform eight-storey concrete apartment buildings, carrying forbidding slogans in Russian and English with texts like, *Long Live the Great Soviet Union* or *The Party and the People Stand United*. The wide main roads were almost empty of cars. There were a few forlorn cafes: no shops or businesses, and very few people. Behind the rain-soaked apartment buildings were leafless bare grey courtyards awaiting the first snows of winter. It all seemed so bleak and hushed.

I had two weeks of handover with my predecessor. We stayed in the Hotel Ukraina on Kutuzovsky Prospekt, near the Novoarbatsky Bridge over the Moscow River. It was a forbidding 1930s neo-Gothic building, one of Stalin's then hated but now nostalgically admired 'Seven Sisters'. It has now been stripped down and internally rebuilt as the luxurious five-star Radisson Hotel: only the remarkable facade remains the same.

The dining-room menus were fly-spotted, yellowing and uninviting. Most dishes were in any case unavailable. The waiters were slow and unsmiling. Upstairs, our *dezhurnayas* (a rotating team of 24-hour floor concierges, grim-faced women stationed on each floor, essentially our watchers) were suspicious and unobliging. We were relieved after two weeks to move into our flat, in a closely guarded, enclosed diplomatic compound at 19 Kutuzovsky Prospekt, across the road from the hotel.

The West already seemed far away. Our new home at apartment 32 was a small, cockroach-ridden third-floor flat. Two bedrooms, a semi-partitioned living/dining area, a small kitchen, a bathroom and a windowless storeroom. We had old and tired flatpack Scandinavian furniture inherited from my predecessors, on drab and worn-out carpet. Our building faced onto an identical building across a narrow bare courtyard of dead grass and muddy dirt, supposedly a children's play area but filled with old dog droppings. The entire compound was surrounded by a high chain wire fence. Stony-faced policemen on 24-hour guard duty at the single gate noted all comings and goings and interrogated anyone who might dare to visit us. Our Russian-language teacher, Lydia Melnikova, and our maid, Lydia Zvyagintseva, were sanctioned regular visitors with security passes, but it would have been a brave Russian who tried to visit us without one – they would have been halted, refused admittance to the compound and interrogated. It was, we were told, all for our own security.

We were a disparate, disconnected group of lower-ranking Western and Third World diplomats and their families. Most of the Soviet citizens' apartment buildings around us were considerably more solid and nicer than ours, at least on the main Kutuzovsky Prospekt, and certainly from the outside. We never got inside any of them, though I remember visiting a similar spacious Soviet-style apartment occupied by a British diplomatic friend in another part of Moscow. We so envied him not to have to live in our dreary fenced compound, though his apartment was still under very visible police surveillance. Our compound was managed by UpDK, the Directorate for the Resourcing of the Diplomatic Corps.

My ambassador, Frederick Joseph Blakeney[1] (1913–90) – 'Blake' to his peers, but 'Sir' to me – was a tall, physically impressive diplomat of the old school. A Catholic from Sydney, he had been a Marist Brothers novice in the 1930s but left the order. He married Margery in 1943. A Royal Australian Air Force officer, he saw active war service in Europe in 1942–45. He joined Foreign Affairs in 1946, at the same time as my father, Charles Kevin. They both rather stood out as Catholics in the then predominantly Protestant department. Blakeney's second posting (after Paris) had been to Stalin's Moscow from 1949–51. A staunch anti-communist, his outlook was set in the Cold War. For Blakeney in his professional years, the West's war against communism never ended.

Blakeney had begun his current Moscow posting one year before me. Only ambassadors were allowed to, or could afford to, import their own senior domestic staff. He had wisely brought with him a quietly competent Italian couple, multi-skilled as cooks, butlers, shoppers and keepers of household budgets, and managers of the Russian kitchen, table service and housecleaning staff. The Residence always worked smoothly under Margery's and their care, and meals there with the ambassador and his wife were always enjoyable. It was part of my official duty to help them entertain larger groups; I learned from them most of what I ever knew about diplomatic protocol and manners.

The Blakeneys lived in a strikingly beautiful Art Nouveau mansion at 13 Kropotkinsky Pereulok (lane), just off Ulitsa (street) Prechistenka. It was built around 1902 by the famous architect Fyodor Schechtel for a very wealthy woman – reputedly the mistress of a rich and generous sugar baron.[2] The main reception hall was a breathtaking three storeys high, dominated by a high, massive arch window through which the winter morning sun would stream in. Opposite was a large white marble fireplace flanked by two stunning carved caryatids that must have been at least eight feet tall. Never lit, it was a fireplace you could lose yourself in. Sipping a pre-dinner cocktail in this marvellously proportioned room, one could easily imagine oneself transported back into a vanished Tsarist world of wealth and grace.

But we would turn back into pumpkins as we drove through Moscow's grim silent night streets back to our dreary compound. We comforted ourselves with the thought that we were living closer to the way ordinary Muscovites lived.

Actually, we were not. We inhabited a sort of weird in-between twilight zone. At least Muscovites had the solidarity and comfort of their common national culture, language, family and neighbourhood ties, and the sense in 1969 that their material lives were slowly improving. We had none of those resources: little real contact with neighbours or sense of community. But we were certainly better resourced and more comfortable in material respects than most of the Russian flat dwellers around us. Most importantly, as privileged diplomats we had freedom and funds to travel to Europe; to read Western books and watch Western movies at home; to import Western food and wines unavailable and barely imaginable at that time to ordinary Russians.

At the practical level, too, we had unusual privileges. When our windows leaked snow in winter, when the plumbing played up, or when cockroaches came scuttling out of the kitchen walls in summer, we would simply ask our landlords, UpDK, to send workers to fix it, and they more or less promptly did so. With the cockroaches, we had to vacate the flat for twelve hours while they fumigated all the rooms and wall cavities with strong insecticide gas. We assumed this was when the KGB's secret listening devices in our walls were checked and updated.

Lower-ranked diplomats made do with modest local domestic staff of various levels of competence and enthusiasm, provided by UpDK as sole supplier (and one had to take whoever was offered). Lydia, our daily cook/housekeeper/childminding help, was young, willing but inexperienced. So were we, on our first posting. We all found our proximity in the small flat awkward and at times embarrassing, but it was the way things were. We assumed Lydia had to report on us; we did not resent her for this.

I threw myself into my work. Valerie soon got to know several other English-speaking wives living in our compound as she awaited the birth of our first baby, Patrick, born in Helsinki three months after we arrived. Through Valerie's friendships with other Western wives living in the same compound – Carol Niles and Sandy Roy from the US Embassy, and Valerie Bryce from the Canadian Embassy – I got to know better their husbands, Tom, Stapleton and Sandy. We were all of similar age and experience, and on our first professionally prized Russia posting. It was easy to make friends in the NATO community. We were all rather proud of ourselves to have scored Moscow, and we comforted our less-than-thrilled wives with this thought. To their credit, they rarely complained, though they pined for nicer surroundings. It was tougher for them than for us, absorbed as we officers were in our interesting work.

Helsinki was the nearest Western leave centre and one of the locations of choice for our wives to give birth: it was close enough for fathers to quickly fly up there. Its hospital at Katiloopisto offered Western standards of maternity and child care. Western embassies did not approve of our babies being born in Moscow; we asked permission, but it was denied. We never used Russian hospitals for security reasons, though we were told there were some good hospitals reserved for privileged senior Communist Party people and approved foreigners.

It was out of the question for me to wait with Valerie in Helsinki for a birth that might still be days away. Sadly, I was only able to get up to Helsinki the day after Patrick's birth. We were a tiny embassy, just three political officers, including my ambassador.

Our Counsellor and Deputy Head of Mission was responsible for Soviet foreign policy reporting. My main duty was to report on internal Soviet affairs. The counsellor and I took it in turns accompanying the ambassador for note-taking and drafting cable reports of his official calls, or helping him draft his own cables. For the rest, we monitored the media and exchanged professional talk with the larger Western embassies. Work soon became an enjoyable routine. My ambassador expected me to limit my absences from Moscow to the essential minimum: he wanted me on call for him full-time. Later in my posting, his early nervousness relaxed as he got the measure of his workload.

For the birth of our second son, Charles, eighteen months later, Valerie wisely arranged to fly home early to her parents, who lived in Belfast. We had an enforced separation lasting around three months. I threw myself into work and remember little of that time. I do remember my delight when Valerie returned to Moscow with Patrick and his newborn baby brother. It had been lonely and scary for her the first time, giving birth alone in Helsinki, even with Valerie Bryce there for company in the hospital.

How did we live? We made the best of life in an environment where we knew ourselves to be alien, under surveillance and friendless. Security concerns dominated our lives. We went with our families on occasional shopping expeditions to farmers' markets, on summertime family walks and picnic excursions to the riverside parks and nearby countryside forest parks, and on delightful cross-country ski trips in winter. We had a car, and there was a lot of unfenced and accessible public forest parkland around Moscow then: it was a much smaller, more compact city, and surrounding land was largely unspoiled and unfenced field and forest, former large aristocratic estates, nationalised but not privatised by developers as today.

We tried to do things in safe NATO-based groups. We used our cars for all city and surrounding travel, avoiding taxis or public transport. We lived in our own diplomatic community bubble, only gradually extending our known road itineraries and picnic spots beyond the most familiar, as our confidence grew in our ability to communicate in Russian or to handle unexpected difficulties driving on the roads. We did not know what we should be afraid of, so we were probably more afraid of everything unfamiliar than we needed to be.

Our wives were braver – the impulse to shop, to meet for coffee in more sympathetic public city places, to explore food and clothing markets, was irresistible. They showed us the way to greater engagement with the city, but it was always very limited.

Because we were all under regular Soviet observation – our car number plates, routinely noted in militia notebooks as we drove by, showed which embassy we were from – any threats to our physical safety would also have doubtless been quickly seen and dealt with. This gave us a paradoxical feeling of physical security. Moscow was very safe for us. But the huge city was a maze of mysterious 'Go' and 'No Go' areas. The American Embassy internally published an indispensable unofficial city road map which they kindly offered to friendly Western embassies, showing the No Go areas. It saved us from a lot of unpleasant encounters with traffic police. There were no proper road maps available for purchase, only a distorted and navigationally useless pictographic tourist panorama 'map' of main sights and landmarks. We learned gradually to navigate our cars around the city with great care, trying not to trespass into closed zones and also not to violate the inscrutable highway code. I don't remember ever riding on the Moscow metro.

I soon reconnoitred a quite pleasant four-kilometre walking route from our flat in Kutuzovsky Prospekt to the chancery compound in

Kropotkinsky Pereulok. I tried to stay fit through walking it regularly to and from work, summer and winter. It passed close by the Kievsky Voksal railway station, a major station for west-bound trains, then crossed the Moscow River over a road bridge, and then through a chilly pedestrian underpass under the major Sadovaya ring road that encircles the city, and out into the historic and prestigious Kropotkinskaya district. Near the Kievsky train station, I would pass a sleazy vodka bar where I avoided the occasional groups of drinking men standing or sitting in the street; and a basic cafe where one could occasionally drop in for a warming snack of boiled or fried *pelmeny* (spicy Siberian pork dumplings). There was a florist shop on Sadovaya not far from the Residence, to buy the occasional bunch of flowers for Valerie.

All the Western ambassadors lived well, especially the British and Americans with whom we had most regular contact. Their residences were large, luxurious compounds, former aristocratic palaces or mansions in Tsarist times. When invited to official functions in these embassies, one briefly forgot one was in Moscow. These two major embassy communities offered the usual range of social pursuits – choirs, drama clubs, reading and craft groups, mother-and-baby circles and so on. One was supposed to keep busy and companionable, and always show a sense of humour and stiff upper lip.

As a group, we were insular. We affected a weary disdain of things in which we probably should have taken more interest. We did a bit of visiting to museums and historic palaces and estate parks, especially when we had Western guests to entertain. We spent a lot of time among ourselves mocking Soviet national propaganda landmarks like the Exhibition of Economic Achievements and the many war memorials. Churches were dilapidated and our visits to them neither welcomed nor enjoyable.

Some of us were quite interested in classical Russian culture, especially those who had done any serious Russian-language training before our postings. I was lucky enough to have had a year's full-time individual language study at the Australian National University (ANU), which had quite a good little Department of Russian Studies – now sadly closed.

I would say in retrospect that we lived in Moscow in a permanent state of alienation and cognitive dissonance – it was probably the only way we could make some sense of what we were doing there. In our closed American and Western European diplomatic milieu, we would draw clear distinctions between Tsarist-era culture (certain aspects of which we allowed ourselves nostalgically to admire) and contemporary Soviet official or popular culture, which we would disparage as vulgar and second-rate, unless it contained elements of political dissidence that would justify us giving it some attention.

We were fundamentally incurious about Soviet or Russian – the terms were synonymous – culture and life. Some of us would allow ourselves to respect the imagined Russia that might have been, had it not been knocked off balance by the communist takeover in 1917. We felt sure that there was no possibility whatsoever of turning the clock back to that more refined, Orthodoxy-based, philosophically reflective pre-communist Russia, the Russia of Tolstoy and Turgenev and Chekhov and Tchaikovsky, that we had learned about in our pre-posting study of Russian history and culture. We could allow ourselves to love this imagined Russia, while despising the Russia where we got up and went to work in our embassies each day.

The Canadians enjoyed ice-hockey matches at the big Lenin Stadium – they and the Russians shared a fierce passion for the game, and Sandy Bryce invited us to see some spirited Canada–USSR games. We played tennis with other diplomats at Luzhniki Park tennis courts, and squash at the Indian Embassy. Once, I swam at Stalin's monstrous city swimming pool where he had pulled down Russia's most historic and revered cathedral (now happily rebuilt).

Classical music was safe, and a welcome relaxation from the routine of political reporting and the diplomatic round. Moscow had, then as now, an abundance of concert halls and theatres. As diplomats we had regular privileged tickets for the best of Soviet musical life at ridiculously cheap prices: high culture was heavily subsidised by the state. UpDK had a generous regular allocation of seats for the Bolshoi Theatre, which they apportioned out to interested embassies. The productions were conservatively done, but the stage sets were breathtakingly opulent and beautiful, and I still remember the vigour and energy of the singing and dancing. I sought out the classic Russian repertoire: Tchaikovsky, Glinka, Mussorgsky, Borodin and so on, in preference to Italian or French works, which the Russians loved.

Orchestral concerts in Moscow concert halls were easy to get into, and always excellent. Concertgoer behaviour was strange: in the intervals, people seemed disinclined to mingle and chat. They formed up into serried ranks of purposeful walkers, who promenaded briskly around the huge lobbies for the duration of intervals in linked-arm groups, always on the move. If people recognised one another, they gave little sign of it. There was hardly any chitchat. I realised, years later, that this was a vestige of prudent practice from the Stalinist terror years. People had learned not to risk casual conversation with acquaintances or strangers in public places, for fear they might be compromising themselves by being seen to be friendly with someone who might already be under security police surveillance.

Thankfully, Bolshoi Theatre audiences were more cosmopolitan and relaxed. One could sip a glass of Soviet wine or cognac or beer and eat an open sandwich during intervals in one of the theatre bars, and usually find people to greet – fellow diplomats, and sometimes Russians from the Foreign or Trade Ministries who were more used to Western-style socialisation.

There were classic plays, too. I had enough Russian from my year at ANU to enjoy going to Chekhov plays after a revisionary pre-reading of my well-thumbed Penguin book of English translations. Modern Russian theatre was more problematical. My Russian was too limited to pick up any veiled dissident messages and undertones in productions at avant-garde theatres like the Taganka. I nodded sagely when my linguistically better-equipped American and British colleagues talked about interesting political messages in the latest play or revue. Similarly, public poetry readings – an art form that had rapidly developed under the Khrushchev thaw,[3] with well-attended readings by popular poets like Yevgeny Yevtushenko, who was pushing the boundaries – were a closed book to me. Films were closely controlled, and heavily into commemorating, with a strong Soviet communist ideological perspective, heroic stories from the Great Patriotic War of 1941–45.

We young diplomats thought the war was already long ago – we could not understand the obsessive Russian interest in continuing to dwell on it. We had no comprehension how hugely Soviet people had suffered in that war, and why descendants would want to remember and honour their parents' suffering. We had no real capacity to imagine the unbearable atrocity of the total war that had been fought by Soviet Russians for four years, mostly on Russian and Ukrainian soil. Somehow, the facts slid by us.

Our wives spent a lot of time planning and mounting reciprocal dinner parties in our flats. This meant a lot of attention to food shopping. We imported most of our alcohol, frozen and canned food by truck from Helsinki. Westerners officially resident in Moscow (but not envious Western students) could purchase foreign currency coupons used to buy fresh food products in the Diplomatic Commissariat – a closed-access large government grocery store. One bought there when items were available. One always kept reserves at home of frozen and canned food for scratch meals. Nobody saved money in Moscow postings. A lot went on food and alcohol.

Only rarely did we enter Russian food stores. The empty shelves and habitually unsmiling and brusque staff, and the archaic three-desk purchasing system, were not encouraging. Supplies were sparse and irregular and some of the processed meats looked and tasted unappetising. But we enjoyed Russian fresh bread, apples, sweet-and-sour pickled gherkins and some of the local Dutch-style or sharper cheddar-style cheeses.

We were inhibited from very much local purchasing by a highly artificial official Soviet banks' exchange rate, around one ruble to the dollar, which we had to use. The real black-market rate in the streets – which we were on pain of expulsion enjoined to avoid at all times for security reasons – was about ten rubles to the dollar. One of our guards broke the rule and was sent home.

The braver and wealthier diplomatic wives ventured out to the private food markets, especially in summer, when one could for cash rubles buy fresh-picked fruits and vegetables, pickles and compotes, jams and cakes, free-range eggs, freshly killed chickens or ducks, all grown or preserved at people's privately owned dachas (weekend cottages) that surrounded Moscow and were an important source of additional food supply and variety – a tolerated, indeed deeply cherished, form of small-scale private ownership and commerce.

These markets also had stalls selling delicacies flown up in large suitcases by private small traders from the Crimea, Caucasus and Central Asia: things like oranges and lemons, nuts, spices, melons and grapes, smoked fish, cognacs, even Caspian caviar.

Eating and drinking quite well was thus possible for diplomatic Westerners living in Moscow, but it took work, time, inventiveness and careful budgeting. Eating at one another's houses or flats was both our major social relaxation and an important way we diplomats exchanged professional knowledge and gossip. One learned the skills of tucking into quite good food and wine while mentally memorising interesting snippets of pre-dinner or at-table conversations to report back to embassy colleagues the next day. Occasionally – not often – one might have picked up some news the ambassador had not. There was a bit of one-upmanship, but people were usually generous with new information: we were all in it together. It was quite a rare thrill when I had something new to contribute to the table talk.

It was hard to find enjoyable spontaneous things for the family to do at the weekend, as a relief from the constant weeknight professional socialising. Walks through city parks pushing babies in prams – or in the winter snow, pulling babies in Russian sledge-prams – were the best fun. There was very little in the way of European-style street life. Good coffee just did not exist. We were not encouraged to visit big tourist hotel lounges or bars like the National or Metropol, because we were given to believe that these were the favourite haunts of prostitutes or honey-traps of both sexes on the books of the KGB, looking for unwary, bored or lonely foreigners to entrap and compromise. For families, there were pleasant summer cafes to go to in riverside parks like Gorky Park, and in winter there were a few better cafes in the fashionable old Arbat district, a shortish stroll across the Novoarbatsky Bridge from our flat. The local favourite weekend afternoon treat there was vanilla ice cream with raspberry compote, washed down with a sweet red port-style fortified wine called *portwein*. I don't know if it came from Portugal; it was more likely a locally made equivalent from the Krasnodar area on the Black Sea, Russia's main domestic wine-growing region. This could be a warming combination on a cold day. Then, of course, there were *bliny* – pancakes in many varieties, sweet or savoury. If we were feeling in a celebratory mood and our wallets were deeper than usual (our junior-officer salary did not go far in legally exchanged rubles), we might treat ourselves to *bliny* with black or red caviar and sour cream, accompanied by a glass of Armenian cognac or red wine.

Out in the narrow European-scale Arbat district streets, on a sunny winter's day, one could almost for a moment pretend that one was living a normal Western European life. There were pretty girls strolling in honey fox-fur coats and hoods, their smiling faces shining pink from the cold. We wondered if they were theatre or movie actresses, or the younger wives or daughters or mistresses of powerful men. Because most of the older women we saw had faces hardened and careworn by years of privation and family grief, the beauty and confidence of these young women shone through all the more brightly. I bought Valerie a honey-coloured fox-fur coat and matching hood in Copenhagen, and she looked just as pretty as any of the Russian girls we saw in Arbat.

We would go into Dom Knigi, Moscow's largest bookstore on the New Arbat Avenue (then called Kalinin Prospekt), to check what might be on offer. Sometimes I would score a set of collected works of one of the great nineteenth-century classics – Pushkin, Lermontov, Tolstoy, Chekhov, Turgenev, or Dostoyevsky. I lovingly took them home and bravely filled my bookshelves with them, vowing to read them one day. They were amazingly cheap for the quality of the binding, paper, print and illustrations. The Russian tradition of good cheap classical book publishing remains alive to this day.

If we were in a mood for records, there was the Melodiya Store just along the road, selling the latest offerings of this famous state-owned record label (which still trades today as a Russian private company). I would look for the names of great Russian opera and orchestral music performers. The discs and packaging were heavy and stiff, the artwork stodgy, but the technical sound quality was good enough, the prices cheap, and the music magnificent. One bought records when one saw them, because they would all be sold out by the next week.

Melodiya also had a good range of popular modern Russian music – balladeer-guitarists like Bulat Okudzhava, gipsy and balalaika orchestras, the shrilly yodelling but to my taste charming Ukrainian female folk choirs (I actually liked them a lot, and still do).

There were a few interesting prestige restaurants in Moscow, specialising in regional cuisines. Better-off Russians went to them for big family anniversary or wedding celebrations, so they were always crowded and convivial. The Aragvi (Georgian cuisine, on Gorky Street, renamed Tverskaya Ulitsa, but the Aragvi is gone) was everybody's favourite for big Russian family occasions: always heavily booked, but somehow a table was usually to be found for allegedly important Western visitors; our invited house guests definitely had their uses here. My favourite dishes were then as now – *shashlikh*, *dolmades*, *khachapuri* (freshly baked soft Georgian cheesy bread) with delicious appetisers, *kuritsa tapaka* (pressed-flat spicy crisp whole chicken). There was a live Georgian band, and exotic singers and dancers.

In the big Soviet hotels, the dining-room menus and prices were all similar. Some central city hotel dining rooms tried out of old-fashioned pride to maintain a professional standard of food and service; others did not bother. I never found anything quite as bad as our early experiences at the Hotel Ukraina, and I enjoyed many better meals, even in standard superior hotels like the Berlin, Budapest or Sovietskaya. Once one got used to the Soviet protocols for eating out – concentrate on the cold appetisers (*zakuski*) and soups (*solyanka*, *borshch*), don't expect too much from the main courses or desserts (basically, beef stroganoff or shashlik), don't ever expect fast service, enjoy the accompanying wines and spirits and fizzy Caucasian *mineralnaya voda*, get up and dance often to fill the long delays – it could be fun!

There was a small range of quite good local wines, brought up from Georgia, Armenia and Crimea. I remember still a very good strong-flavoured Georgian dry red called Mukhuzani, and an almost as good dry white called Tsinandali. Armenian and Georgian cognac were excellent. Russian *champanskoe* was cloyingly sweet, and we never drank it for pleasure. Stolichnaya vodka in those days was sold strong, 50 per cent proof, and it did not take too many toasts with Russians at official functions, which had to be drunk *do dnya* – to the bottom of the glass – to become literally legless once the cold air hit your lungs outside the restaurant. We learned to pace ourselves sipping our more familiar imported duty-free whisky soda and gin and tonic.

Low-life night clubs? There were none. But there were one or two permanently moored riverboats of dubious repute, retired Volga passenger cruise ships, with gipsy-kletzmer or jazz orchestras, torch singers and dance floors, and card games. One went to them for a bit of Bohemian life and they could be slightly scary fun. They were said to be frequented by prostitutes and cruising gigolos or gay men. Dark stories were told of drinks being spiked and unsuspecting lonely male or female embassy staff members waking up later drugged in an onboard cabin, confronted with incriminating photographs and KGB blackmail attempts.

NATO embassy administrations were utterly obsessed with personnel security. Britain had been shocked and frightened by the Burgess, Maclean and Philby affairs, in which people at the heart of the British foreign service establishment turned out to be committed communist double agents for the Soviet Union. Kim Philby had fled to Moscow only in 1963: he was living in Moscow while I was there.

The British Embassy was determined to keep a very tight ship. We Australians had obligatory regular security briefings there. We were instructed, firmly and emphatically, to avoid local entanglements of any kind – sentimental, romantic or even simply friendly – and to promptly report all non-official contacts with any Soviet citizens. Anything other than short superficial conversation with Russians we met could get us and them into trouble when the KGB got wind of the contact. We were told that any Russian 'licensed' to fraternise with foreigners would be a 'crocodile', almost certainly required to report to the KGB on those he had befriended. Contact with a Russian could not be taken at face value, and anyone keen to make friends with us was probably up to no good – or soon would be, when the KGB got to know of any developing friendship and decided to exploit it. If they were stupidly naive, they were a danger to us as well as themselves.

Sex – covert, security-compromising sex – was seen to be central to potential vulnerabilities. Our young men and women were bluntly given to understand – 'Do what you like, we know it is a tough posting here and you may need to let off some steam sometimes, but *stick to the Golden Rule, keep whatever you do within NATO'*. And so we did – there were no compromising incidents to my knowledge involving any NATO embassy staff and Russians while I was there.

We were urged to live our 'private' lives as if we were not being listened to or monitored. We were assured that all our domestic conversations – even in our most personal moments at home – were actually profoundly uninteresting to Russian monitors, whom we would never meet, and whose interest was solely in checking for any spies or targets of opportunity. They had heard it all before. Unless one were silly enough to relay at home to one's spouse and to the possible listeners in the walls anything confidential from the day's work, it could simply be shrugged off as another intriguing aspect of diplomatic life in Moscow. We got used to it being the first question our house visitors asked us.

We were also taught not to behave in 'clandestine' or provocative ways when we thought someone might be following us in the city in a car, or on foot. It was important not to show awareness of or sensitivity to such things. After all, we were not doing anything improper, so we should never turn and try to catch out possible followers, nor should we look as though we were trying to shake them off. The rule was – be normal, pretend nothing is happening here, and eventually they might be satisfied and leave you alone.

It was not hard to have quite a good non-professional social life. Every NATO embassy had its social club and there was a Friday-night drinks circuit around the embassy clubs. One rarely got bored because there were always new staff arriving at posts, people to farewell, or visiting house guests to show around and introduce. Our popular Australian Embassy club – naturally called the Down Under Club – operated out of a spare basement in the Residence. We had a regular volunteer bar roster and there was always a good Western crowd there. It was not at all rank conscious: it was Australian in the best egalitarian sense.

Thirteen Kropotkinsky Pereulok was a busy, multipurpose compound. The main mansion housed the ambassador's reception rooms, his private family apartment upstairs, and a cramped but secure chancery on the third floor. In the basement were the club and storage cellars. A large (originally for stables and carriages) set of buildings at the back of the property housed the Consular and Administrative Section, which had Australian managers and staff and their supporting locally engaged English-speaking Russian staff. No Russian was ever allowed into the secure upstairs Chancery Section, which was guarded by three very bored Australian federal police officers on 24-hour rotating shifts (these were the years before secure electronic locking). When the ambassador had important Soviet Foreign Ministry visitors, he received them in his large reception room downstairs.

In the back outbuildings area, there was a cosy upstairs flat for the Deputy Head of Mission – John Brook, a bachelor, enjoyed it, but it was cramped for a family. All in all, it worked well enough. These days, the Chancery and Administrative Sections have moved to a separate building about four kilometres away on the other side of Red Square, in the Kitay-Gorod area.

In addition to our three political officers, our two consular and administrative A-based staff downstairs, and our three guarding policemen, we had three Australian women support staff – the ambassador's secretary and two cipher clerks. All three were fully security-cleared and the embassy could not have functioned for one day without them. They took shorthand, typed memoranda and cables, prepared diplomatic bags for weekly dispatch with British couriers, and coded and decoded secure cables. Because all secure messages had to be manually encoded and decoded using one-time coding pads, it was a laborious and physically tiring business to send and receive secure cables. One learned to be economical with words.

Let me describe our 'safe room' – I am sure after forty-five years of technical development, I am not giving away any secrets that would matter in so doing. It was the place we used for discussions we wanted to be quite sure could not be overheard by our Soviet landlords. Actually, it was a freestanding cubicle within a larger room, resting on four large transparent perspex cubes. The adjacent, above and below free air space was regularly walked and crawled around by our guards to ensure that no wires had been pushed through from outside. Once we went inside the room, a cocktail party chatter tape was automatically turned on, intended to muffle our conversations from any powerful noise-detecting microphone nearby. It was

World War II technology, but I guess it worked, because there was no superior Soviet listening technology at the time. At any rate, we felt secure in our stuffy little safe room, and we quite enjoyed the drama of going in there to talk, as long as it was not for too long or too often.

Encounters with any dissidents or asylum seekers attempting to come into the embassy would have presented a particular operational problem. There were Soviet guards posted at the front gate in any case. Even if that gauntlet were run, our experienced and tough consul, John Colquhoun-Denvers, would have been quick to smell trouble and shoo away potentially embarrassing visitors.

We were taught that any approach from a person claiming to be a dissident should be treated with extreme suspicion. They might be trying to entrap or compromise the embassy person they approached. If they looked genuine, they should be directed away to larger Western embassies.

It was thus a curiously constricting experience to live as a diplomat in Moscow representing a small Western alliance member at the height of the Cold War. No doubt Soviet embassy staff had similar life experiences in Canberra, where they were isolated and closely watched. Australian–Soviet diplomatic relations had been severed by Moscow in 1954, after Western exposure of Soviet spying in the Petrov affair, and did not resume until 1959. There was a lesser test of relations over the Skripov affair in 1963, but fortunately it did not lead to ruptured relations – both sides had learned not to push such incidents to the brink of disruptive embassy closures – and so Australian occupancy of the Kropotkinsky Pereulok property was not lost. Nor were relations severed much later over the Combe–Ivanov affair in 1983.

Visits to the chancery by Australian visitors to Russia were rare. Family reunion visits to Russia for Australians of Russian origin were difficult and expensive to arrange, and those who did manage to get such visas would not have wanted to draw the KGB's suspicious attention by frequenting our embassy. There was almost no trade. Our embassy did not conduct a cultural-relations program. There was a trickle of visits to Moscow by Australian communists and left-wing or non-aligned writers like Manning Clark, Judith Wright or Geoffrey Dutton, but these visits were usually assisted by the twin

Australia–Soviet Friendship Societies in both countries. Our embassy was rarely if ever involved. I once was asked to attend a function put on by the Friendship Society in Moscow, representing my ambassador, who was diplomatically indisposed; it was an odd, awkward evening and I don't think anybody enjoyed the contact.

The Soviet Government supported the system of such reciprocal 'friendship societies' with Western countries, as vehicles for unofficial diplomacy, reaching out to more sympathetic communities in the West and bypassing official channels. There were branches in all major Australian cities. In Canberra, we strictly avoided these venues: we knew the best way to get onto an ASIO file was to attend an Australia–Soviet Friendship Society function. Yet – as I can see now in retrospect – there were many good, well-meaning and non-political people in these societies, with genuine interests in the other country, and affections going back to family links and shared experience in World War II.

Such was the iron logic of the Cold War. Our role in Moscow was a very special, narrowly defined kind of diplomacy. Canberra's main concern was that the embassy staff should keep our heads down in Moscow and stay out of trouble to avoid any pretext for tit-for-tat expulsions,[4] and should keep our premises and personnel secure.

Why were we there at all? I surmise for reasons of solidarity in the US-led Western alliance; and perhaps because Canberra felt that our Foreign Affairs Department should make some sort of visible effort to develop independent knowledge and understanding of the Soviet Union, as a major world power and Permanent Member of the UN Security Council; that we should not rely totally on the intelligence reports being provided by our major allies, the United States and United Kingdom. In our own very modest way, we were possibly an additional Western listening post – at least, so we liked to believe. I think the truth is that we were diplomats on training wheels: we had little real idea of what was going on in Moscow, we just pretended that we did, and we relied on the vastly superior reporting capabilities of our American and British friends. And we tried to work on improving our Russian.

Looking back, I wonder to what extent we made worse our own isolation in Moscow. Would it have really been so risky to try to make a few Russian friends outside our diplomatic round? Could one not have found people with genuine common interests, not 'crocodiles', to escape from the strains of the Cold War for a while, get to know people with dachas, help them to dig or pick fruit in their home gardens, drink their homemade mead or spirits with them?

The Cold War isolation of our NATO circle of embassies was complete and airtight. The best I ever got to in Moscow was a mutual smiling greeting and a moment of shared small talk when meeting Russian strangers on a ski track deep in the woods, or a few minutes' friendly talk on a long-distance train – never prolonged, and never followed up.

My melange of bittersweet memories of Moscow – of living behind an unbreakable soundproof plate-glass window, looking in on a society of which I could never be any part – is perhaps why I get such vicarious pleasure out of reading Le Carré novels, with their intimate first-hand knowledge of the worlds of Cold War diplomacy and spying. His body of work tells the story of how the Cold War was being fought at the human level through so many years, and how it gradually dissolved in the late 1980s, to be replaced by new adversaries – international crime, corruption, terrorism.

The problems were far from only on our side. There was the assumption instilled in all Russians, through books, films and plays (I actually saw one in which the villain was an Australian diplomat!) that all Western diplomats in Moscow were duplicitous spies, people to be avoided. It always got a good laugh when I went back this time, in explaining to Russians I met who asked where and when I had learned such good Russian, to reply, 'I was a diplomat forty-five years ago' – meaningful pause – 'a spy'.

The younger Russian Foreign Ministry officials, professional career diplomats like me, with whom I had regular working contacts to arrange official visit programs and so on, were as apprehensive as we were about breaching security guidelines and drawing the attention of the KGB. I remember two of them – Mr Poseliagin and Mr Ustenko. The former was a jolly man, I am sure delightfully warm and funny with his family and friends at home, but nervous and shy with us.

The latter was a good-looking, athletic, also rather shy man. Maybe he was KGB? Or just rather big and strong for his claimed role? We would invite them to dinner parties at our flat and they came once or twice, always a tense and strained professional pair, never with their wives. They never invited us back to their homes or for lunches in their own ministry. But they were always happy to come to our big formal embassy receptions for Australian high-level delegations or on Australia Day and tuck in. Clearly they were constrained by tight security protocols, too. They did their job well within those ground rules.

Lydia Melnikova – our charming regular Russian home teacher with whom we became friends – invited us once to afternoon tea, but only at the very end of our posting when she must have finally felt it appropriate and safe to do so. It was a nice visit, and she and her husband were gracious hosts. They lived with their children in a bright and sunny flat in a modern white-painted apartment complex in the newer south-western suburbs, surrounded by parkland with flower beds, real green grass and ponds. But I felt sad that we only ever saw the way Lydia and her family lived just before we left.

There were a few Australian postgraduate students in Moscow who had a very different experience to ours, thrown into the bureaucratic rough-and-tumble of Moscow State University student life, and very poor indeed at the official dollar–ruble exchange rate. They did meet ordinary Russians – they attended courses conducted in Russian and lived in rooms at the imposing university building on Lenin Hills, but there were privations. Basic pharmaceuticals and toiletries were hard to get – we became an appreciated alternative source. Our student friends welcomed whatever little luxuries we could offer. The young Robert Dessaix and his charming wife, Elizabeth, were valued regular visitors, and a window for us into another side of Moscow life. We always admired their courage, curiosity and good spirits.

We enjoyed weekend breaks in Leningrad – easily accessible by the comfortable sleeper train the Red Arrow, and in a refreshing local country resort for diplomats called Zavidovo, about 100 kilometres north of Moscow on a peninsula surrounded by a sharp bend of the Volga River. Zavidovo was administered by the UpDK. It comprised a small central restaurant and hotel building, and around a dozen surrounding basic but charming dachas available for short-term rental by families. It had been built after World War II as a superior prisoner of war camp for captured German generals. Each had been allowed his own dacha and batman. It still had the aura of a comfortable prison. In summer we would have barbecues on our dacha lawn, swim or sail in the Volga, or in cold winters ski across the wide frozen river to wander on skis in pleasant forest hills on the other side. I enjoyed the peace and space of the place. And its views on a summer or winter day, of fields and forests and rivers and faraway village church golden domes shining in the sun, could be quite magical. It felt like the old Russia, though it was in some ways quite artificial.

We – especially our bored and confined wives and children – looked forward to our leave in Western Europe every few months. In our first leave, in early summer, Valerie and I and our baby, Patrick, took a relaxed three-day Russian sleeper train trip all the way to Venice, through Ukraine, Hungary, Serbia and Croatia. In autumn, we drove our German car up to Helsinki and rented a lakeside cottage in the Finnish lake district for a few days. We were pining just to have a normal sort of family holiday in our own world, at a price we could afford.

Did we know or care how the Russian people were faring under Brezhnev, whether life might be getting better or worse for them? Not really: this was not our primary reporting focus. We were not part of any Soviet Union aid project. We were more interested in who was on top in the Kremlin and what that might signify for Russian foreign policy. We were engaged in a Cold War with them, after all.

Still, we were friends with research specialists in the larger embassies who studied socio-economic questions. They told us it was clear that the economy was becoming better off, but coming up against real resource constraints as it tried to diversify and offer a better quality and range of cars and household goods. People were pressing hard for Western-standard cars and appliances, Western clothes, Western music and lifestyles. They were sick of second best, and they despised their own competing standardised Soviet products. They imported whatever and whenever they could.

Work-wise, there were so many other interesting things to monitor as well. How were the strategic arms-limitation talks going? The CSCE process in Helsinki? What was the real policy towards outspoken dissident writers: was it easing or hardening? Boris Pasternak had died in 1960, but Alexander Solzhenitsyn was still writing scorching *samizdat* (underground-published, illegally circulated) novels in Moscow. He was awarded the Nobel Prize for Literature in 1970 but refused to go to Stockholm to receive it for fear he would not be allowed back into his beloved homeland. Starting in 1970, dissident nuclear scientist Andrei Sakharov came under increasing pressure from the government. More and more Soviet Jews were openly behaving as a faith-based community and pressing for the right to emigrate to Israel, and Washington had made clear that a new Soviet policy not to impede this emigration would be an essential condition of détente. The system still seemed so strong and self-defining, and yet...

As for me, I had acclimatised to the life I had mapped out for myself in Moscow – perhaps too well. I had learned to enjoy its modest pleasures and predictability, to live quite simply and routinely, to enjoy our books, records and concerts, to grow red geraniums and herbs in pots in summer on our small balcony at home, to walk with our baby sons, and to ski in winter with diplomatic friends. I was making myself too much at home in Russia, committing the cardinal sin for a diplomat – *localitis*. Though I always behaved safely and followed security guidelines punctiliously, I was perhaps imperceptibly and without knowing it becoming to a degree 'Sovietised', in that I was coming to terms psychologically with the strange world around me.

For each time I went back West on leave, I felt more and more sharply the contrast of my now familiar grey Moscow with the bustle and bright lights and colours of Western cities. I found it almost physically painful to return on holiday to the West, until I adjusted back to Western pace, affluence and consumerism. I know I was not alone in this – some of my colleagues confessed to similar reactions. Flying to the West was a shock, like surfacing too quickly in a diving chamber – one needed time to decompress.

The department, in its wisdom, decided not to extend my posting beyond two years: the normal duration of a 'hardship post', as Moscow was designated. We had asked for an optional third year because I felt we were enjoying Moscow and I was doing well there professionally. Then my beloved grandmother, Josephine Schick, died of a heart attack in Sydney days before we were due to leave Moscow in September 1971, and I lost my poor mother, Minnie, in a road accident just a month later, so in retrospect it was a good thing that we were posted back to Australia when we were. But I felt a real sense of dislocation and loss when we left Moscow. Despite the constraints, it had been a uniquely interesting and rewarding two years.

Chapter 3

Laurie

Laurie Matheson (1930–87), Australia's Trade Commissioner to the Soviet Union in 1969–71 and subsequently founder of the private trading firm Commercial Bureau, which for a few years dominated Australian–Soviet trade, is a vivid Moscow memory for me. We were good friends and embassy colleagues. He was a mentor, a significant influence on my personal and professional growth. His unusual career is a story worth telling, because of his larger-than-life influence on Australian–Russian relations, and also on my own later life. Laurie made a difference in so many ways.

He was an impressive, enigmatic person. About a year after my posting ended, we lost personal contact as our life paths diverged. What I know of the last fifteen years of Laurie's life comes from Canberra gossip, and from more serious media reporting of the 1983 Hope Royal Commission into the Combe–Ivanov spy affair, in which Laurie played a reluctant major role.[1] David Marr's book *The Ivanov Trail* (1984) tells what is publicly known of the story of Prime Minister Bob Hawke's decision to expel alleged KGB spy Valery Ivanov, and the subsequent Hope Royal Commission into the circumstances surrounding that expulsion and David Combe's involvement. Marr's book presents Laurie's role in a quite negative light, reflecting left-progressive Australian opinion at the time. But this was not the Laurie Matheson I knew.

Laurie was a private man who hated publicity. There are very few photos of him. The best I have found is in Marr's book, a Fairfax press photo taken when he appeared as a witness in the Hope Royal

Commission in mid-1983.[2] The photo shows a still handsome but careworn face. I could only just recognise the Laurie I knew in happier times twelve years earlier.

The years 1982–83 were, I would guess, the most distressing in Matheson's life. He was forced by circumstances to denounce in an Australian Royal Commission a Soviet diplomat in Canberra, Valery Ivanov, as a probable KGB spy, an action contrary to all the rules of privacy and discretion by which Laurie had conducted his Australia–Soviet trade business. He knew his testimony would destroy his livelihood, which depended above all on discretion and maintaining good personal relations with senior Soviet Government trade officials. They would never trust him again. I am sure Laurie's early death from cancer in 1987 at the young age of fifty-seven was linked to those two years of public and private hell he would have endured during the Combe–Ivanov affair.

Laurie's phenomenally successful business career as an entrepreneur and middle man for Australian primary produce exports to Russia began when he opened the Heine Brothers office in Moscow in December 1972. When Heine Brothers withdrew from Moscow three years later to concentrate on its China trade agency, he took over the business, opening his own firm, Commercial Bureau Australia, in Moscow in January 1976. For the next six years, his firm enjoyed an effective monopoly as broker for Australian primary produce exports to the Soviet Union. From almost zero trade, he generated hundreds of millions of dollars' worth of new Soviet markets for Australian primary products, very quickly making Russia one of Australia's biggest agricultural customers. He rapidly became wealthy from brokerage commissions.

In 1982 a bitter legal dispute erupted between Matheson and a former employee and briefly junior partner, Bruce Fasham, who had now started a rival company, PACTRA (Pacific Commerce and Traders Company). PACTRA had very good political contacts within the NSW Labor Party and government, and wanted a piece of the action. Matheson felt the new firm was out to take over his business. Also, Prime Minister Malcolm Fraser's harsh anti-Soviet rhetoric and

Olympic Games sanctions over Afghanistan had damaged Australia's standing as a trade partner in Moscow. Commercial Bureau's business was eroding and it was now facing debts. Matheson was preparing for legal action against Fasham.

On 4 November 1982, Matheson engaged lobbyist David Combe, a former Labor Party National Secretary (1973–81) who boasted of his continuing strong Labor Party links, as a consultant to try to help him protect Commercial Bureau's public standing and business in Australia.

Over the next few months, Combe told Matheson about his developing friendship with Valery Ivanov. Combe apparently did not know that the Australian Security Intelligence Organisation (ASIO), tasked to protect Australia and its citizens from espionage and other threats to national security, already had Ivanov under surveillance as a suspected KGB spy. Thanks to a Soviet defector, the British had a list of names of KGB agents in London whom they were preparing to expel. This defector had also named Ivanov, and ASIO was building its own expulsion case against him.

Ivanov had presented himself to Combe as a diplomat interested in discussing politics and trade. ASIO soon became convinced that Ivanov was grooming Combe to be a KGB 'agent of influence', and to provide him with information and forecasts on Labor Party policies. No evidence was ever publicly cited by ASIO against Ivanov, beyond his so-called habits of 'clandestinity' in his friendly cultivation of Combe, indicating to ASIO that he was using the typical tradecraft of a KGB spy. This information had come to ASIO partly from its own observations of Ivanov – for example, his evasive driving habits, and partly from what Combe had told Matheson, who in turn told ASIO.

Was Matheson an ASIO 'operative', or was he a source of information who became useful to ASIO in building their case against Ivanov? The way Marr tells the story points towards the latter view, though Marr's opinion is not clear from his book.[3] There was no shortage of people who accused Matheson of being an ASIO operative.

It was routine ASIO practice to debrief any Australian businessman returning from Moscow, according to its counter-intelligence mandate. Matheson was obviously of keen interest to ASIO. Marr says that 'throughout the Moscow years, Matheson had provided

ASIO with information', but that he 'had broken with ASIO at the time he returned to take up permanent residence in Melbourne' in 1981. At some time very soon after Matheson engaged Combe on 4 November 1982, 'Matheson began once more to debrief ASIO'. Marr suggests a number of reasons why an always cautious Matheson would have thought it prudent to make sure he kept ASIO informed of his current dealings with Combe: 'Matheson wondered if ASIO was helping Fasham and PACTRA. He even wondered if Combe had been set on him by ASIO'.

Over the ensuing months, Matheson held at least two more meetings with his ASIO case officer. At one, he said, 'Combe suspected Ivanov was KGB'. At a second meeting on 15 April, he gave ASIO 'a version of the Russian's clandestinity warning' to Combe.[4]

On 5 March 1983, Bob Hawke became Labor Prime Minister. On 20 April, the Director-General of ASIO, Harvey Barnett, requested an urgent meeting with Hawke, at which he recommended Ivanov's immediate expulsion from Australia. Marr writes that Ivanov's observed 'clandestinity', and the informant report from London, seem to have been the main grounds for Barnett's case. A week later, Ivanov was duly expelled. Hawke was keen to convince the United States that his new government could be trusted to be a loyal US ally: he was not going to reawaken the American suspicions of the Labor Party dating back to Gough Whitlam's years as Australia's previous Labor Prime Minister (1972–75).

The Ivanov story was now leaking badly: the media quickly gleaned the background, including the roles of Combe and Matheson. Following mounting disquiet among senior Cabinet ministers, in particular the well-regarded, left-leaning Foreign Minister Bill Hayden, over the credibility of ASIO's clandestinity case which had now destroyed Combe's reputation and livelihood, Hawke decided to set up the Hope Royal Commission.

Matheson was the key Crown witness. Much of his testimony was presented *in camera* in a vain bid to protect his privacy, but his name and former career in Australian naval intelligence and then in Moscow soon became public knowledge. He was bitterly condemned by the Australian Left as part of its general suspicion of ASIO. In August 1983, a former South Australian Attorney-General denounced

Matheson in the South Australian Parliament in the strongest terms that would have been defamatory unless protected by parliamentary privilege. Matheson could not defend himself.

The Hope Commission reported in December 1983. It cleared Combe and ASIO, while endorsing Prime Minister Hawke's decision to expel Ivanov. Marr comments ironically that this was 'a difficult enough task, fraught with contradictions'.[5] Hope declared it was 'clear beyond argument that Ivanov was an active KGB agent cultivating Combe...to act, wittingly or unwittingly, as an agent of [Soviet] influence'.

This was exactly the outcome that Hawke wanted to have judicially endorsed. He soon organised a safe consolation prize for Combe – a minor Trade Commissioner job in Canada.

The real victim of the Hope Royal Commission process was Laurie Matheson. It left his public reputation and business in ruins. Laurie sold Commercial Bureau to Elders IXL in July 1984, and then seems to have retired. He died three years later. He left his widow, Christine, and their two young children, as well as three children from his first marriage to Ginny.

Laurie came into my office a week or so after my arrival in Moscow in 1969 and introduced himself. A compact man of middle height and easy good manners, he was thirty-nine at the time. He had neatly combed sandy hair and wore a smart navy wool overcoat and a grey Caspian-style Astrakhan lamb's wool cap. His voice was medium-pitched and pleasant: a 'navy' voice, British-accented with a slight hint of Scots brogue in the background. I can still hear that voice even now, even though it was so many years ago. In appearance, he could have been British or Scandinavian or Baltic German – he had the sort of clear, good-looking face that could be that of any well-educated official, businessman or military officer from a Northern European country. Think of Robert Redford at around the same age, and you will have a mental image of the man. He smiled easily, and had the casual charm and good manners of the former naval officer that he was.

Laurie had been stationed in Vienna since early 1969 with his wife, Ginny, and their three young children. Initially, he worked out of the Australian Trade Commission post there, headed by Rudi

Schneemann, who had the task of promoting Australian trade within all of Central and Eastern Europe.[6] Laurie initially held the official rank in Vienna of Assistant Trade Commissioner responsible for trade with the Soviet Union. His job was to build an intergovernmental base for the expansion of Australian primary produce exports to the Soviet Union, which were still very low in the cold diplomatic climate of Australian–Soviet relations after the Petrov and Skripov spy cases. But Britain had joined the European Union, and traditional Australian primary produce export markets in the United Kingdom were now under pressure from protectionist EU policies. Trade Minister and Deputy Prime Minister John McEwan was keen to build new markets in communist East Europe to replace the declining traditional British market. The resources boom was far in the future: Australia still relied heavily on food and fibre farm exports, and had chronic balance-of-payments problems.

The old Soviet economic autarky was beginning to break down. Soviet collectivised agriculture was chronically inefficient, and dependent on the vagaries of Russian weather. Brezhnev wanted to improve the food security of Soviet citizens. His government was looking to open up reliable low-cost sources of supply from the West to help it overcome harvest failures and food shortages. Though the Soviet Union had been unwilling to use its large foreign currency reserves for non-essential imports, and traditionally aspired to balanced bilateral trade, it was now able to sell gold abroad in quantity from its Siberian mines, developed at huge human cost by Gulag prison labour in the harsh Stalin years. It was ready to pay for essential imports – which now for the first time extended to reliable well-priced food commodities. The United States, Canada and Australia were the most obvious potential suppliers, as experienced growers and international exporters. McEwan saw a moment of opportunity to develop dependable, large new markets for Australian food exports. Canada and the United States were Australia's competitors.

On both sides, the legacies of Cold War mistrust, the fact that the Soviet Union produced sub-standard industrial goods of little export appeal to Western markets, and the bureaucratic conservatism and inertia of the Moscow trade bureaucracy, were major impediments to trade. It needed an unusual entrepreneurial man of charm, imagination, dogged persistence and good Russian cultural skills to do the hard yards of breaking open this huge potential market for Australia, by building sound relations with the suspicious, slow-moving Soviet trading bureaucracy. Laurie was that man.

His spectacular success can be measured by published trade statistics. Just in his first three years of work as Trade Commissioner, Australian exports to the Soviet Union trebled from $20.3 million in 1966/67 to $62.7 million in 1970/71. Over this same period, Soviet exports to Australia stagnated at around $2 million. When Laurie then went into private business as an Australia–Soviet commodities trader, first with Heine Brothers and then with Commercial Bureau, Australian exports to the Soviet Union grew even more dramatically, and by the end of the 1970s, they had risen to over $270 million.

Laurie's employer in 1969 was an unusual organisation. The Australian Trade Commissioner Service was proudly independent of the Department of Foreign Affairs. In 1969–71, the head of the Trade Commissioner Service reported directly to the formidable Trade Minister and Deputy Prime Minister, John McEwan. Trade Commissioners – their status at a zenith in the 1960s – did not easily accept the authority at post of Foreign Affairs ambassadors over their work in countries where both agencies had missions. They wanted the protection and prestige of Australian diplomatic status, but they also wanted a free hand in their trade work.

In 1958, Australia opened a Trade Commission in Sweden with responsibility for developing trade with communist Europe. Australia still had no diplomatic relations with the Soviet Union after the Petrov breach, nor did Foreign Affairs have an Embassy in Sweden. McEwan wanted the new Trade Commissioner in Sweden to have full diplomatic status to be able to do his job. Foreign Affairs prevaricated. McEwan insisted that Trade Commissioners had to have diplomatic status, because trade-promotion work in communist countries involved extensive negotiation with governments which control the import policies that determine access of Australian products to their markets. Also, he reasoned, contact at ambassador level with host country ministers would enable a trade post to better report on developments in agricultural policies likely to affect Australian interests.[7]

McEwan won the battle. In 1961, the Trade Commissioner in Sweden was given the diplomatic status of Chargé d'Affaires, Australian Embassy, Sweden. Foreign Affairs got the message that it had to get its ambassadors more involved in trade work if it wanted to remain on top. It demanded acceptance by Trade that Trade Commissioners could not be a separate independent Australian official presence. Their obligation was to work under resident ambassadors and keep them fully informed and involved in all important work contacts.

In September 1969, shortly before my arrival, Schneemann and Matheson had spent a month together touring the Soviet Union, mostly in Moscow. The purpose was to introduce Laurie formally to Soviet trade officials as Australia's Trade Commissioner Designate in Moscow. Schneemann had recommended to McEwan that a full resident Trade Commission be established in Moscow as soon as possible, with Laurie in charge of it.

The official history, which praises Schneemann for his contribution to developing Australian–Soviet trade, is more tight-lipped about Laurie:

> An essential part of this process was the opening of a trade post in Moscow in accord with Soviet wishes. Cabinet approval was obtained in 1970, but opening of the post was delayed until 1972 to allow time for suitable accommodation to be found. Matheson, a fluent speaker of Russian with a background in naval intelligence, was appointed the first Trade Commissioner. His appointment was unusual in the sense that his experience was limited to several years with Schneemann in Vienna, and he remained in Moscow as commissioner for only a short period. Language proficiency was not always given priority by the Trade Commissioner Service, but, in this case, it was the overriding consideration. Matheson resigned from the Service for personal reasons in 1973 but continued to be active in Australian–USSR trade in a private capacity.[8]

Ambassador Blakeney accompanied the two visitors to their first high-level meetings with the Ministry of Foreign Trade and with

Soviet export organisations. From then on, says Schedvin, 'gradually the trading relationship deepened'. During my two years in Moscow, Laurie visited every few weeks, staying in a hotel, building up his official contacts in the Soviet Trade Ministry and in Soviet export organisations. He was trying to help potential Soviet exports to Australia, and to promote Australian wheat, beef and wool exports to the Soviets. He had no contact with the Soviet Foreign Ministry. He used embassy transport and based himself (when in Moscow) at a spare desk in my office. He did not send many cables through the embassy classified system. Most of his communication back to Canberra or Vienna was conducted independently, using open telephones or telegrams. He wanted to show the Soviets that he was hiding nothing from them.

As I got to know Laurie, it quickly became clear to me that he was playing by very different rules to the rest of our embassy. Cold War talk and Kremlin hierarchy speculation did not interest him at all. He was, bluntly, his own man with his own agenda. He and the ambassador observed the office civilities, but I sensed a tension between them. They basically mistrusted each other's agendas, for good reason, which I was soon to discover.

It never occurred to me to doubt Laurie's story that he had been a Royal Navy submarine officer, who had taught himself Russian during long cruises at sea. But Laurie's Russian was just too good to have been learned as an off-duty hobby in submarines. It was fluent, almost accent-free, and to my ear, good enough for him to pass as a Russian speaker from the Soviet Baltic States. Laurie had a command of Russian idiom and literature, suggesting that he had attended a good Russian-language school for an extended period of study. But when, where and why?

Out of the Combe–Ivanov Royal Commission would come more detailed, authoritative public disclosures.[9] Laurie had had a tough childhood, brought up in orphanages and agricultural boarding high schools in New South Wales after his parents separated in 1938 when he was eight years old; he had joined the navy as a junior seaman at age seventeen; he had changed his surname from Phelan to his mother's maiden name of Matheson in 1948, aged eighteen; he had done an intensive Russian-language course at Point Cook Royal Australian

Air Force Languages Academy, Victoria, in 1954; he had become a commissioned naval officer in 1959; he had then worked as a 'supply officer', suggesting that he was 'a member of naval intelligence'. In 1967 he was secretary to the Commander of HMAS Cerberus, the naval station outside Melbourne. In that senior role he had helped on the beach, as a qualified diver, in the unsuccessful search for disappeared Prime Minister Harold Holt, though he was not one of the thirty-two frogmen officially engaged in that operation. In 1968 he had resigned from the navy at the rank of lieutenant, having been offered a position in the Australian Trade Commissioner Service.

The 2008 official history by Schedvin repeats what by then must have been public knowledge in Canberra – that Laurie was a fluent speaker of Russian with a background in naval intelligence.[10]

Had Laurie been using his Russian-language skills professionally over 1954–67, while working in naval intelligence? Was his claimed service on submarines something of a 'legend' (in Le Carré's term of art for a spy's cover story) to cover years of undeclared Western intelligence work? It would have never occurred to me at the time to ask such questions. It was not good manners to question one's colleagues' pasts. I did not even know Laurie was thirty-nine. I assumed he was just a few years older than me, and I was twenty-six.

Did the Soviet officials with whom Laurie dealt in Moscow believe his 'legend'? Possibly not, but it might have suited them to behave as if they did. There is, after all, a long tradition in Russia of people moving forwards and backwards between different kinds of career path, including between intelligence work and commercial work, and reinventing or burying past careers. As long as Laurie was doing a good job as Australia's Trade Commissioner, in ways that advanced Soviet objectives to secure access to high volumes of good low-cost Australian agricultural commodities, they would not have wanted to embarrass him by inquiring into his past. If the KGB was monitoring him, it would not have seen any reason to interfere with his duties, once they had satisfied themselves that he was doing nothing 'clandestine' in Russia now. And I do not believe he was, in the time I knew him there.

Ambassador Blakeney was an austere, authoritarian man, with a strong sense of proper lines of command and obedience. A few years younger than my father, Charles Kevin, who had died in 1968, he had great fondness and respect for my father. That affection translated into benevolence towards me, which I felt duty bound to reciprocate. Also, I quite liked him.

Blakeney's strong view was that Laurie could have no secrets from him about his work in Moscow, under the standing protocols that ambassadors needed to know what all embassy staff – including attached staff from other departments – were doing. That included Laurie, until an incident which completely destroyed their working relationship.

Laurie felt that the ambassador was locked into outmoded Cold War ways of thinking, and had no understanding of the importance for Australia of his trade-promotion work in Moscow. For Laurie, the Cold War was rapidly becoming old history: Russia was becoming a consumer society, and Australia was moving into a world of globalised trade and ruthless competition for new commodity markets; a game in which our closest political allies were also our sharpest trade rivals. Australian exporters and the entire economy desperately needed to develop major new markets and it was his job to help them do so. Laurie told me his commercial-in-confidence work to develop trust and cooperation with suspicious Russian trade officials had nothing at all to do with Blakeney's Cold War focus. Laurie was confident he would have Minister McEwan's support for such strong views.

Laurie told me that he had tried repeatedly to explain to Blakeney how vital it was not to discuss his trade-promotion work at all with other Western ambassadors. The ambassador just did not get it.

For Blakeney, the real business in Moscow was the Cold War high-diplomacy discussion he shared with his NATO colleagues – Kremlin leadership gossip, European and American ministerial visits, the SALT talks, the Helsinki process, the latest dissident news, Jewish emigration and proxy wars in the Third World. The sad thing was that Blakeney would not have had a great deal to offer his colleagues in return. Canberra was far away, and we were too small an embassy to produce useful at-post independent research. There was just not enough happening in Australian–Soviet diplomatic relations to share with his colleagues. Ministerial visits were extremely rare, if ever. We were really only a spectator in the great Cold War game. The temptation for Blakeney must have been very high to just drop a few hints – very little detail, he would have assured Laurie – about what his energetic young Trade Commissioner was doing in Moscow. The US and Canadian ambassadors were no doubt curious, and would have been urged by their parent trade-promotion agencies back home to try to find out more. And so the crisis brewed.

Meanwhile, Laurie and I were having something of a bromance. I was proud of my new friend. I missed male friendships my own age. Laurie became a sort of an admired older brother. He enjoyed my company, too, or seemed to. Certainly, it was a break from his Moscow round of appointments with Soviet trade officials for meetings, business lunches and dinners, which must have become quite exhausting and tedious. And the hours alone afterwards in his hotel room would have been lonely, too. He helped me build a Mirror sailing dinghy from a British flatpack kit, in an unused attic above the consulate, and we sailed it together on nearby lakes on some summer weekends. We found we both had shared enthusiasms for Russian history and literature and culture, and for good food and wine. He quoted Pushkin verse with ease and enjoyment, and much of what I learned about Russian food and wine and public behaviour I learned with Laurie – he introduced Valerie and me to some of the hotel restaurants off the usual diplomatic beaten track, to the riverboat nightclubs, to some walks and picnic places. With Laurie, going out in Moscow even for a weekend walk was a bit of an adventure. I felt that with him I was breaking out a little from the stodginess of my regulated diplomatic life, tasting some of the reality of Moscow.

Valerie was generous and hospitable – we often invited Laurie around to our home for a family dinner when he had a free night – but she did not have the same enthusiasm for his company that I did. I think she could see with her feminine intuition that I was a bit out of my depth with this charming and sophisticated new older friend, and she wanted to keep some restraints on the friendship. She did not trust his urbanity and smoothness, and at times he talked down to her, which irritated her. We visited Laurie and his family in Vienna on an early trip to the West to stock up on things we needed for our flat. We all got on well and it was good to see that our wives liked each other.

One day about halfway through my posting, Laurie came into my office in an icy rage such as I had never seen, saying words to this effect:

> That fool at the other end of the corridor is making my job impossible. I am pursuing secret negotiations with the Russians to develop new markets for our wheat and beef, potentially worth millions of dollars to Australia. I keep him informed as he insists I do, but now I know for certain that he passes everything I tell him to the Americans and Canadians. They give him diplomatic titbits of no importance, and in return he gives them secrets about my trade discussions that are of huge commercial importance, which could allow them to undercut us in negotiations and take away Australian business. I am not going to tell him anything from now on about my work!

I am sure Laurie took his complaint to his superiors in Canberra, and that McEwan would have instructed the Trade Department to take it up with Foreign Affairs. My guess is that there would have resulted Foreign Affairs guidance to Blakeney to leave Matheson more professional space. From then on, Laurie's relations with the ambassador were correct but minimal. They had nothing more to say to each other.

And I had an interesting early experience in learning how to live with and manage conflicting professional and personal loyalties. Laurie was by now a good friend, and I respected the strength of his grievance, yet I continued also to respect my ambassador's expertise and judgement in East–West relations, and his authority over me in the embassy. Both men were right, by their own lights.

I see now that Laurie's rage was not just about the content of anything Blakeney might have revealed to his American or Canadian colleagues. For Laurie, literally his whole new career as a trade diplomat was on the line. He had burned his navy career boats, and he was trying to build the confidence of his Soviet trade interlocutors. He must have known that the KGB would have guessed at his former naval-intelligence background and would be watching him for any questionable behaviour. He had to convince the Trade Ministry that he was a genuine trade diplomat now, and nothing more. The last thing he needed was for his name and activities to be bandied about in NATO cables or conversations that might be picked up and reported back to Soviet intelligence. The Cold War was still very much a reality. Laurie did not want his new career to be sacrificed to it. He had a unique job to do and it was in the Australian national interest that he be left to get on with it. He was an angry man because he thought Blakeney just could not see these realities.

Years later, I read the excellent memoir by Robert Bruce Lockhart on his dramatic years as British 'Agent' (Chargé d'Affaires) in Moscow after the 1917 Bolshevik Revolution, which had left traditional Foreign Office diplomats in Saint Petersburg completely unprepared and ineffective.[11] I suspect Laurie might have read and been inspired by this book. He saw how the Soviets had come to trust and engage with Lockhart, though they well knew his intelligence background and his loyalty to the British Government of the day, because they knew Lockhart had come to love Russia and was trying to understand the agonies the country was going through; and, within the limits of his job, trying to help Russia, as well as serving his own country. I think that was what Laurie was aspiring to do.

When I went home in October 1971, I was replaced by Christine Salvaris – a vibrant, well-regarded young Australian diplomat. She inherited my flat. Laurie was still commuting in Moscow hotels, waiting to be offered suitable accommodation befitting his status. They fell in love. Their relationship became public knowledge and both were summarily recalled home in disfavour. The new Australian ambassador in Moscow refused to have Laurie back at the post. Laurie tried to repair his marriage, but it did not work out. He resigned from the Trade Commissioner Service and joined the Melbourne trading firm Heine Brothers. Christine resigned from Foreign Affairs and they soon married. Laurie was offered a spacious family apartment in Moscow (with the support of the Soviet Trade Ministry), where he set up with Christine their new home and office.

To the envy of the Americans and Canadians, Australia now had the inside track in the Soviet agricultural import trade. Heine

Brothers, and its successor Commercial Bureau, negotiated several years of huge contracts for the supply of keenly priced Australian primary products to the Soviet Union. In just a few years, Laurie had fulfilled John McEwan's dream of a new East European market.

I hope that one day there may be a proper, sympathetic assessment of Laurie's life and contributions to the public interest. He was harshly judged in Australia in his sad final years. Marr did as well as one could with the material available to him from the Hope Commission, and in the contentious spirit of the times. But one day, free of the bitter Left–Right passions of those years, someone should try to do justice to Laurie's remarkable life: his tough childhood, his ascent from seaman to officer, his naval-intelligence career whatever it was, his genuine affection for Russia, his complex relationships and loyalties, and how he dealt with it all according to his own conscience.

The nicest memory I have of Laurie was of an overnight train journey we made one weekend to Kharkov and Poltava in the Soviet Ukraine. Kharkov, the second city in Ukraine, was a miniature Moscow of no particular interest. Poltava – which had monuments and a museum set in a lovely country area – was the site of the last major Russian–Swedish battle in 1709, when forces led by Tsar Peter the Great defeated an invading Swedish army led by King Charles XII. The battle is said to have marked the end of Sweden's European Empire, and the real beginning of Russia's European Empire. It was a site Russians revered.

It was my first train trip in Russia and I was pretty apprehensive and ill-at-ease. Laurie wasted no time. I soon found him reciting Pushkin verse to a pair of admiring tea ladies at the end of our sleeper carriage. From then on, they could not do enough for us.

When Laurie died in 1987, his widow had erected on his gravestone according to his wishes a specially commissioned life-size stone sculpture by an artist friend, of a shapely reclining naked woman. It was a fitting memorial to a man who had defied convention and who had loved poetry, art and beauty in his sadly short life. Rest in peace, Laurie. *Pokoysya s mirom.*

PART TWO

THERE...

Chapter 4

Quiet Days in Moscow

Moscow Home Hostel in Khamovniki was a small family business: several former apartments on two floors, ingeniously repartitioned into a low-budget hostel. It was perfectly suited to my needs and budget, at around US$30 a day for a basic private room with a tiny shower and WC. It was always warm and secure, and was usually quiet. The reception staff were always ready to help with local advice, arranging a pre-dawn taxi to the airport or in-house laundry, or just to chat.

Most of the guests were young Russians and Ukrainians starting or looking for new jobs in the city. They would gather in the street outside the front door to smoke and gossip (like all Moscow public buildings, the hostel banned smoking indoors). They must have found my comings and goings wrapped in my woollen overcoat, gloves, scarf and fur hat or cap as odd as I found them, bare-headed in their spartan young people's all-year uniform of quilted parka, tee-shirt, jeans and sneakers. They did not seem to register the cold, and after a few weeks of acclimatisation I felt it less, too, starting to shed layers of clothing. It was an unusually warm winter in Moscow: an intense heat island sat over European Russia, driving February temperatures in Moscow up to 10–15 degrees Celsius above the long-term average. Moscow really did not have a winter in 2016 – not a winter as Muscovites remember it. Christmas and New Year had been entirely snow-free until a twenty-centimetre snowfall in late January a few days before my arrival, and this snow had already disappeared from the streets by late February.

I took the metro up to the city centre to see what was playing at the Tchaikovsky Conservatorium Hall, Moscow's best concert venue. I was so lucky – this evening offered a testimonial concert in honour of a famous Bolshoi Opera grande dame, soprano Yelena Obraztsova, who had passed away in 2015. In Canberra I had seen a YouTube video of her 75th Birthday Gala Concert at the Bolshoi Theatre in 2014, attended by Prime Minister Medvedev and featuring top-line Bolshoi opera artists like Dmitri Hvorostovsky and Anna Netrebko, and I knew how well-loved she had been by Moscow opera-goers. At the conservatorium ticket office I managed to score one of the few good seats left, for 1200 roubles – about fifteen dollars. I found it helps to be alone – pairs of seats are harder to come by for popular concerts, but the odd single can usually be found.

It was a lovely concert – around twelve well-known soloists on the Moscow opera scene, accompanied by a very good house orchestra. They sang a mixed repertoire of operatic favourites – Gluck, Mozart, Rossini, Donizetti, Verdi, Puccini, Mussorgsky, Tchaikovsky, Rimsky-Korsakov, Dvorak, Gounod, Bizet, Bellini, even Lehar: something for everyone. The singers came from many parts of the former Soviet Union – Abkhazia, Georgia, Moscow, Saint Petersburg, Stavropol, Ukraine, and even neighbouring Mongolia. The Georgians, a soprano and a tenor, were especially popular. This concert might have been a moment of nostalgia for the rich musical life of the former Soviet Union – Obraztova's musical career began around 1960 and spanned fifty years.

I was struck by the broad age spread of the audience – it included many young people, teenagers and children; also by the general enthusiasm and civility; and by how well dressed everyone was. It was a lively, sophisticated concertgoer crowd.

I was to find this was the normal Tchaikovsky Conservatorium scene. Midwinter is high season for live classical music in Moscow – during my three weeks there, I attended six more top-class concerts featuring five different orchestras and three soloists:

- The New Russia State Symphony Orchestra, highlighting the Mozart *Requiem*.
- Pianist Alexander Shtarkman playing Beethoven, Brahms, Scriabin and Prokofiev sonatas.

- The Musica Viva Moscow Chamber Orchestra performing Vivaldi's *Four Seasons* and *Gloria*.
- The State Academic Symphony Chamber Orchestra of Russia and pianist Andrei Korobyenikov playing Rachmaninov and Mahler.
- The Russian National Orchestra playing Wagner's *Siegfried Idyll* and more Mahler.
- Violinist Vladimir Ivanov with the Moscow Conservatorium Chamber Orchestra playing Bach violin concertos.

After the concert I dropped in at the next-door Coffeemania cafe. This was the favourite after-theatre watering hole of conservatorium performers and guests. It had a real inner-city buzz, interesting food, and was filled with beautiful people of all orientations. It was such a pleasure to dine there, and I was made very welcome despite being alone and older than most of the regular crowd. I tried to think of what it reminded me of – maybe a little of the feeling of Renoir's famous 1880 painting *Luncheon of the Boating Party*? Elegance, beauty, youthful energy...eventually I tore myself away and made my way home. But I made a point of going there often, and became a known regular.

I had planned to spend much of my Russian sojourn based in Moscow, allowing myself days for short overnight trips away. I wanted to allow myself time to settle into a routine as a temporary resident of this huge, fast-moving city. I hoped that as a solo traveller with some degree of Russian-language ability, I might taste something of life as lived by Muscovites. My two visiting friends, Grahame and later Julian, were keen to share the big sightseeing trips with me, which left me a few quiet days alone to wander the city, absorb its moods and meet a few people. Even while Grahame and Julian were in town, I had a little time on my own each day commuting to and from their hotels, often dropping in to one of my local cafes for a late-night coffee or cognac on my way home to bed.

I stayed in Khamovniki, the area south-west of the Kremlin where the Moscow River makes a huge loop around the Luzhniki Sports Complex and the Novodevichy Convent and famous cemetery.

Khamovniki is a quiet residential district of better-quality older apartment buildings, much favoured by young financial district workers because it is only a few stops away on a direct metro line, the No. 1 Red Line, into the Lubyanka–Kitay-Gorod business district. This Red Line, opened in 1935 under Stalin, was the first Moscow metro to be constructed. It runs north-easterly from the Moscow State University district west of the Moscow River, across the river and through three stops in Khamovniki, then on through the central city out to beyond Sokolniki Park. It stops at some of Moscow's most important city locations – Kropotkinskaya near the huge newly rebuilt Cathedral of Christ the Saviour, Biblioteka Imeni Lenina (Lenin Library) near the main public entrance into the Kremlin, Okhotny Ryad near Red Square and the Bolshoi Theatre and the top four city hotels (Four Seasons, Metropole, National, and Ritz-Carlton), Kuznetsky Most near Lubyanka and Kitay-Gorod, and Komsomolskaya near the main Saint Petersburg railway station. Because I used this metro line more often than any other to go into the city for concerts or to meet Grahame in Okhotny Ryad, or Julian in Kuznetsky Most, I got to know its character at different times of the day.

The metro system continues to grow, opening new stations and extending lines far out into the Moscow suburban regions. This metro is one of the wonders of the modern world. Modelled on the London and Paris metro systems, it is much larger in scale. The distances between stations are long, up to twenty minutes of walking. The system is made up of eight separate intersecting radial lines and one circular line (with an outer ring line being planned). They cross one another at different depths underground, and some go very deep. The deepest stations were used as air-raid shelters during World War II. Sometimes lines intersect at stations with a single name as at Park Kultury, with simple escalator connections between lines, but more often there are connecting underground passageways between up to three nearby stations, each station having its own name and line-identifying colour. It takes time to get to know the complex geography of these interwoven subterranean mazes.

The trains – there must be thousands of them – run at two- to three-minute intervals all day every day around the whole system, closing only between 1.00 am and 5.30 am. They are noisy but reliable. The stations are warm, clean and well policed. The older central city stations are decorated with murals, statuary, columns and arches. There is almost no advertising. Despite the noise and bustle of clanging trains and the huge numbers of commuters moving around, people feel safe in the metro: they crowd onto busy platforms, seemingly secure in the knowledge that they will not be shoved under an oncoming train. I saw no hooliganism in these metro stations or on the trains. Entrance turnstiles were policed carefully, to pick up anyone who might look like a potential troublemaker on the way in. All suitcases or large bags had to go through airport-style security scanners at entrances. Escalators were constantly monitored for threats by watchful guards sitting at the bottom.

The flow of people at peak hours was breathtaking: the long open escalator galleries were filled with people, commuting purposefully up and down. Sure-footed people in a hurry ran up or down on the left-hand side of the escalator, even wearing high heels, as the rest of us stood patiently on the right.

Early mornings I would see service workers (cleaners, hotel workers and the like) and groups of smartly uniformed military and police in fur hats, on the way to work or training courses. Then between 8.30 and 10.00 am, shop and office workers and business people in suits (most shops and offices in central Moscow open at ten and close at six). Later in the morning, I would see well-dressed ladies going into the city for shopping or lunch, and retired folk like myself moving around. Early in the evening there was the theatre and restaurant crowd heading into the centre. And always, students. Most Moscow residents use the metro, supplemented by local regional trains, electric trolley-buses and motor buses and walking, for all their daily and weekend transport needs. One really does not need to take taxis, much less to own a car, in this densely populated city that is so well served by public transport.

From about 8.30 am, the crowd catching the train at my local station, Park Kultury, was predominantly made up of young city workers in their twenties to forties. The young women were a treat to the eyes: mostly tall and slim, attractively made up and hair-styled, beautifully dressed in fur coats or well-tailored wool overcoats with fluffy fur collars, polished leather boots, handbags or briefcases, gloves, hats or scarves and muffs of every kind. I was surrounded by so many young people of high fashion sense and elegant appearance. If these were the daughters or wives or mistresses of rich oligarchs, I can only say there must be many rich oligarchs in Moscow. I would say rather that most were young women in middle-class jobs or professions who wanted to look their best at work: an impression confirmed by the large numbers of pharmacies, beauty and hairdressing salons, spas, and clothing boutiques and drycleaners around Khamovniki and nearby Prechistenka.

And the way they moved: that lovely, long-legged purposeful young Russian women's stride, with nothing coquettish or flirtatious about it at all. They walked like women who knew where they were going and were determined to get there as fast as possible, and with the same hundred-mile stares. Every morning on the Park Kultury platform was like a Paris winter fashion show.

The men were less style conscious but still neat and tidy. Younger businesspeople favoured smart parkas with fur collars rather than overcoats. They usually went bare-headed except on the coldest days, or at most wore a Gatsby-style tweed cap: I rarely saw the old-fashioned *shapka*s (fur hats with earflaps), except on older people and uniformed soldiers or police. I saw quite a few beards. I was struck at how many slim, tall, good-looking young Russian men I saw: very few had the squat stocky build that I remembered from Soviet times. Better diets and medical care since childhood had encouraged, at least in the young Moscow better-off, a taller more Northern European physique.

Ethnicity was mixed: more Slav than anything else, I would say, but by no means uniformly so. I saw many faces I would guess to be Jewish, Georgian, Armenian, Baltic German or Scandinavian. And Turkic, Tatar, Central Asian or Siberian. Maybe because it was winter, but I saw or heard few recognisable Western Europeans or Americans, either as tourists or resident expatriates. I am told that the number of Westerners living and working in Moscow has declined considerably in recent years from its peak in 1995–2000, and what I saw on the metro confirmed this. Almost all the voices I heard around me, regardless of ethnic appearance, were speaking fluent Russian. And more and more, when I was walking or on the metro, as I always dressed smartly, I was assumed to be a retired local: people started asking me the way in Russian.

Where were the older people and children, whom I did not see in large numbers around Khamovniki? A lot of them apparently live in family-owned dachas, in the outer suburban or nearby rural areas. I saw many of these dacha communities on train journeys out from the city: they are not slums, but well-laid-out and serviced rural village settlements often close to a commuter train station, comprising timber houses of varying sizes, from basic small kit homes no bigger than a garage, to quite spacious two-storey homes on quarter-acre blocks in neat snowy streets. I could see snowed-in orchards and glasshouses and vegetable plots, garages and hobby workshops, pickling kitchens – this is how many retired Muscovites spend their days: reading, cooking, walking in the forest, watching television, while their children go to work in the city, and live in flats in places like Khamovniki that were formerly (and perhaps still legally are) their parents' home properties by title deed since the 1990s privatisation.

Families come together at the weekends, when parents come into the city or the kids go out to the dacha to see their parents. Some younger children would live with their grandparents in the dacha areas and attend local preschools or primary schools; when teenagers, as they become more independently mobile, they would move back to the family flats in Moscow to attend high schools. I saw something of this in the Khamovniki area. On weekends, I saw a lot of three-generation families.

In places like Presnya–Barrikada or the northern urban districts around the Dostoevsky metro station and the Gulag and Jewish Museums, I saw more of a mix of older and younger people and children. I did not have time to see all of metropolitan Moscow, so these impressions don't claim to be scientific. I am sure there are many poorer areas, and my upper-middle-class area of Khamovniki would not be representative of an average. But then, every city has local variations in income and amenity and 'street feel'.

Under the post-communist privatisation process, many people were simply given legal title to the state-owned flats in which they had been living on low rents for decades. And this, I believe, is what has solidified in Khamovniki and the nearby Prechistenka, Arbatskaya and Kropotkinskaya districts their special middle-class character, even today. For these were the preferred residential areas of the better-off urban professional middle-class and academic and political intelligentsia, both in Tsarist and Soviet times. Dotted with palaces and churches and museums, these older districts are also graced with beautiful early twentieth-century Russian Art Nouveau and constructivist-style high-end apartment buildings. Much has been demolished and replaced by lesser-value, more modern buildings, but a lot of the old character survives.

These were the areas where the 'children of the revolution', or the 'Children of the Arbat', the Soviet intellectual and cultural elite, enjoyed quite comfortable lives in the early communist years.[1] And these streets have their own dark Stalinist memories, too: so many innocent formerly privileged young people were arrested here, from these same apartments, for concocted or minor security offences, to disappear into the Gulag and often never return. Their parents' high party status did not protect these young people from Stalin's paranoia or from Beria's harsh secret police teams, who hated well-off or educated people and were free to draw up their own interrogation and arrest lists.

The old huge Communist Party motivational signs were all gone, but a large Coca-Cola sign towered over the fourteen-lane ring road, Zubovsky Boulevard, near my hostel, as if to say, 'Look, the West is here!' But there wasn't a lot of in-your-face advertising. In European style, streetscapes were generally free of advertising apart from discreet business and cafe shopfront signs.

The buildings were in generally good repair, freshly painted and rendered. There were construction cranes visible around the city, but it did not feel like a construction boom. Even the construction sites had safety screens around them, painted to look like classical facades. Near my hostel, I soon found all that I needed for a comfortable urban life: a shoe-repair kiosk, a dry-cleaning depot, a tailor for clothing repairs, a bank to change dollars, a grocery supermarket and street-food kiosks and cafes.

Zubovsky Boulevard, the nearby Ring Road, was daunting – sixteen lanes of busy peak-hour traffic wide, with just forty-four timed seconds to walk briskly across on pedestrian green. No time to dawdle or stumble on the icy road. Such timed pedestrian crossings were numerous in central Moscow and motorists respected them, with on-the-spot-fines police keeping watch.

A lot of effort went into keeping the major streets and pedestrian pavements swept clean of snow and black ice chipped away. The old good housekeeping tradition to keep one's street frontages free of snow is still in force. Moscow takes even heavy snowfalls in its stride. One sometimes has to walk warily and watch for mini-avalanches and falling icicles from roofs, and standards of snow-clearing fall away in quieter side streets. But even in winter, I found Moscow a walker-friendly city. And when one got cold, there was always a nearby cafe to slip into and get warm.

I spent a fair amount of time relaxing in warm cafes. These are private businesses, often franchised, but each has its own character. With my Russian chip in my iPad giving me 3-G coverage throughout Moscow and the other cities I visited, and many cafes offering wi-fi, I could while away the spare hours sipping coffee, writing email letters to my family and friends in Australia, sending photos to my Facebook page and catching up a little on Australian news. I would browse favourite international news sites – the *Guardian*, *New York Times*, *Moscow Times*, *Russia Today* and *Russia Insider* (www.rt.com and www.russia-insider.com), and check the latest weather on the accurate local Russian weather channel, www.gismeteo.com. I felt connected to the outside world, yet free of it. As the snow drifted down, I sat snug indoors, happily nursing a coffee or a glass of wine or cognac: winter life, Moscow-style. Not a bad place to be, if one was retired and with enough money and time to enjoy these simple pleasures.

As on the metro, I was struck by the civility and politeness of waiters and customers in the cafes. Some people were busy with their mobile phones, but there were also conversing couples and groups. Sometimes mothers dropped in with small children for an after-school treat. People were well dressed and spoke softly – I rarely heard loud or raised voices. They seemed fairly self-contained, reserved people, who would smile rather than laugh. Personal space was respected in the cafes I frequented: I was never stared at, much less hassled. It was easy to exchange pleasantries with staff, without being obtrusively questioning.

One of my nearby favourites was a wine bar on Prechistenka called Obraz Zhizny (Way of Life). It did indeed have an extensive wine list, including surprisingly a d'Arenberg Stump Jump shiraz from South Australia, which had travelled well, and some equally good South African reds. But all the wines were expensive, and Russian vodka was by far the most economical way to drink alcohol. And I discovered vodka went so well with blini and smoked salmon or red caviar, or herring on black bread...so I finished up drinking rather more vodka than wine in Russia. Obraz Zhizny offered their own house vodka by the flask in an excellent 'business lunch' menu. They were originally an Israeli restaurant and the menu still had an Eastern Mediterranean flair, with dishes like felafel.

There were some excellent French-style cafes and bakeries. One of the best was Paul's, near the Foreign Ministry. Also, Pain du Jour near my metro station. For a larger meal, the Kuznetsky Most Brasserie was excellent. The lounges of big prestige hotels like the Metropol and the National were a pleasure to visit for morning or afternoon tea. Because I did not look like a tourist, I could come and go as I pleased in these places favoured by locals. I was lucky the exchange rate was so favourable to me, that I could enjoy them within my budget − a few years ago, this would not have been the case.

The old Moscow of the 1960s seemed a distant bad memory. This was a bright, elegant European city now, and it was all accessible. Having some Russian helped me enormously to overcome initial feelings of strangeness as I moved around the city, and opened all doors for me. I had been expecting to encounter many people wanting to practise their English as in so many parts of the world these days, but this proved not to be the case − perhaps a sign of how far and how fast Russia is now withdrawing from any excessive enthusiasm to get close to the West. It seemed an assured, self-sufficient culture. It was not that I ever felt personally disliked or feared as a Westerner, but rather that I picked up a calm attitude of 'you are in our country, and we really like it − and you − when we see you are clearly making an effort to speak our language'.

The dourness and unfriendliness that Western visitors so often speak of encountering in Russia melts away, if one can succeed in communicating in Russian even a little. Initially guarded faces relax and light up in smiles. Finally, I understood what Laurie Matheson had been trying to do all those years ago with his recitals of Pushkin verse to the carriage ladies on trains.

I would think this has to go beyond just mechanically learning a few token guidebook phrases, memorised Berlitz-style. Russian is a highly structured grammatical language that takes some groundwork effort, but for anyone planning to spend any time in the country, the mental effort to reach a basic street-conversation level of facility is well worth it. And then it builds…and builds.

I was fortunate to have had a good grounding back in 1968 at the Australian National University Russian Department. Now, during 2015, I was able to resurrect that buried knowledge with the help of the *New Penguin Russian Course*,[2] an excellent and thorough course book for beginners. I practised my accent and speed-reading using a cheerful inexpensive conversational Russian online audiovisual course, offered by Babbel. I watched many popular Russian melodrama films (without subtitles) on YouTube, to get used to the rhythm and speed of real spoken Russian. These YouTube films were actually a good introduction to contemporary Russian life and values. Their predictable romantic or crime-film plots gave me the (initially false but gradually more assured) confidence that I could pick up on what was happening on-screen. It all must have helped, because after my first two weeks of fairly stilted efforts in Russian, my language facility finally clicked in during my weekend in Yekaterinburg in Siberia. It was like a key being turned in a door. At last, I was fluent enough to chat easily with hotel receptionists, bartenders, waiters, taxi drivers and casual acquaintances. It was so enjoyable to break through the language barrier.

Food is an interesting subject. I had wondered, after reading reports for two years of escalating tit-for-tat European and Russian sanctions over Ukraine, and remembering the dire warnings of my friends, just how much good food would be left in Moscow? But my friends need not have worried. My local mini-supermarket was stuffed full of recognisable brands of European foods and wines, along with local brands at cheaper prices. Although midwinter, there was plenty of fresh food from the south. Armenian and Georgian cognac and wines were on sale, alongside French, Italian and local Black Sea–region brands. Pellegrini mineral water was everywhere. The deli section was excellently stocked with a wide range of hams and meat smallgoods and fish products and varieties of fresh and pre-packaged cheeses, both Russian and imported. Plenty of teas, coffees, chocolates and biscuits and takeaway frozen dinners...I saw no sign of any food shortages or queues or price inflation. I wanted for nothing. Admittedly, this was in Park Kultury district.

Similarly in restaurants, I was pleased to see my local Georgian restaurant, the Guria, was serving the same fine Georgian wines that I remembered from the Aragvi in 1970.

Everything in Moscow just felt pretty safe and normal to me. Tourists want to see as much as possible of a city's major historic and cultural sites, and those sites are well and conspicuously guarded by police as potential terrorism targets. But off the beaten tourist track, it was easy just to kick back and relax into local communities. To me, Moscow now felt like a welcoming city, and I never felt watched by anyone.

I encountered just one political street demonstration, an important and worthy one, on a busy bridge near the Kremlin, where veteran liberal politician Boris Nemtsov was murdered in 2015 by unknown assassins who shot him from a passing car as he strolled home with his girlfriend. Clearly, it was a politically motivated professional killing and the murderers have so far not been found or arrested, though they are suspected of being Chechen security agents. A standing human rights activist presence was being maintained at the site, with daily fresh flower wreaths in profusion. I have no doubt this demonstration will continue. Activists were quietly explaining to interested passers-by what it was about, and people were engaging with them. They told me they were hopeful justice would eventually be done. I saw no obvious signs of police surveillance of the demonstration, though numbers were constrained by law to two or three activists at a time on this narrow pedestrian walkway.

Chapter 5

Peredelkino and Boris Pasternak

On my fourth day in Russia, I caught an early-morning Moscow-region train out from Kievsky Station, on my way to Boris Pasternak's country home at Peredelkino. For many years I had loved his famous novel *Doctor Zhivago*. I wanted to learn more about his life, and to get some personal sense of the family home in which he spent his last twenty-five most creative years (1935–60), and where he wrote this masterpiece. I knew that *Doctor Zhivago* – especially after the popular David Lean film (1965) starring Julie Christie and Omar Sharif brought it a mass world audience – had been influential in the collapse of Soviet communism and the resurrection in Russia of a society aspiring to respect individual values. In his life and work, Pasternak had become a key symbol of passive resistance, first to the harsh autocracy of Stalin, and later to the much softer autocracy of Khrushchev.

Today, sixty years after its first publication, Pasternak's novel is still a key to better East–West understanding. It has the power still to introduce a new generation of Western readers to Pasternak's feelings about his beloved Russia, and its travails under civil war and communism – 'I made the whole world weep at the beauty of my land' – and about the authoritarian forces against which he quietly but valiantly contended in his later years. It is a tragic, complicated but at the same time inspiring story of a very brave Russian, and the difference he made in the world. Pasternak indeed was Doctor Zhivago.

At Maxim Gorky's suggestion (Gorky, a highly esteemed and utterly loyal communist writer, was president of the powerful Soviet Writers' Union), Stalin in 1934 approved the establishment of a new 'writers' colony' in a quiet forest area near Moscow, with around fifty comfortable new wooden dachas imported from Germany. Lifetime low rents for these country homes were to be granted to the most prestigious and favoured members of the Writers' Union, as a way of rewarding their loyalty to the Soviet state and ensuring their continued adherence to socialist realist values in their work.

Peredelkino was chosen: a small village in a quiet and beautiful forested area on a former large aristocratic estate, about 25 kilometres west of Moscow, with its own station on the regular Moscow–Kaluga railway line. Pasternak, aged forty-five and then at the height of his popularity as an approved Soviet poet, was one of the lucky few. From 1935 onwards, he lived here quietly with his family in a modest two-storey timber dacha on a five-acre block until his death in 1960 aged seventy, his writer's peace seemingly undisturbed until his last four stressful years.

In 1988, the house was proclaimed as a state memorial ('*Dom-muzei Pasternaka*') by Gorbachev. Until then, it had been insecurely inhabited by Pasternak's widow and children. Now, the family's tenure of a heritage-protected private home/museum and surrounding small park is apparently secure. Or so one hopes, as Moscow's new rich increasingly move into this now sought-after area and its small estates and farms become suburbanised. Most of Gorky's writers' cottages have now been bulldozed and replaced by streets of new large houses in what is becoming a prestige outer Moscow garden suburb. Much of Pasternak's beloved forest is gone. Busy roads thread the area, and the multi-storey apartment buildings of 'New Peredelkino' loom on the horizon. But I hope that Pasternak's immense political and cultural significance will continue to protect his former home and estate as a literary museum. His is one of only two of the original fifty writers' dachas still open to the public as a house-museum.[1]

I had never been to Peredelkino during my posting, though American Embassy colleagues had done so and returned enthusing over its political significance and beauty. The whole subject of Pasternak was still pretty raw politically in Moscow, only ten years after his death and with his name still in official disgrace. I had thought it prudent under our embassy guidelines not to visit. I was at last able to rectify that omission.

It was early morning, around zero degrees, and snowing lightly. The pavements were slippery with black ice underfoot, but I hoped to find colder, deeper snow and easier walking outside the city at Peredelkino. I picked my way carefully through the streets from my hostel to the Moscow River, and across the new covered pedestrian bridge to Kievsksy Voksal. At the station, my Russian not yet being reliable, after managing to buy the correct ticket I found myself directed onto the wrong platform, catching in haste a departing Kaluga express train, which I soon discovered was not stopping at Peredelkino. Fortunately, I was able to alight from the train at the only intermediate stop and wait there on a cold platform for the right local train, half an hour later. From Peredelkino station, I followed the guidebook walking instructions and found the nearby village cemetery without difficulty: a large old cemetery behind a gleaming blue-and-gold church on a hill. I could not find Pasternak's grave. There were no markers or directions to it, and nobody around to ask. But I caught the mood of the cemetery – calm, religious.

I had read that his funeral in 1960, which the authorities had hoped to manage as a quiet police-supervised family ceremony, had somehow attracted by word of mouth a massive dissident presence. Ineffective official attempts to control proceedings were overwhelmed by hours of spontaneous eulogies, recitals of Pasternak's poems, and of Russian songs and hymns sung by hundreds of Pasternak's friends and admirers.

The gravesite soon became a place of pilgrimage and for quiet meetings of like-minded dissident Russians. Yevgeny Yevtushenko in 1997 told the story that a garden bench thoughtfully placed near the grave where these visitors could sit and talk was found years later to contain a hidden microphone in a hollow leg, to help the security police to keep closer track of dissident contacts.[2]

I walked the kilometre or so from the cemetery to Pasternak's house. With help from passers-by, it was not hard to find. Across the road from the house, in what in his time had been a field devoted to growing potatoes and beets, and which he used to cross on foot as a shortcut to the church and village on the other side of the small river, now sat a row of imposing new concrete mansions behind high masonry walls with guard dogs. New trees had been planted around the house's perimeter to protect something of its former rural privacy.

The house was lovely – a modestly proportioned brown timber two-storey cottage in the snow, not at all a country mansion. It felt more like the family home it was than a museum. I was the first guest of the day and was warmly welcomed by the lady attendants. I was invited to wander on my own, but after a while a guide with some English came to help show me around a little. She was refreshingly non-reverential.

The house was quite minimalist in style and furnishings: there were few memento display cases and no keep-off guard ropes. It wonderfully evoked Pasternak's austere, simple life as a mature writer. The room that most interested me, where I could best sense his presence, was his large study/bedroom/library upstairs, which extended across the whole width of the building to catch breezes from either north or south, and the adjacent sunroom with its round bay window facing south, which must have been an oasis of light and warmth on cold sunny days. I sat at his desk where he worked on his poems, translations and his major work, *Doctor Zhivago*. It was a simple, strongly made utilitarian desk and wooden chair. I looked at his monastic iron-framed narrow single bed, and his modest-sized bookcase, filled with classics in several languages, and the large dictionaries that he used for his literary translations into Russian. On a side hook on a small wardrobe hung his overcoat, tweed cap and walking stick, all very English-style. A handsome large portrait photo of him was on the opposite wall, I would say taken when he was about forty-five and had just moved into the house.

The guide told me that Pasternak had lived in this room until he was too weak in his last months of illness to safely get up and down the rather steep stairs. He then moved to a small maid's bedroom at the foot of the stairs, where his wife, Zinaida, nursed him and brought him meals. He died in that bed, at home with his family. In answer to my question, 'So who was Lara?', the guide replied that Lara was a combination of Pasternak's second wife, Zinaida, and his mistress, Olga Ivinskaya. Respectfully, she would not criticise either woman or Pasternak himself, saying simply, 'He was a complicated man'.

Downstairs was a warm and cosy bay-windowed south-facing dining room, with a large oval table where the family and guests would meet for meals, set as if for afternoon tea. Zinaida had her own bedroom on the ground floor next to the kitchen, and this area is not part of the exhibition – maybe it is still in use by the family. There were also outbuildings that the family seems to occupy.

Much commentary has already been written about Boris Pasternak and *Doctor Zhivago*, most of which was penned secretly at Peredelkino between 1945 and 1956, the years of his long relationship with his beloved mistress, Olga. Recently reading the book again, and seeing Peredelkino, has prompted in me new reflections on the remarkable public and personal life of this great man. I was assisted by several published internet sources.[3]

I cannot think of *Doctor Zhivago*, both as the original novel and in subsequent creative interpretations on film and stage, without emotion. I feel close to Pasternak – this all-too-human, flawed man of genius and courage – and to the women and children he loved and tried to protect in dangerous years to the best of his ability.

The publishing history of *Doctor Zhivago* became a bitter East–West culture war that was fought ruthlessly by both sides, both in public and clandestinely. The hapless Pasternak found himself through no fault of his own at the centre of this conflict. We now know that the CIA secretly facilitated and financed the book's translation, publication and worldwide promotion, seeing it correctly as a powerful means to discredit and demoralise the Soviet communist system. But the CIA could not have done so if the book had not itself been so true and so compelling, and if Pasternak had not taken the first steps to get the book out to the world. The book's own literary merits justly earned it the 1958 Nobel Prize for Literature, and have ensured its now permanent place in Russian and world literature. Millions have read and loved it in its many translations. It has rightly joined the canon of Russian classics.

Pasternak first smuggled the Russian text out of Russia in 1956, in the Khrushchev era, after its rejection by *Novy Mir* literary magazine as contrary to socialist realist ideology. The reviewing editors condemned it as irretrievably anti-Soviet, as indeed it was. Pasternak was bitterly disappointed, and desperate that his major work should somehow still see the light of day. He deliberately passed a copy to a visiting Italian Communist Party journalist, saying with a laugh, 'You are hereby invited to watch me face the firing squad'. It seems Pasternak took a calculated risk, hoping naively that the book's publication in Italian in 1957 by an Italian communist publisher, Feltrinelli, might force the Soviet authorities' hand to reconsider allowing its publication at home: after all, Russia under Khrushchev was becoming more liberal, having left behind the worst brutalities of Stalin.

But the CIA moved first, having quickly recognised the political value of the book in the Cold War, and threw its large resources behind its rapid global re-publication. The Italian-language edition was soon followed by an excellent and highly successful English translation by Max Hayward and Manya Harari, published in 1958 by William Collins. The award of the 1958 Nobel Prize for Literature took the world by storm but enraged Nikita Khrushchev's government and in particular the KGB, which in retaliation made Pasternak's last two years of life at Peredelkino a misery. Then, shockingly, the KGB arrested Olga again after Pasternak's death, accusing her of assisting his 'treason' in publishing abroad. It was her second arrest. She had already served four years in the Gulag from 1949 to 1953, in an early KGB effort to force her to incriminate Pasternak. Olga had not cracked then, and nor had he. After her release in 1953 in the first year of the Khrushchev thaw, she was able to enjoy seven happy years with Pasternak at Peredelkino until his death.

When *Doctor Zhivago* was awarded the Nobel Prize, Stalin had been dead for five years. His successor, Khrushchev, had been steering a careful line, pursuing moderate political reform: he condemned Stalin's excesses, closed the gulags, began to rehabilitate their victims, and allowed more cultural freedom. Yet he was still committed to maintaining an authoritarian one-party Soviet communist system.

He saw his nation as in bitter Cold War competition with the United States (I recall his famous taunt to Western ambassadors, 'We will bury you'). The last thing he wanted was a *Doctor Zhivago* literary censorship scandal.

Over the next few years, *Doctor Zhivago* sold millions of copies in many languages around the world: all the while being banned in the Soviet Union as a seditious, disloyal book. It could not be otherwise.

I have the 1997 retrospective Folio Society edition of the Hayward–Harari text, with evocative illustrations and a perceptive new introduction by poet Yevgeny Yevtushenko.

David Lean's 1965 movie with Julie Christie, Geraldine Chaplin and Omar Sharif in the lead roles of Lara, Tonya and Zhivago (filmed mostly in Spain, Finland and Canada) was immensely popular and is still a movie-classic favourite. This film was never allowed to be shown in the Soviet Union: it was first shown in Russia only in 1994, under Yeltsin.

In Russia, unauthorised versions of the original book, published by Russian-language émigré publishers with CIA support and smuggled back in from the West, circulated for years clandestinely as *samizdat*. By the time Pasternak died, there must have been tens of thousands of such copies in illegal circulation. The first authorised printing, initially in serial form in the literary journal *Novy Mir*, the journal that had originally rejected it, came out in 1988 in communism's twilight years. The book is now freely available in Russian bookshops and kiosks in good low-cost editions of the classics. I bought my copy at Peredelkino, but I also saw it freely on sale in Moscow and Saint Petersburg bookshops. There are even fridge magnets on sale, of famous quotes from *Doctor Zhivago*. The book was filmed in Britain as a television miniseries in 2002, and as a Russian television series in 2006. Lucy Simon composed an excellent musical version, *Doctor Zhivago – a New Musical*, which premiered in Australia in 2011.

Pasternak, who by 1935 had secured his fame and official favour in the Soviet Union as a brilliant young revolutionary poet, will now live on through *Doctor Zhivago*. The suffering Pasternak and those most dear to him went through in the last years of his life in uncanny ways reconfigures plot lines he had already mapped out in his novel. It is as if Pasternak foresaw in his writer's imagination his own family's future real-life travails.

The story begins in 1954, when the Soviet literary journal *Znamya* published some of his newest poems under the title *Poems from a Novel*, actually then referred to by name as *Doctor Zhivago*. These poems later appeared at the end of the book as some of *Zhivago's Poems*.

But it really begins long before, with Pasternak's own family history. Boris Pasternak was the first-born son of an artistic, well-connected, comfortably off, ethnically Jewish but secularised intelligentsia family whose roots lay in Odessa. The Pasternak family history is in some ways a *Buddenbrooks* story.[4] Boris's father, Leonid Pasternak, was the son of a prosperous Odessa hotel keeper. Leonid moved to Moscow to study art. Handsome, talented and socially accomplished, he became a successful post-impressionist painter and professor at the Moscow School of Painting. He was a friend of the Tolstoys and moved in their fashionable literary and musical circle. He illustrated many of Tolstoy's books. I later saw some of Leonid's art displayed in the museum at the Tolstoy estate Yasnaya Polyana, and very good it is.

Boris's mother, Rosa Kaufman, was the daughter of wealthy Jewish Odessa industrialist Isadore Kaufman. She was trained as a professional concert pianist. She and Leonid were a happy couple – they stayed together for life and had four children – two boys, Boris and Alexander, and two girls, Lydia and Josephine.

Up to the age of twenty-four in 1914, Pasternak had a secure childhood and youth in Moscow, growing up in a politically liberal, cultured, artistic and well-off secular Jewish-origin household. His young life in the prewar and pre-Soviet Russian intelligentsia – golden years for those fortunate enough to have belonged to this privileged stratum of society – is glowingly recalled in the early chapters of *Doctor Zhivago*. The novel offers one of the few literary pictures we have of Moscow in the early twentieth century before the communist revolution, years of industry-generated wealth and high culture for the well-off, who enjoyed comfortable and gracious lives, while the currents of socialist revolution swirled in the deprived and angry working classes below. The best and brightest of the middle-class youth – including presumably Pasternak – sympathised with the revolutionaries. Some even joined them on the barricades of the suppressed 1905 workers' rising in Presnya, then a poor industrial suburb of Moscow. We see all this portrayed in *Doctor Zhivago*.

We also see the early social and economic impact of the two 1917 Revolutions and the Civil War on Pasternak's family and friends – on this class which had initially welcomed the revolutions as liberating.

Pasternak had originally aspired to a musical career and for a while, no doubt encouraged by his mother, attended the Moscow Conservatory School of Music. But he shifted his focus to writing when he concluded that he lacked sufficient musical talent. From 1910 to 1914 he studied neo-Kantian philosophy at the German university of Marburg. During World War I he taught and worked at a chemical factory near Perm in the Urals. Perm was later portrayed as the fictional town of Yuryatin in *Doctor Zhivago*; it was a town and region Pasternak got to know well in these years.

Pasternak spent the Civil War years in Moscow. He did not go to the front. During these troubled years, he was poor. He sold off family books and antiques to survive. He began to write and publicly recite poetry in support of the Revolution, living precariously off his recital collections.

A huge trauma in Pasternak's life must have been his parents' decision to emigrate permanently from Russia in 1921, when Lenin allowed middle-class people the choice after the Civil War ended either to commit to the new communist society, or permanently to emigrate. They never returned to Russia. Boris and Alexander, then young men aged thirty-one and twenty-eight, must have chosen to stay in Russia. They did not try to follow their parents and sisters to the West, and as far as I can tell, they never saw them again. The politics of the Soviet Union under Lenin's successor, Stalin, made any such family reunions – even maintenance of contact through letters or phone calls – dangerous and finally impossible. In 1938 under the Nazi threat, Leonid moved with his wife and daughters from Berlin to safer refuge in Britain. They ended their lives peacefully there, many years later.

So much of *Doctor Zhivago* reflects the pain Pasternak experienced as a young man, of permanent separation from his parents and sisters under the implacable pressures of revolution and civil war. In Zhivago's imagined life, there are so many cruel unwilling farewells between parents and children, husbands and wives, and lovers. No one is blamed for these desperately sad separations: Zhivago accepts them stoically, as things that life threw up, and had to be lived through. This must be how Pasternak dealt with the emigration of his parents. He could have gone with them, but he made his choice to stay in his beloved homeland, knowing he might never see them again.

For Pasternak, the permanent loss of his parents and sisters – especially, I would guess, the loss of contact with his mother – was a wound for which he would always seek through his wives and lover to compensate. Did he think they had deserted him? Or did he feel guilt that he and his younger brother had chosen motherland over family, and had not gone with their parents and sisters abroad, as so many in their class did? The photographs of Boris as a young man show so much sadness and loneliness in his face. And it explains why Pasternak was so desperate later in life to stay close to the women and children who mattered most to him: above all, not to be forced into punitive lonely exile by the Soviet Government after he was awarded the Nobel Prize in 1958. He declined to go to Stockholm to collect the prize because he knew he would never be allowed back home if he did. And he could not bear that thought.

In youth, he was a strikingly handsome dark-haired man who must have been attractive to women. It was not a conventionally masculine face – it was quite delicate, even feminine. It hardened and became more craggy and patriarchal as he grew older.

Pasternak certainly had a complicated personal life. He had a son, Evgeny, by his first wife, Evgeniya; they had married in 1922. Ten years later he fell in love with Zinaida Neigauz, a married woman and mother of two sons. They both divorced their spouses, and married in 1934. Pasternak had a second son, Leonid, with Zinaida. Throughout his Peredelkino years, he lived with Zinaida and their four sons. Both Evgeniya and Zinaida were strong, beautiful, intelligent women at the time when they married Pasternak, but the subsequent years were not kind to them.

In 1946, Pasternak began his famous affair with Olga Ivinskaya, a single mother of two children who worked as a writer at *Novy Mir* magazine. Zinaida knew about Olga but chose to turn a blind eye, focusing her life on the four boys. According to Keck:

Pasternak was married twice and had several affairs; he supported his two sons, his two stepsons [from Zinaida], and the [two] children of his mistress Olga Ivinskaya, with whom he began a relationship in 1946, from her previous marriages.[5]

So love of children, and duty of care to so many children, were permanent features of Pasternak's home life. Pasternak could not have been an easy husband to live with, though he was no casual philanderer or seducer either. His contempt for such men is vividly manifested in the character of Komarovsky in *Doctor Zhivago*. He was racked with guilt about his long affair with Olga, yet neither he nor she could bear to end it even under intense emotional pressure from Zinaida. I would guess that as with Zhivago, Pasternak's women chose him rather than the other way around.

Zhivago falls helplessly into his three important relationships with women − driven by uncontrollable emotions on both sides: with Tonya, with Lara, and (not in the film, but importantly in the book) with his third wife, Marina, who falls in love with him at his lowest ebb after he has lost everything, and puts him back on his feet, and with whom he has two more children. None of Zhivago's personal relationships is the product of lust or calculation. I am sure that Pasternak's relationships with Evgeniya, Zinaida and Olga were not either.

Around the time his relationship with Olga began, Zinaida ceased to live with him as his wife. They agreed, for the children's sake, perhaps also out of their own mutual respect and loyalty, not to break up the family home: they kept living under one roof, ate and entertained together as a family, but slept thereafter in separate rooms. He met Olga by day, in Moscow or in Peredelkino village, where she had rented a cottage as his literary secretary. It must have been an open secret, known to all but not mentioned. Pasternak would walk through the fields to her house by day, and return to his extended family at night. He must have had his hands full balancing all his obligations.

Their lives were otherwise calm and simple, but enlivened by regular lunch parties of visitors from nearby writers' dachas or from Moscow and, increasingly in the last years, visitors from abroad.

Pasternak kept up a cultured circle of friends and he and Zinaida gave them all a warm and lively home welcome. There must have been many happy moments in that household, despite its stresses.

So much of what Zhivago experienced, Pasternak could only have imagined as a writer. He did not go to the World War I front. He did not get caught up in the Civil War in the Urals. But like Zhivago, Pasternak was haunted by guilt. Like Zhivago, he delighted in nature's beauty and the beauty of human life and love, and was like him a poet. Like Zhivago, Pasternak could not hate his enemies: he loved and forgave them all.

Pasternak's Jewish family origin is a subject that I cannot bypass. There is a story that he was secretly baptised as an Orthodox Christian as a small child by his nurse; whether true or not, it is clear that by the time he was an adult he thought of himself as a member of the Russian Orthodox Church, with whose beliefs and liturgy he was thoroughly familiar. For him, Orthodoxy was part of being Russian, part of the life choice he had made, and in a sense his parents had made for him. He received Orthodox last rites and had an Orthodox burial. *Doctor Zhivago* is full of Orthodox liturgical references and discussion of Christian resurrection theology. It is not a Jewish book.

There is a revealing rumination by Zhivago's best friend, Misha Gordon – the only clearly identified Jewish character. Gordon argues that the only way to end the recurring waves of anti-Semitism and Jewish suffering in the Russian Empire is by total assimilation of Jews into Russian society – effectively, the route Pasternak's parents Leonid and Rosa had chosen, and the route so many Jewish communists chose. Says Misha:

Why don't they [Jewish community leaders] say to their people: 'That's enough, stop now. Don't hold onto your identity, don't get together in a crowd. Disperse. Be with all the rest. You are the first and best Christians in the world...'[6]

How Pasternak could have reconciled this view with the Nazi Holocaust in occupied European Russia – which, as he surely must have known, spared neither Orthodox Jewish *shtetl*-dwellers (*shtetl* meaning 'village') nor assimilated urban secular intelligentsia Jews like his parents – we do not know.

Life at the dacha should have been idyllic for Pasternak, but it was no 'walk across a field' for him.[7] Writing and translating poetry was his officially recognised full-time occupation. In the Soviet Union, every healthy person had to have a paid job, or be subject to arrest as a social parasite. Pasternak, like all full-time writers, had to belong to the Soviet Writers' Union, the powerful state-compliant professional union which maintained discipline over its members through various inducements and sanctions.

Pasternak tried to stay completely out of politics: he kept his head down, writing and translating poetry; his translations of Shakespeare's plays were renowned. But under Stalin, the apparent security of his Peredelkino years was always an illusion, and could have been shattered at any moment by arbitrary arrest and dispatch to the Gulag, as happened to many of his fellow writers (Isaac Babel was arrested in a Peredelkino dacha in 1937 and sent to the Gulag, never to return).

It seems Pasternak was favoured by Stalin because of his already famous body of work as a Soviet poet, and his popular translations of foreign poetry. It is said that Stalin especially admired his translations from classic Georgian poetry, and that this may have helped to shield Pasternak from the purges of writers in the years of the Great Terror. In 1937 Pasternak bravely and dangerously declined to co-sign a Soviet Writers' Union mass denunciation of the purged and arrested poet, his friend Osip Mandelstam. He was thereby placed on a security police list submitted to Stalin for approval of arrest. But Stalin is said to have annotated the file, 'Leave that cloud-dweller in peace'.

Did Stalin, a former Orthodox seminarian, sentimentally see Pasternak as a sort of 'holy fool', as the half-ironic epithet 'cloud-dweller' suggests? In fifteenth- and sixteenth-century Moscow, the tsars under Orthodox religious law had to respect holy fools' freedom of speech and protect them from harm, despite their apparent madness and anarchic rejection of social hierarchies. A holy fool plays an important dramatic role in Mussorgsky's opera *Boris Godunov*, a work both Pasternak and Stalin would have known well.

In her article *Holy Foolishness as a Key to Russian Culture*, Priscilla Hunt comments that in old Muscovy, holy fools had special access to rulers and served as their 'walking conscience'. Russian holy foolishness was a 'culturally productive antipode' to the 'potential for alienation and violence of the autocratic and bureaucratic state'.[8]

Stalin, so another story goes, rang Pasternak without warning soon after Mandelstam's arrest to ask him menacingly what he thought of Mandelstam's approach to poetry. Pasternak tried haltingly to explain the differences between his own and Mandelstam's philosophies of poetry. At the end, Stalin said mockingly, 'I see, you just aren't able to stick up for a comrade', and put down the receiver. A quaking Pasternak waited for the security police to come to arrest him.

Yet Pasternak was never arrested, and his years at Peredelkino were quiet and productive. He lived the prewar and postwar years as a Stalin-protected writer: writing, going for walks, growing fruit and vegetables in his large home garden, inviting friends out to visit him, and after 1946, spending private time with Olga Ivinskaya. Prudently, he pretty much abandoned writing original poetry for publication, concentrating on his translations into Russian.

He was too old (fifty-one) to serve in World War II, but he welcomed the outbreak of that war in 1941 as a chance for Russia to leave behind the years of Stalinist terror and to begin to cleanse itself morally:

> It was not only felt by men...in concentration camps, but by everyone without exception, at home and at the front, and they all took a deep breath and flung themselves into the furnaces of this deadly, liberating struggle with real joy, with rapture...'[9]

Pasternak wrote patriotic war poems, worked as an air-raid warden in Moscow, and in 1943 was allowed to begin motivational poetry recital visits to the frontline. This was his experience of real war that he used in *Doctor Zhivago*.

After the war, particularly after Stalin's death in 1953, Pasternak hoped for better times. He had long since ceased to believe in communism's promise of future happiness, having seen how it created so much present-day cruelty and fear and falsehood. Meeting and falling in love with Olga, and writing *Doctor Zhivago*, had changed his life. Zhivago's fears, miseries and precarious survival in the Civil War and under Soviet rule were also the realities of his own life. Like Zhivago and Lara in their last ecstatic weeks together at their country retreat in Varykino, Pasternak never knew when the authorities would come to arrest him. He knew he was living in the eye of Stalin's raging storm, and that his domestic peace and settled ways at Peredelkino could be swept away in an instant.

When Olga was arrested in 1949 and sentenced to prison for ten years, the KGB hoped she would denounce Pasternak, but she never did. Early in her sentence, she miscarried under abusive treatment and lost their unborn child. He was mad with grief. He expected never to see her again. Yet he went on stoically writing *Doctor Zhivago* in secret. She was released by Khrushchev in 1953 but arrested again in 1960 after Pasternak's death. Again, life had imitated his famous words:

> One day Lara went out and did not come back. She must have been arrested in the street, as so often happened in those days, and she died or vanished somewhere, forgotten as a nameless number on a list which later was mislaid, in one of the innumerable mixed or women's concentration camps in the north.[10]

But Olga did come back. She was released in 1964 and never arrested again. In 1978 her memoirs were smuggled abroad and published in Paris. She was legally rehabilitated in 1988. She died peacefully in Russia in 1995. What a heroic and loyal woman she must have been.

The subsidiary characters in Doctor Zhivago are also revealing of Pasternak's initial welcoming of the Soviet 'new dawn', and his later disillusionment with Soviet communism's cruelty and mendacity. They also offer clues to the different strategies by which he and his friends tried to survive the years of unpredictable autocracy.

Pavel Antipov, the gentle and idealistic left-wing student who becomes the fanatical and ruthless revolutionary leader Strelnikov in the novel, is without doubt a communist. Pasternak knew that he could not identify him as such in the book, if he were ever to hope to have it published in the Soviet Union. So he labels Strelnikov rather unconvincingly as an 'independent revolutionist' whom the party eventually sees as a threat and purges. But Strelnikov's whole ideology and style is recognisably communist: like Stalin, Mao and Pol Pot, who deliberately used violence, starvation and terror to intimidate and control their helpless subjects. Russian readers would have recognised Strelnikov's measures as those of Stalin's henchmen in the Ukraine, Caucasus and Urals – forced collectivisation of farms, razed crops, burnt villages, people left to starve or forced to flee their homes.

Zhivago's friends Gordon and Dudorov are interesting characters, too. Soviet intellectuals, both must have been modelled on Pasternak's many friends in the Writers' Union: men who were humanist in their inner-core values, but prudent, even cowardly, accommodators to state power and to the prevailing political line – men who had learned to think in 'pious platitudes...in the spirit of the age...Men who are not free, he [Zhivago] thought, always idealise their bondage'. Yet when war with Germany comes, these same 'desperately commonplace' men whom Zhivago in one way rightly despised, find their courage: they fight bravely for the motherland and in the end are redeemed as decent men, who mourn Zhivago's death and share his hopes for Russia's brighter future. It would have been a redemptive message not lost on Pasternak's Russian readers.

Zhivago's mysterious beneficent half-brother, Yevgraf Zhivago, the half-Kyrgyz KGB General (well played by Alec Guinness in the movie) seems just too good to be true. He is a convenient deus ex machina in the plot who repeatedly appears unexpectedly when all seems lost, to protect Zhivago or put him back on his feet. He arranges with Lara a decent funeral for Zhivago. The description of Lara's impassioned mourning over Zhivago's coffin is Wagnerian in its emotional force.

Yevgraf retrieves and publishes Zhivago's writings. He helps Lara and later Tanya, Zhivago's and Lara's abandoned child. Did Pasternak ever know any KGB generals like this in life, who protected him and his family? Or is Yevgraf a metaphor, an imagined wish-fulfilment KGB figure? Might Yevgraf have been Pasternak's silent appeal to the KGB to treat Olga and Zinaida and all the children decently after Pasternak's death? If so, in the case of Olga, the appeal went unheeded. From Olga's memoir, we know that the KGB officers under whom she suffered were cruel, crudely abusive, misogynist and unforgiving. But Zinaida and the children were left in peace.

Yevgraf's real significance – and Guinness in the film captures this well – may be that he represents Pasternak's unquenched faith in Russia's future: that out of all the pain and misery and oppression of the Bolshevik Revolution, Civil War and Stalinist years, would come at last a better, happier, more decent and humanist Russia.

As for Komarovsky, Pasternak would have known many men like him in the unstable, dangerous years after 1917. Komarovsky is the type of opportunist who exists in every society in transition, alert to manipulating and profiting from fluid political situations to his own personal advantage, and ready to use his power over others for his monetary or sexual gain. Ironically, Russia's second 'time of troubles' in 1985–2000 would be another opportunity for men like Komarovsky to find ways to feather their own nests at the expense of more worthy but powerless people.

Doctor Zhivago – completed, let us remember, as early as 1956, with over thirty years of Soviet communism and Cold War tension still to come – ends with a sense of cautious optimism, that both the book and the film capture symbolically in the character of Zhivago's and Lara's daughter, Tanya – a bright, emotionally resilient young Russian woman with everything to look forward to in life, despite her lonely, deprived and traumatic childhood. Tanya is a metaphor for Russia itself. Pasternak ends his lovely book on a note of forgiveness and hope:

> Although the enlightenment and liberation which had been expected to come after the war had not come with victory, a presage of freedom was in the air throughout these post-war years, and it was their only historical meaning.

To the two ageing friends [Gordon and Dudorov] sitting by the window it seemed that this freedom of the spirit was there, that on that very evening the future had become almost tangible in the streets below, and that they themselves had entered that future and would, from now on, be part of it. They felt a peaceful joy for this holy city and for the whole land and for the survivors among those who had played a part in this story and for their children, and the silent music of happiness filled them and enveloped them and spread far and wide. And it seemed that the book in their hands [the book of Yuri's writings which Yevgraf had had published] knew what they were feeling, and gave them its support and confirmation.[11]

What a noble ending. Only a man who had grown up in the gracious middle-class world of late imperial Russia, and then survived the long traumatic years of war and communist autocracy, and yet still somehow kept his faith alive that Russia could look forward to a better future beyond communism, could have written such words. Herein lies Pasternak's huge importance. Other writers like the émigré Ivan Bunin had eulogised the late imperial years, or like Andrei Rybakov and Alexander Solzhenitsyn and Vasily Grossman had portrayed the evils of Stalinism. But Pasternak had in *Doctor Zhivago* foreseen a brighter future as well, bridging all three periods.

In 1997, six years into the post-communist transition under Russia's President Boris Yeltsin, eminent poet Yevgeny Yevtushenko summed up Pasternak's importance thus:

Ideas tossed into the air of humanity prematurely, at great risk to their authors, do not vanish without trace. They turn into magnets, as it were, hovering in the air and gradually attracting more souls. So it was in the ancient Roman stone quarries in early Christian times, and later in those Soviet asylums of freedom, the cramped communal kitchens where the Russian intelligentsia used to huddle over faded, tattered typescript copies of Pasternak's banned novel. Its clandestine readers not only inhaled the novel with the air they breathed, they also exhaled it. And its thoughts became increasingly part of the air of Russia as the country prepared itself for change.[12]

Pasternak was an imperfect hero – a man like the rest of us. But he was also a writer of sensitivity, compassion and genius. He lived his life on a moral knife-edge, trying to protect his family, to honour his love for his motherland, and to remain loyal to his principles of universal human values and individual freedom of conscience. This constant tension, especially in his embattled later years, must have hastened his death from cancer. The Nobel Prize he had to decline in 1958 was finally accepted long after his death by his eldest son, Yevgeny, in a ceremony in Stockholm in 1989. Cellist Mstislav Rostropovich played a Bach serenade there, in Pasternak's honour.

The deeply emotional valedictory poem Pasternak wrote in 1959, *Nobel Prize*, epitomises how he felt at the time of the Nobel award:

> Like a beast in a pen, I'm cut off
> From my friends, freedom, the sun,
> But the hunters are gaining ground.
> I've nowhere else to run.
>
> Dark wood and the bank of a pond,
> Trunk of a fallen tree.
> There's no way forward, no way back.
> It's all up with me.
>
> Am I a gangster or murderer?
> Of what crime do I stand
> Condemned? I made the whole world weep
> At the beauty of my land.
>
> Even so, one step from my grave,
> I believe that cruelty, spite,
> The powers of darkness will in time
> Be crushed by the spirit of light.[13]

Chapter 6

Suzdal and Russian Identity

There is one place in Russia that, more than anywhere else, defines who Russians think they are. It is Suzdal: the most iconic of the five historic towns in the Golden Ring, a region of historic old city-states a few hours to the north-east of Moscow. The other four are Sergiev Posad (renamed Zagorsk in the Soviet period, which I visited in 1970 – a shabby and run-down place then, but no longer so, now being the proud centre of the renascent Orthodox Church), Yaroslavl, Kostroma and Vladimir. Unlike the other four which are now large populated towns, Suzdal remains a sleepy country village dominated by churches and monasteries, nestling in a fertile river valley, and with a population of only 12,000 people who live mainly by tourism and market gardening. It is also now a popular place to retire. Suzdal was bypassed by the Trans-Siberian Railway line which ran eastwards through nearby Vladimir, and it was somehow not touched by nineteenth-century industrialisation. Now it is the jewel of the Golden Ring: an unspoiled little town of the fifteenth to seventeenth centuries. It epitomises the Russian soul.

Grahame and I experienced Suzdal on a cold, calm and sunny midwinter day. The brightly painted church domes and spires, predominantly in blues and yellows but many other colours and patterns besides, stood out vividly in a blanket of fresh white snow under a crisp blue sky. There were hardly any tourists as it was off-season. The river and its surrounding grassy flats were completely snowed in, and the whole town looked like something out of an old Russian fairytale.

Suzdal had been an important town for several centuries in the early history of the Moscow-based Russian state. After my first few days in Moscow, I was keen to experience an overnight stay there. Grahame was to join me the next morning.

It was around 180 kilometres from Moscow to Vladimir, a comfortable two-hour afternoon journey. The train soon left the city high-rises behind and entered deep snowy countryside. From Vladimir train station I got a local taxi for the last 16 kilometres to Suzdal, arriving at dusk at the Kremlyovsky Hotel, a charming two-storey country inn, a short walk across the river from the main Suzdal town and churches.

The history of Russia begins in the pre-Christian era with the Scythians, or Sarmatians, a fierce mounted nomadic people of Iranian Caucasian origin, said to be red-haired and blue-eyed, who roamed the open grassland Eurasian steppes north of the Black Sea, warring and trading with Greek and Roman colonies on the coast. They were talented goldsmiths but never produced a settled civilisation.

The recorded history of the eastern Slav peoples, the ancestors of today's Russian nation, begins in the ninth century of the Christian era. They inhabited a huge zone of mixed field-and-forest country between the Baltic and the Black Sea, north and north-west of the treeless steppes. They were free peasant farmers living simple lives in villages. They were animist and had no written language.

The first important towns in this region were Novgorod on the Volkhov River in the far north, not far inland from present-day Saint Petersburg, and Kiev Rus' on the Dnieper River to the south on the edge of the steppes. The Volkhov flows north to the Baltic via two large lakes, Ilmen and Ladoga, and the Dnieper south to the Black Sea. In this flat well-watered country, there were easy water linkages between these two river systems. In around the ninth century, Vikings or Varangians from the Baltic – maritime pirates and traders – developed Novgorod and Kiev Rus' as their fortified supply depots on these long river routes, which were easily navigable by their shallow-draught longships all the way from the Baltic to the Black Sea and onwards around the Black Sea coast to Byzantium,

modern-day Istanbul. The Varangians – known by then as the 'Rus' –
raided Byzantium several times, but by 945 AD had made peace and
established profitable trade links with the Byzantine Greeks.

Varangian Rus chieftains and their clansmen settled in Novgorod
and Kiev Rus', and quickly became Russified as a warrior caste
ruling over the Slavonic-speaking local Slav peasantry, who became
their serfs: rather as the Vikings, Danes and Saxons were moving
into Britain as feudal ruling castes over the native Britons. A loose
'federation' of east-Slavic states developed under the rule of the
Varangian Rurik dynasty, occupying the river lands extending from
the Baltic to the Black Sea.[1]

From around 900 AD, Orthodox Christianity brought by
missionaries from Byzantium became the dominant religion of Kiev
and Novgorod. Saints Kirill and Methodius developed for religious
use the first written Slav alphabet. It was based on the Greek alphabet
(many of its letters and sounds are identical to Greek) but with
several newly invented letters to represent unique Slav sounds not
found in Greek: letters like *zhe* and *tse* and *che* and *sha* and *shcha*.
This language is known as Old Church Slavonic. It is the precursor
of all the modern family of Slav languages or dialects written in
Cyrillic alphabets (Russian, Ukrainian, Byelorussian, Bulgarian,
Macedonian, Serbian, Montenegrin, and – though it adopted a
Romanic script – Polish).

By 1000 AD, Kiev Rus' had grown into a wealthy and flourishing
trading city. Its influence extended southwards towards Byzantium,
westwards into Galicia (the area now shared between south-eastern
Poland, Slovakia, Hungary, Moldavia and Romania), northwards
to Novgorod and the Golden Ring towns, and eastwards as far as
Crimea, Georgia and Armenia. Kiev Rus' thrived, forging links
through dynastic marriages with Western European states. Its golden
age was in the eleventh century under its Prince Yaroslav the Wise
(1019–54). It then fell into decline, weakened by internal disunity
and increasingly destructive attacks from steppe nomads. The Rus'
civilisation gradually retreated northwards into the colder and safer
forested areas, where it was harder for nomadic mounted armies to
pursue them. Small independent city-states, speaking Russian and
practising Orthodox Christianity, emerged in the north as successors

to the collapsed civilisation of Kiev Rus': especially around Novgorod in the north-west, and in the Golden Ring region in the north-east.

In the thirteenth century, these surviving Russian principalities very nearly themselves succumbed to further invasions from the west and south-east. Strong forces first of Swedes, and then of Teutonic knights and Estonians, attacked Novgorod in 1240 and 1242. Both armies were narrowly repulsed by defending Russian armies, gathered and led by Prince Alexander of Novgorod (1220–63). His victory in the first battle in 1240 on the River Neva earned him the honorific surname 'Nevsky'. The subsequent battle on the ice of Lake Peipus in 1242 was immortalised in the famous film by Sergei Eisenstein, *Alexander Nevsky*.

The Golden Ring principalities were in the same period conquered by a new formidable nomadic invader from the south-east: the Mongols or Tatars as they were known, led by Batu, a grandson of Genghiz Khan. But the Tatars, disliking the dark cold forests of the Russian north, soon withdrew to the sunnier open grassland steppes in the south-east and south, where they established three long-lived 'Golden Horde' Tatar kingdoms – Kazan, Astrakhan, and Crimea. The conquered Golden Ring principalities and the newer nearby city-state of Moscow paid tribute to the Tatars for 200 years, in return for which they were largely left alone. In 1480 Moscow stopped paying the tribute, knowing the Tatars were no longer militarily strong enough to enforce it.

Gradually, Moscow through skilful diplomacy and judicious use of force had brought all the nearby independent Golden Ring towns under its rule. Under its Prince Ivan III (1462–1505), Moscow also annexed Novgorod and thus acquired its extensive northern lands, stretching from the Finnish border to the Urals. Ivan III made a shrewd dynastic marriage to the niece of the last emperor of Byzantium before it fell to the Turks. From this time onwards, Moscow presented itself to the world as the heir to Kiev Rus', Byzantium and Rome. Moscow, an Orthodox Church-based expanding Russian state, saw its destiny as to be the 'third Rome': Rome and Byzantium, former capitals of the Western Roman Empire and of the Orthodox Church and Eastern Roman Empire, had fallen, but Russian monks prophesied that Moscow would not fall. Around this time the prince of Moscow, previously known as *knyaz* (prince), adopted the grander title *Tsar* (Caesar).

More troubles were in store for this confident and expanding new Christian state on the north-eastern fringe of Europe. Tsar Ivan IV ('Ivan the Terrible') was crowned in 1547 and ruled till 1584. He conquered the now weakened Tatar kingdoms of Kazan and Astrakhan to the south-east. He enforced the cultural absorption of their ethnic Tatar populations and thus cleared the way to Russia's amazingly rapid subsequent eastwards colonisation through sparsely populated, politically inchoate Siberia. Russian military-trading expeditions first claimed possession of Siberia's Pacific coast in 1647 with the establishment of Okhotsk. Russian political control over the whole of Siberia was firm by the early nineteenth century, and they even for a time colonised and claimed Alaska, until the United States purchased it from them.

Ivan's long reign was marked by his growing paranoia and cruelty towards his people, nobles and his own family. He launched a pitiless war of extermination against the boyars – nobles who resisted his autocratic power. He founded Russia's first secret police force answerable only to him – the dreaded Oprichniki. When he died in 1584, he left his deeply scarred country in trauma. A catastrophic thirty-year 'time of troubles' (*smutnoye vremya*) ensued, with warring pretenders to the throne, including Boris Godunov (who tried vainly during his short reign to restore national peace and stability – as movingly portrayed in Mussorgsky's great opera), and a subsequent opportunistic invasion from the nearby Polish–Lithuanian Commonwealth, then a great Polish-led kingdom at the height of its powers. For a time, a Polish army occupied Moscow and a son of the Polish king Sigismund III was installed on the Russian throne. It seemed as if Russia might be absorbed as an eastern frontier province of Poland, its ethnically fellow Slav but by now fervently Catholic and Western-leaning neighbour.

A national Russian patriotic resistance developed, based in the Golden Ring towns of Vladimir and Suzdal, and in Nizhny Novgorod, a Russian trading and fortress town 250 kilometres further east, reinforced during Ivan the Terrible's campaigns to conquer the Kazan Tatars. An unlikely duo, Prince Dmitry Pozharsky, from the

Suzdal area, and Kuzma Minin, a butcher from Nizhny Novgorod, became joint military leaders, heading a patriotic Russian insurgency, which after a two-year campaign finally expelled the Polish occupiers from Moscow in 1613.[2]

An assembly of boyars then elected a new Russian Tsar, Mikhail Romanov: the founder of the Romanov autocratic dynasty which lasted an amazing 304 years until the political murder of Tsar Nicholas and his whole family by order of the communists in Yekaterinburg in 1918, after the Tsar's forced abdication and imprisonment in 1917.

The seventeenth century, until around 1712, when Tsar Peter the Great moved Russia's capital from Moscow to his new city on the Baltic Sea, Saint Petersburg, was Suzdal's Golden Age. On the main carriage road from Moscow to Nizhny Novgorod and beyond to Siberia, Suzdal became wealthy from Moscow's growing trade with Asia. Its 400-odd merchants competed with one another to build family-owned churches of increasing splendour. Even today there are 300 listed architectural monuments in Suzdal, mostly churches and monasteries.

This was the century when Russia was at its most uniquely 'Russian'. The culture – Russian-speaking, using a Cyrillic alphabet, fervently Orthodox in faith and liturgy – was highly exotic to visiting Western Europeans. It felt almost as foreign as Turkey or Persia. This was before Tsar Peter the Great's modernising reforms and move to his new capital created a new, more westward-looking Russia.

In the nineteenth century, as new main roads and railway lines bypassed Suzdal, the town fell into lethargy, becoming a sleepy place of interest only to religious pilgrims, tourists and market gardeners. It was neglected in the Soviet period: the communists saw its churches as dead historical museums, not – as the Russian Government does today – as living national treasures and symbols of Russian identity and national pride.

The churches have been reoccupied by Orthodox monks, with generous state subsidies for their rehabilitation as practising churches and national heritage sites. Sitting in green fields, or as

I saw them covered in snow, they are breathtakingly beautiful: a photographer's paradise.

Suzdal township itself is being restored, as wealthy Muscovites buy the large rundown old timber merchants' houses, with their beautifully carved windows and doors, and restore them authentically as restaurants, guest houses, and weekend and retirement homes. This house-restoration industry, plus the ongoing restoration and maintenance of church properties, keeps many artists and craftsmen busily employed in Suzdal. I am sure that this lovely town, so close to Moscow, has an assured heritage-based future, because it so perfectly represents Russia's romantic vision of itself.

Here one can still get a real sense of what Russia was before Peter the Great forcibly dragged his nation into eighteenth-century Europe, and before its nineteenth-century state-capitalism-led industrialisation. Suzdal is a living museum.

I found the story of Pozharsky's and Minin's successful military campaign to expel foreign invaders from Russia in 1611–13 fascinating in many ways. First, because the story so well expresses Russia's already strong sense of its deep differences from Western Europe, Catholic or Protestant. What made the Poles finally unacceptable to Russians as conquerors of Moscow was that they were Catholic and used the alien Romanic alphabet – otherwise they might well have been accepted and assimilated, as the Varangians had been accepted and assimilated by the Slavs as the ruling caste of Kiev Rus'.

Second, Pozharsky and Minin came out of Russia's expanding eastern frontier towards its Siberian future. Pozharsky and Minin were defending Russia's dream of its great future Eurasian destiny. They were determined not to allow their great nation to become a mere border province of the Polish–Lithuanian Empire.

Third, this unlikely but steadfast alliance of a prince and a butcher as co-leaders, who always stayed friendly allies and never competed with each other. Minin was subsequently ennobled by the new Tsar, Mikhail Romanov, in gratitude.

Fourth, that neither Pozharsky nor Minin ever sought the throne for themselves: such selfless patriotism was what Russia desperately needed after the decades-long Time of Troubles, to restore the nation's faith in its destiny.

It is thus no accident that the epic story of Pozharsky and Minin has been so attractive to all Russian governments ever since. A statue of Pozharsky and Minin stands in front of Saint Basil's Cathedral in Moscow, erected in 1818 soon after the defeat of Napoleon. The main square in front of the Kremlin in Nizhny Novgorod is named after them, and has an almost exact copy of the same monument, erected in 2005.

The communists emphasised the fact that Minin was a genuine working-class hero. Tsarist Russia, and again Putin's Russia today, emphasise the two leaders' selfless patriotism and ability to work together in the national interest across class boundaries. So it was a made-to-order national story that has maintained its power through the centuries, and has renewed force now.

As it did in Stalin's Russia during World War II. I saw the famous pair of Great Patriotic War inspirational posters in a little museum at the Saint Euthymius Monastery in Suzdal. In each poster, a small band of Soviet soldiers stands with drawn bayonets and guns blazing, fighting under the Red flag, resisting Nazi invaders, while above and behind them stand the supporting ghostly images of Pozharsky and Minin doing battle against the enemy invaders of their era. Both pictures carry the same exhortation: 'May the courageous model of our great forebears inspire us in this patriotic war'. One carries a quote from Pozharsky, 'Our armies will fight to the death', and the other a quote from Minin, 'There is no force which can triumph over us'. In this nationally sacred museum, I could so feel in these two posters the power of that message of resolute Russian resistance to invasion.

And Russia has been invaded so often: in the beginning by the Varangians and steppe nomads; then in the thirteenth century by the Teutonic Knights, Estonians and Swedes from the west, and Mongols (Tatars) from the south-east; then by the Polish-Lithuanians in 1611–13. Sweden would invade again in 1706–09, France in 1812, Britain and France and Turkey in the Crimean War of 1853–56, and Germany in 1914–17 and 1941–45.

Russia, because of its flat, open terrain, hard-frozen icy roads in winter, easily navigable waterways, and absence of natural frontier barriers like seas or mountain ranges, has always been dreadfully exposed to large invading land armies at times when it was politically and militarily weak. Most of its major wars were fought as defensive wars on its own soil: with the exceptions of Russia's own steady colonial expansions eastwards and southwards into the Tatar lands, Siberia, the Caucasus and Central Asia.

What does Suzdal say to Russians now about their national destiny? For four centuries, there have been two opposing tendencies within Russia, arguing passionately over Russia's identity: the Slavophiles and the Westernisers.[3] The argument has never been decisively settled, and is still important today.

The Golden Ring towns absolutely symbolise Russia's Slavophile identity. Saint Petersburg represents Russia's quest to Westernise itself. Moscow is historically conflicted, always having had an undecided foot in each camp.

Slavophiles affirm that Russia has a unique culture, fundamentally defined by its core Slav ethnicity, Cyrillic language, Orthodox Christianity and Tsarist imperial history. All these things, they say, set Russia firmly apart from the mainstream Western European identity, based on the Roman Empire, Romanic alphabet, Catholic and Protestant Christianity, and the Enlightenment. Russia did not experience these things at first hand. Its destiny, they say, is inevitably different.

Slavophilia can be narrowly chauvinistic, centred on race-based doctrines of Slav exceptionalism. This ethnically based version of Slavophilia has historically been linked with a sense of cultural identity and political 'duty of care' for the related smaller Slav nations in the Balkans: Bulgarians, Serbians, Macedonians and so on. Russia's sense of guardianship over the welfare of these Slav peoples under Turkish or Austro-Hungarian imperial rule was a major factor in pre-1914 European imperial tensions building up to World War I.

There is also a more expansive, more ethnically pluralistic version of Slavophilia, a more culturally based Russophilia as I call it, that draws strength from Russia's history of successful absorption into the Tsarist 'Empire of all the Russias' of so many non-Slav peoples:

Tatars, Finnish and Baltic peoples, Jews, Poles, Greeks, Georgians, Armenians and so on, through the Siberian, Caucasian and Central Asian imperial conquests or colonisations. Under this more inclusive 'imperial' interpretation of Slavophilia, Russian civilisation has been an inspiration and a boon to surrounding peoples who have through the Tsarist Empire come under its beneficent political and cultural influence. This is a not dissimilar view to the nineteenth-century British Empire view of its benign global mission – 'the white man's burden' – or the French Empire's self-proclaimed '*mission civilisatrice*'.

With one important difference: Russia's growing colonial empire was always advancing into contiguous places and nations, often with pre-existing advanced cultures like the Georgians and Armenians, Central Asian Islamic states, or the Tatars. So there was always a degree of respect for Russia's imperially absorbed former neighbours. One can see this in the orientalist-themed paintings in the Tretyakov Gallery. Russians as imperialists did not usually display the blatant racism of the old British Empire. They were developing a Russian form of multiculturalism over centuries of expansion, and their literature, music and art clearly shows this.

There was, from the beginning, a higher degree of ethnic inter-mingling and enrichment than in Western European colonial empires. Russia was already absorbing large Tatar populations of Islamic faith from the sixteenth century onwards. Either Napoleon or the Marquis de Custine once quipped, 'Scratch the Slav and find a Tatar'. Russians have taken this either as an admiring compliment to their fiercely wild and free nature, or as an insulting claim that their Western civilisation is only skin-deep. There must be Tatar or Mongol DNA in so many Russians, from their centuries of living side by side, invading each other and intermarrying.

Russia's Westernisers start from another cultural place altogether: an anxious perception of Russia's weakness relative to the West, not its strength. They argue that Russia will always be vulnerable to invasions and domination from the more advanced European nations to its west, unless and until it learns from their example how to run a successful modern state and economy. Westernisers argue that Russia needs to learn how to beat the West at its own game if it is not to become a Western dependency, even if it has to sacrifice some of its own unique Russian identity in the process. Only then will the West respect Russia's strength and admit it into the Euro-Atlantic community of advanced national cultures. China, India and Japan all underwent similar important debates about their national identity, in the wake of their initial humiliating failures to resist Western imperialist power.

The first important Westerniser in Russian history was Tsar Peter the Great. We have a benign view of him as a man bent on modernisation – the nice king who learned from the West how to build and sail boats as an incognito carpenter in Holland, and so on. But we overlook how ruthless his methods were. He modernised the Orthodox faith and suppressed the Old Believer Orthodox sect with great force and cruelty. Under threat of arrest and confiscation of estates, he made Russian nobles shave off their beards, wear Western dress, and adopt Western court manners. He dreamed of his new capital Saint Petersburg becoming 'the Venice of the North', a masterpiece of classical Western art and architecture. But the city was built on the backs of serf labour and pitiless taxation of the people: the death toll was huge.

Peter's successors, the German-origin empresses Elizabeth and Catherine, assiduously pursued his Westernisation project, though Russia remained a society based on serfdom until the emancipation of the serfs in 1861. Western skilled immigrants – professional soldiers, engineers, architects, bankers, textile weavers, steelmakers, teachers and doctors, from Germany, France, Britain and Italy – were welcomed into Russia as immigrant settlers, to help accelerate its Westernisation. Parts of the Russian aristocracy actually lost fluency in their native language, so determined were they to educate their children in French language and culture. Russia became two nations – a Westernised cosmopolitan elite, and a conservative Slav Orthodox peasant serf underclass, with smaller merchant, clerical and Jewish classes occupying intermediate social roles.

Only the Orthodox Church, fervently loyal to the Tsar and the Russian language, over time brought together again these otherwise very divergent levels of Russian society. The Napoleonic Wars were a great national unifier, as Tolstoy's *War and Peace* expresses so well. But in most respects, the Westernisers were still ascendant through the nineteenth century.

Napoleon's almost successful invasion led to a revival in the educated elite of Russian national pride and Slavophilia. Their argument with the Westernisers raged on. Most state officials, philosophers, political scientists and industrialists, whose names are now not well remembered outside Russia, were Westernisers. But those we honour as Russia's greatest nineteenth-century writers and artists and composers – like Tolstoy, Dostoyevsky, Turgenev, Chekhov, Repin, Tchaikovsky and Mussorgsky – identified with the Slavophile tendency (though Turgenev, typically, saw merit on both sides).

In both *War and Peace* and *Anna Karenina*, Tolstoy offers us characters and attitudes representing both sides of the argument. Tolstoy gently mocks the francophone elite in *War and Peace*. One of the loveliest moments in the book is when Natasha Rostova, who has only ever been taught French-style ballroom dancing in Moscow, is shown how to dance Russian-style to the music of balalaikas by the peasant-background woman who is the housekeeper-mistress of one of her father's bachelor neighbours. Natasha is entranced, as her buried nursery memories of Russian folk music and dancing come flooding back, and her feet instinctively know the steps. In *Anna Karenina*, the modernising Western-oriented landlord Konstantin Levin has a similar epiphany spending a day in the fields wielding a scythe, harvesting wheat in the traditional way with the local peasants – his family's former serfs, now free men. He glories in his sense of shared Russian identity with them. Tolstoy on his estate, Yasnaya Polyana, was Levin: he wore peasant costume, farmed the land, and opened and taught in a free school for local peasant children.

In the second half of the nineteenth century and into the twentieth, the Russian intelligentsia were rediscovering and falling in love with their previously suppressed Russian identity. This was the cultural milieu Boris Pasternak grew up in. It was a time of revival of long-disparaged Russian architecture, culture and handicrafts. Whole schools of painting grew up, based on the Russian landscape (prior to the nineteenth century, Russian landscapes were not considered interesting enough to paint – Russian painters had to go to Italy to paint landscapes), and on great dramatic moments in Russian history.[4] In music, a national romantic school went back to old Russian historical themes and fairytales, and incorporated church anthems and hymns and folksong tunes into their orchestral music, operas and ballets.[5]

When the Bolsheviks came to power, they found it difficult to situate themselves in this unending national debate. They were Westernisers in the sense that they knew Russia needed Western technical and social models to continue to industrialise, in order to compete politically and militarily with the West. Also, they wanted to do away with the Orthodox Church, which they saw as obscurantist, archaic, Slav-hegemonist and irredeemably tied to old Tsarist values. Finally, Trotsky and those who thought like him aspired to Soviet-led world revolution.

Yet the communists could not deny the authenticity and motivating energy of peasant and working-class Russian culture. And they could see the huge latent mobilising power of Russian national culture if Russia were again to be threatened in war, as it had been in the Civil War of 1917–20. Winning that war had forced the Bolsheviks to espouse – or pretend to – Slavophile values.[6]

The challenge to the Soviet communists on winning the Civil War was: how could they rebuild the old Tsarist Empire as a new Soviet Union of freely uniting national communist parties? Despite facts to the contrary, it was a tenet of Soviet communism that the Soviet Union was to be a voluntary and equal association of national communist republics freely exercising self-determination to come together.

They tried to square the circle: to generate a new public ethos of Soviet patriotism, by promulgating unconvincing propaganda tropes like, 'the Soviet People' or 'the New Soviet Man'. But such ideas were always in fundamental contradiction. How could Russians ever give loyalty to a 'Soviet' motherland? *Rod* means 'family, kin, clan' and *rodina* means 'Russian motherland' or 'Mother Russia' – it can have no other meaning. A *soviet* is a council, a political gathering or association: definitely not a people or a motherland.

Stalin quickly found this out in the Great Patriotic War, when he saw that Soviet communism just was not motivating the people to fight. The Red Army was reeling back, demoralised under the ruthlessly efficient Nazi blitzkrieg assault. Stalin resorted quickly to the old values of Russia – the Russia of the tsars, the Orthodox Church, Pozharsky and Minin – to generate the necessary patriotic zeal and courage to throw back the Nazi invaders. Defence of the Russian motherland – the *rodina* – was the indispensable message to inspire the Russian people to fight for victory in the Great Patriotic War.

This was now the expansive version of Russophilia – with both its huge pride in Russia, and its message that non-Slav Soviet citizens were also invited to share in Russia's great destiny. We see in the final chapters of *Doctor Zhivago* Boris Pasternak's fervent loyalty to this now widely shared concept of Russia.

Communist central committees and political bureaus were always careful to include representatives of minority nationalities – Ukrainians, Byelorussians, Jews, Georgians, Armenians – to strengthen the myth of an emerging Soviet national identity. And of course Stalin and Beria were Georgians. Ukraine, particularly, was regarded as Russia's brother nation in the Soviet Union, and Ukrainians played major roles in every national endeavour, as the Scots have done in the United Kingdom.

But the inner contradictions in the Soviet national idea were again exposed in the Gorbachev and Yeltsin years, when national chauvinism re-emerged as the dominant tendency under perestroika – in the majority Russian as well as in the Soviet minority nationalities.

Gorbachev was a communist, a Westerniser and a fervent believer in the New Soviet Man trope. Yeltsin by contrast was a Russian nationalist, thoroughly disenchanted with Soviet ideology, and willing to harness to his political ambition the widespread popular Russian belief that Russians had been exploited by the Soviet communist power elite to subsidise the other poorer Soviet republics. Yeltsin set out to liberate the Russian people from what he saw as the tyranny of the Soviet bureaucracy. His nativist vision of Russia was wildly popular with ordinary Russians, at least initially.

Alexander Blok, a famous Russian romantic symbolist poet of the late nineteenth and early twentieth century, wrote a really important and disturbing political poem in January 1918, *The Scythians*. He composed it just as the Bolsheviks had taken power in Saint Petersburg and were preparing to sign a humiliating peace with Germany, under which Russia would have to abandon long-held imperial territories in the Baltic States, Byelorussia and Western Ukraine. It was a moment of great national demoralisation and soul-searching.

His defiant, passionate poem asks the old question again: *So, who are we Russians? What is our destiny?* Blok – a Saint Petersburg intellectual – put forward in his 1918 poem a startling proposition: that today's Russians are the proud heirs of the original wild and strong Scythian nomads of the steppe. Their day will come again, when the world will once again come to fear and love Russia's 'Scythian' culture.[7]

The genius of Blok was to cut through the already rather tired Slavophile–Westerniser polemic by going back to the Scythians: these heroic semi-mythical steppe nomads with whom many Russians felt some spiritual or sentimental affinity. His poem, historically wildly inaccurate, is premised on how utterly different Russia is from the old Europe – that the old European world will never solve the riddle of the Russian Sphinx, or prevail over Russia, but should instead link arms with Russia as a friend, before it is too late. Eurasian Russia's 'barbarian lyre' calls Europe to a feast 'of peace and brotherhood'.

And what of today? How is Vladimir Putin addressing Russia's perennial Slavophile–Westerniser conflict?[8] It seems to me that as president, he is pursuing the more inclusive 'Russophile' version of Slavophilia. After the Gorbachev and Yeltsin years of ideological colonisation by Western agencies and values, weakness and corruption, and loss of national morale, the Russian people were ready for Putin's carefully chosen words in his annual presidential message (Poslanie) of 15 December 2012:

> For centuries, Russia developed as a multi-ethnic nation (from the very beginning), a state-civilisation bonded by the Russian people, Russian language, and Russian culture native for all of us, uniting us and preventing us from dissolving in this diverse world.

Putin continues to resist xenophobic excesses of Slavophilia, though he pays lip service to it when it suits him politically, such as in his public warmth towards the Night Wolves, a proto-fascist Slavophile bikie club.

Putin has strongly pursued Yeltsin's vision of warm mutual support between the Russian state and the national Russian Orthodox Church. In this sense, Putin has gone right back to the Tsarist-era concept of Russian national identity. But he also shows a greater respect for Russia's other religious and ethnic-based communities. Putin advocates religious and ethnic pluralism in the way the Tsarist state never did: for the Romanovs as for the communists, anti-minority campaigns were cranked up for reasons of state when considered useful. In his seventeen years in power, Putin has not done this. Today, Russia is a secular state, as affirmed in Yeltsin's 1993 Constitution, although the Orthodox Church has certainly been gaining increasing prominence, resourcing and protection by the state under Putin's rule. Clearly, Patriarch Kirill expects to be heeded when he pronounces on moral issues, and he condemns as heresy some cherished Western human rights values.[9]

When Putin mourns what he calls 'the greatest historical catastrophe of the twentieth century' – the breakup of the Soviet Union – he is not mourning the failed communist attempt to create an artificial Soviet national identity, the New Soviet Man. He is mourning more concrete things: the loss of some of the best, warmest, most fertile and most strategically important places in the former Union, and some of its most creative and dynamic peoples. Above all, I think, Putin regrets the loss of Ukraine. He thinks that the whole Soviet communist ideological experiment abused, and finally under his immediate predecessors fecklessly threw away, the hard-won Russian imperial inheritance from the Tsarist Empire of all the Russias. He thinks that with wise leadership, Russia could have by democratic methods held onto that entire shared inheritance. For him, the old Soviet Union was all in the end 'Russian', in the inclusive sense of imperial patrimony by which he defines it, and for him it is a historical catastrophe that in 1989–91 Russia gave so much of it away – when it really did not need to.

Through my brief exposure to Russia's artistic and musical heritage, I got a sense of how such an expansive view of Russian identity sits easily in the educated class. There is a real puzzlement and pain about why Ukraine's parliamentary leaders turned so violently against Russia – 'after all, Ukrainians are our brothers'. There is real warmth towards non-Slav artists performing in Moscow from former Soviet neighbouring republics like Georgia and Armenia. And some of the 'orientalist' art I saw in the Tretyakov shows a similar mutual respect and admiration between Russians and the adjacent nations they absorbed through imperial conquest into their political and social community.

One can form a much deeper understanding of the nature of the choices Russia faces today, of either becoming more like the West or of holding onto something uniquely Russian, if one keeps in mind this complicated cultural–political history: going back all the way to the Scythian nomads and the Vikings, Kiev Rus' in the tenth century, the expansionist Slav Duchy of Muscovy, the Tatars and the Siberian, Caucasian and Central Asian peoples whom Russia later conquered and more or less absorbed, and the continuing repercussions of Peter the Great's imperial European project. Russia has had to digest so much history.

Something unique was created that exists in Russia today – a complex cultural matrix. Putin and his advisers understand this. But neither the doctrinaire liberal market-economy Westernising faction, nor the narrowly Slavophile crypto-fascist faction which has some minority support in Russia, would understand it. My own view is that Putin is trying to steer Russia, and some of the fragile countries and cultures in its neighbourhood, between these opposite extremes: and that he is doing a good job of it.

Chapter 7

Nizhny Novgorod and Andrei Sakharov

Nizhny Novgorod, named Gorky in the Soviet era after the writer and Writers' Union boss, is the fifth-largest city in Russia, with a population of 1.26 million. A centre of advanced engineering and the aviation industry, it was strictly closed to Western visitors for national security reasons throughout most of the Soviet period. I hoped to find answers in Nizhny Novgorod to these questions: Was Moscow the true face of Russia, or had it become an exception – a rich urban fantasyland, a Westernised playground for wealthy oligarchs and their affluent metropolitan office workers? Would I find a less attractive Russia out here in the provinces – poorer, hungrier, shabbier, more intolerant and xenophobic? More Soviet, in other words? I thought this major industrial city might be a good place to test these questions. I had also read that its surrounds and historic city centre were quite beautiful.

So on my fifteenth day in Russia, a Tuesday, I caught a *Strizh* fast train to Nizhny Novgorod at 7.15 am from Kursk station. A 420-kilometre journey, it took just under four hours, with the new Spanish-built train reaching speeds at times of up to 150 kph on the smooth track. My second-class carriage was clean, well appointed and well served. There were just two stops. I ordered a taxi by internet phone from the train, which met me on arrival in Nizhny. My driver, who I booked for the next day also, was on the station with a hand-written sign showing my name in Cyrillic letters. He took me to the Azimut, a functional three-star business hotel in a commanding scenic location high on the city's natural escarpment above the junction of two mighty rivers, the Volga and the Oka. From my second-floor river-view window it was a magnificent sight over the old town on the riverbank below, with huge landscapes stretching eastwards beyond the wide frozen Volga.

I began to walk around the top of the escarpment towards the historic Nizhny Kremlin, built in the fifteenth century and never conquered by an enemy. It was very beautiful, and the below-zero air was crisp and refreshing. I passed groups of kids excitedly tobogganing on the snowy upper slopes under their carers' watchful gaze, and gingerly picked my way down a slippery icy road into the lower town. I admired the many brightly painted churches there, before tackling a steep pathway and staircase up to the Kremlin. It was all so lovely in the winter sunshine.

The climb was rewarded. I reached the Pozharsky and Minin Town Square and walked through a gateway in a massive stone wall into a large enclosed fortress area, with interesting war memorials scattered around neat gardens amidst government buildings. The Nazi invasion never reached this far, but the war is well remembered in this city, which was a powerhouse of Soviet arms manufacture against Hitler's Germany. On display was a T34 tank. I was struck by its brute strength, its tons of rough-forged crude steel, evoking the desperate urgency of its war production. It had absolutely no frills, no polished surfaces or insignia. They cast and assembled these T34s in their tens of thousands and threw them straight into battle. I also saw a fighter aircraft, one of tens of thousands built here. Like the tank, it was heavily built, squat, with small fixed wings – one wonders how it ever got off the ground, let alone manoeuvred in the air. There was a nearby Monument to the Unknown Soldier with its eternal flame, and a functioning Orthodox memorial church, overlooking the river Volga. I saw the statue of Pozharsky and Minin in the main square and then walked along Bolshaya Pokrovskaya Street, the beautiful pedestrian main street running along the ridge, across the city centre to Gorky Square. Many of the buildings looked to be early nineteenth century or older, going back to Nizhny Novgorod's heyday as a major trading city. This was the old centre – most of the industrial plants and residential areas are out in the newer suburbs.

Nizhny Novgorod – 'Lower Novgorod' – was founded by Russian merchants in 1221. Kazan, the capital of the Tatar Kazan Khanate, conquered by Ivan the Terrible in 1552, was 390 kilometres to the east. The Volga, a great river which starts far to the north-west of Moscow, winds down through this rich fertile area, which over the centuries has been home to an incredible patchwork of peoples, states, languages and religions, all the way south to the Caspian Sea. Orthodox Christians, Buddhists, Muslims and animists are all native to this huge fertile middle Volga region. To live here is to experience Russia's diversity.

I bought some local fine angora-wool scarves and painted brooches in a well-stocked souvenir-and-handicrafts shop. At dusk, lots of people were strolling along Pokrovskaya, despite the encroaching chill. There is a live tradition here of the early-evening promenade, as in Mediterranean countries (and also, as I was to find later, in Saint Petersburg). The street lights came on, glittering on the snowy street, and it all looked quite lovely. People were well dressed, though perhaps rather more conservatively than in Moscow.

On Wednesday I was keen to ride the aerial cableway to the satellite industrial town of Bor, 3 kilometres away across the Volga. From my cable car high in the sky, I looked down at large numbers of people fishing through holes sawn in the ice. Some fishermen were well set up with tents and charcoal braziers on legs – others just toughed it out, sitting huddled on stools or boxes and wearing warm winter tracksuits and beanies.

I met a fellow in his forties on the funicular who had lost his industrial job in a factory in Bor recently. He said the factory had been sold and the new owners had sacked the old workforce and brought in their own people as workers. I asked how he was faring, and he said fortunately his wife had a well-paid job in town. They had a low-mortgage flat in Bor, to which they owned the title from his previous factory job. He said the city government did not spend enough money on keeping the streets clear of snow, and they did not do enough to create jobs for people. Basically, they looked after themselves and their cronies.

When I got to Bor, I wandered around the town. It felt very quiet and rather bleak, maybe because it was still early in the morning.

There was a pedimented council building of typical classic Russian design, light brown, with a big statue of Lenin out in front: in Bor, it felt as if I was back in the USSR. Across the road, treed avenues radiated out, lined with sedate apartment buildings – no shops to be seen, few signs, few cars, even fewer people. In the distance were factory chimneys. I was quite glad after a beer in a cafe to take the cableway back across the river to the much more lively city centre.

I visited a nineteenth-century rich merchant's mansion on the prestigious embankment road high above the river, now a museum – the Rukavishnikov Mansion. It was impressive. I could readily imagine the busy commercial and social life in this house 150 years ago. The three-storey house had its own ballroom and salons for sitting out, all ornately decorated and furnished. The office with its huge mahogany desk and bookcases filled with leather-bound books bespoke wealth and power and strong imperial connections. One felt the raw commercial energy and massive resources of this rich merchant family dynasty.

I lunched at the Vitalich, a recommended restaurant on Bolshaya Pokrovskaya. I was told it was Nizhny Novgorod's best, founded in 1992, and favoured by the city's political and business elite. It was a restored private house, with cosy interconnected dining rooms of moderate size. It was well furnished, and the food was excellent – as was the local house vodka. Vintage paintings and photographs and hunting trophies adorned the walls. My waiter was a real professional, an older man experienced in and proud of his job. The tables were quite full, mostly business lunch groups, and smartly dressed ladies lunching together. I was the only non-Russian there.

After lunch, my taxi driver drove me to an outer suburb, around fifteen kilometres from the centre. I was going out to see Andrei Sakharov's place of enforced exile from 1980 to 1986, a small two-bedroom flat which has been turned into a mini-museum (the main Sakharov Museum, which I did not get to see, is in Moscow).

Andrei Sakharov (1921–89) is another huge and heroic figure in Russia's painfully slow democratisation after Stalin. Drawing on his domestic and international prestige as a leading Soviet nuclear-weapons scientist in the 1950s – he is known as 'father of the Russian H-bomb' – Sakharov, in his last twenty-two years of life, became a leading figure in the international movement towards East–West peaceful coexistence. He devoted these latter years to the search for ways to reduce East–West tensions and the existential risk of thermonuclear war by design or miscalculation. Sakharov reluctantly became, along with Solzhenitsyn, a focus of dissidence in the long struggle for human rights and liberation of the peoples of the Soviet Union from communist repression. The fictional Russian scientist Yakov Savelyev, in Le Carré's *The Russia House*, is a character in some ways modelled on Sakharov. But with one important difference: Sakharov never betrayed his country.

The importance of his intellectual and moral leadership, heroism and personal sacrifice cannot be rated too highly. The older he got, the braver he became. Together with Nelson Mandela and Martin Luther King, he was one of the modern world's great heroes of conscience.

Sakharov married in 1943, aged twenty-two. A photo of him at this time hints at his intense energy and brilliant mind. He and his wife, Klavdia, raised two daughters and a son. Klavdia died young, in 1969, when he was still just forty-eight.

Sakharov had obtained his doctorate in nuclear physics in 1947 at the age of twenty-six. The next year, he started work on the Soviet top-secret nuclear-bomb project. The first Soviet bomb was tested in 1949. Sakharov continued to work on the development of higher-capacity thermonuclear devices, leading up to the 50 megaton Tsar Bomba, tested in 1961, the most powerful nuclear bomb ever detonated at that time. Sakharov in his later years defended his work in developing Soviet nuclear weapons, saying, 'After more than forty years, we have had no third world war, and the balance of nuclear terror...may have helped to prevent one'. It is clear that he believed his years of urgent scientific work to create a credible Soviet second-strike nuclear response weapon helped to deter the United States from ever being tempted to try to 'take out' or blackmail the Soviet Union from a position of unassailable first-strike nuclear capability. He did not assume American goodwill or restraint towards his country, then or later.

Yet he believed that the system of Mutual Assured Destruction (MAD), which he had helped to establish through building a credible Russian second-strike capability, needed to be made safer and less prone to war by accident or miscalculation, and his ideas on how to do this (through Moscow–Washington emergency telephone 'hot lines', early warning systems of accidental launches, and mutual agreement not to deploy 'tactical' nuclear weapons that would blur the distinction between conventional and nuclear war) positively influenced the strategies of both nuclear superpowers. He was thus the architect of a more stable Cold War.

From the late 1950s, he became more concerned about the moral and political implications of nuclear weapons. He opposed nuclear proliferation and pushed for an end to superpower atmospheric nuclear testing, which was halted by the 1963 Partial Test Ban Treaty signed in Moscow under Khrushchev.

In 1967, Sakharov, now aged forty-six, began to urge the Soviet Government to accept American proposals for a bilateral ban on developing anti-ballistic missile-defence systems. At this time, the Politburo foolishly thought Russia could survive a nuclear war if it installed sufficiently strong and numerous defensive missile systems. Ironically, sixteen years later US President Reagan succumbed to the same folly with his vaunted 'Star Wars' Strategic Defense Initiative.

Sakharov, understanding the crucial importance for peace of maintaining a stable nuclear-deterrent balance, wrote an article in 1967 intended for publication in a leading Soviet journal, explaining why he supported a bilateral ban on anti-ballistic missile-defence systems. The Soviet Government (then led by Brezhnev) suppressed its publication.

This suppression fatally provoked him into taking his next, irrevocably defiant step: writing his famous comprehensive essay on world political and environmental challenges, *Reflections on Progress, Peaceful Coexistence and Intellectual Freedom*.[1] He first circulated this essay by *samizdat* in the Soviet Union in May 1968. It was, inevitably, soon smuggled out to the West and published in English translation, in full, in the *New York Times* in August 1968, one year before I arrived in Moscow.

It is a powerful, captivating argument, in a dense, wide-ranging manifesto: one of the most important political statements of the twentieth century. It makes relevant and prophetic reading even today. One is struck by how many of its criticisms of the then Soviet political elite are as pertinent to attitudes in parts of the US political elite today: of superpower exceptionalism disdain for UN Security Council–based global peacekeeping orders, and indifference to the urgency of the global warming crisis. I recall that my dominant impression from my first reading of it in 1968 was how profoundly it challenged Soviet Government policies. Now I read it as having universal relevance in its challenges to short-sighted, ignorant and parochial-minded governments anywhere.

Retribution was swift. Sakharov was banned from any further military-related research, which meant isolation from his scientific community. In 1970 he co-founded the dissident Committee on Human Rights in the USSR.

In 1972, aged fifty-two, he married Yelena Bonner, a medical doctor and fellow human rights activist. A former Communist Party member, she had been disillusioned by Brezhnev's suppression of the Prague Spring democracy movement in 1968. They met in 1970, a year after the death of Sakharov's first wife Klavdia. Yelena, two years younger than Andrei, was beyond child-bearing age: she had two grown-up children from her first marriage. She was the daughter of a high-ranking Armenian communist father and a Russian Jewish communist mother. Her father was executed in Stalin's Great Purge and her mother served eight years in the Gulag, followed by nine years of internal exile. Both were 'rehabilitated' under Khrushchev following Stalin's death.

From 1972 on, Soviet official and media attacks against Sakharov and Alexander Solzhenitsyn became more intense. Both men were now alleged to be traitors to the Soviet Union. In those years, Sakharov came to realise more fully the utter dysfunctionality of the Soviet communist political system. He famously compared it to cancer cells in an otherwise healthy organism. The more he was anathemised by the Soviet authorities, the more his fame and popularity in the West grew. Yet Soviet people in general knew little of this.

He now saw respect for human rights as the only proper basis for any politics. He was awarded the Nobel Peace Prize in 1975 but was not allowed to leave the Soviet Union to collect it. Yelena went to Norway and read his speech 'Peace, Progress, and Human Rights'.[2] It argued that peace, progress and human rights are indissolubly linked to one another: that it is impossible to achieve one of these goals if the other two are ignored. Here are some of his closing words:

> Without losing sight of an overall solution of this kind, we must today fight for every individual person separately against injustice and the violation of human rights. Much of our future depends on this.
>
> In struggling to protect human rights we must, I am convinced, first and foremost act as protectors of the innocent victims of regimes installed in various countries, without demanding the destruction or total condemnation of these regimes. We need reform, not revolution. We need a pliant, pluralist, tolerant community, which selectively and tentatively can bring about a free, undogmatic use of the experiences of all social systems. What is détente? What is rapprochement? We are concerned not with words, but with a willingness to create a better and more friendly society, a better world order.
>
> Thousands of years ago tribes of human beings suffered great privations in the struggle to survive. In this struggle it was important not only to be able to handle a club, but also to possess the ability to think reasonably, to take care of the knowledge and experience garnered by the tribe, and to develop the links that would provide cooperation with other tribes. Today the entire human race is faced with a similar test...

Five years later, he was arrested under the Brezhnev regime in 1980, following his leading role in public protests against the Soviet decision to send troops to Afghanistan in support of the locally unpopular pro-Soviet Government there. This military intervention was massively condemned as an invasion by the UN General Assembly, under strong urging from the Western powers, by a vote of 104–18 (but had it ever gone to the Security Council, the Soviet Union would have vetoed any resolution under its veto right). Afghan Muslim mujahedin insurgents, forerunners of the Taliban and al-Qaeda, received massive amounts of arms and covert military support from the United States and Pakistan, and soon gained control of most of the country. The

Soviet Union took heavy casualties in this long unwinnable war, which became increasingly unpopular at home. It was the Soviet Union's and Russia's worst strategic disaster: their Vietnam. Finally, between 1987 and 1989, Gorbachev took the hard but necessary decision to withdraw all Soviet forces from Afghanistan. Sakharov had been right all along.

Sakharov was never convicted of any crime – he had huge international prestige, and under the Helsinki Accords it would have been impossible credibly to convict him in any open Soviet court. Instead, he was in 1980 administratively silenced: sent by government order to indefinite internal exile in Gorky, a city off-limits to foreigners. The terms of his exile as stated to him by the Gorky Procurator were: 'overt surveillance, prohibition against leaving the city limits, prohibition against meeting with foreigners and "criminal elements", prohibition against correspondence and telephone conversations with foreigners, including scientific and purely personal communications, even with [his own] children and grandchildren'.[3] His apartment was kept under tight KGB surveillance from an apartment opposite, maintained 24/7 by tag teams of KGB officers tasked to monitor all his movements and visitors. He recalled later that they repeatedly searched and harassed him. His phone was cut off.

For his first four years in Gorky, his wife, Yelena, was still free to travel internally. She was his lifeline, his only tenuous connection to the outside world through Moscow. But in April 1984 (with Chernenko now Soviet President), Yelena was herself arrested. In response, Sakharov went on his first hunger strike. He was force-fed. The next month, Yelena too was ordered to five years' exile in Gorky. Picture their situation now: they had no phone, no local friends. They were in complete isolation, and every rare message they smuggled out involved danger for themselves and their clandestine helpers.

In March 1985 Chernenko died and Gorbachev became Soviet leader. In April 1985 Sakharov, now sixty-four, again went on hunger strike, demanding that his wife be allowed to travel to the United States for necessary medical treatment for her serious heart condition. Again he was force-fed in hospital for months, until October 1985 when Gorbachev finally allowed Yelena to go to America for heart surgery. She returned to Gorky, cured, in June 1986.

In December 1986, twenty-one months into Gorbachev's rule, Gorbachev blinked first. He ordered the reconnection of Sakharov's phone line, and he made the first self-congratulatory phone call to him in six years, to pass on the 'good news' that Sakharov and his wife were now permitted to return to Moscow as free citizens. He had spent six years in exile in Gorky and undergone at least two risky and life-shortening hunger strikes.

If Gorbachev expected Sakharov to live quietly and gratefully count his blessings back in Moscow, he misjudged the man. Able at last to speak and write again, Sakharov's accounts of his and Yelena's ordeals gained him renewed public recognition and respect. In March 1989, Sakharov was elected to the new Soviet Parliament, the People's All-Union Congress of People's Deputies, where he co-led the democratic opposition against Mikhail Gorbachev's Communist Party. In December 1989 he died of a heart attack, aged sixty-eight, while preparing an important speech to deliver the next day, critical of Gorbachev's indecisive and half-hearted implementation of perestroika. Yelena Bonner lived another twenty-two years: she died in 2011 aged ninety-two, an indomitable human rights activist until the end. She must have been as brave and resolute as Sakharov himself, but physically she proved stronger than he.

There can be no doubt that Sakharov's death was hastened by the stresses of the official mistreatment meted out to him and to Yelena between 1972–86, and especially the last six years of punitive isolation in Gorky in 1980–86. Journalist David Remnick recalled that by 1989 Sakharov's heart was failing: he was breathless and could barely walk up short flights of stairs, and he looked fifteen years older than his age. His gaunt face in photographs in his last year shows the toll it had all taken on his health.

In December 1999, Boris Yeltsin – now President of Russia – nominated Sakharov to *Time* magazine as his choice for 'Person of the Century'.

The ground-floor flat was drab and tiny, as I expected. But it was moving to walk through it, wondering what sort of constrained life this brave, formerly highly privileged, middle-aged couple had suffered in their cruel and anachronistic Gorky exile, for the sake of their abstract principles of humanism and human rights. Most of us would not have had their courage. Yes, it was not as bad as the Gulag – but this was long after the era of the Gulag, in modern times, and after the Soviet Union had promised to observe the Helsinki human rights accords.

It must have been a kind of slow death. I suppose they could cook and read and listen to music on the radio and enjoy some basic warmth and domestic comfort in their little flat, but it would have been soul-destroyingly lonely. But they never cracked, right through the final years of post-Stalinist communism and well into the Gorbachev era. In the end, it was Gorbachev who gave way. A fact that would surely have not escaped Boris Yeltsin, already measuring his own strength against Gorbachev in their deepening battle of wills.

It is interesting to trace important political connections between Sakharov, Gorbachev and Yeltsin in the crucial years of change of 1987–91. Conor O'Clery offers clues.[4] He writes that the first ten-day session of the new People's Congress in May 1989, a Gorbachev perestroika initiative that was televised throughout Russia, made a powerful impact on Yeltsin, as he watched democratic reformers venting 'anger and vitriol' against the Soviet communist system. O'Clery writes:

> Yeltsin himself became a different person through his exposure to the radical reformers who gathered around him in the Kremlin foyer. Andrey Sakharov especially made a strong impression.
>
> Sakharov did not like Yeltsin, but he saw in him a leader for the emerging democrats, one who had a level of support among the proletariat to which members of the intelligentsia could not aspire. The Congress marked the real start of Yeltsin's political evolution from communist 'stormer' to anti-communist democrat.[5]

On this reading, Sakharov's final year of life (1989), spent in perestroika-inspired Moscow politics, was a major influence on Yeltsin's decision to challenge Gorbachev in 1991, and all that has followed since in Russia.

Could Sakharov have foreseen that, just two years after Gorbachev's repeated public humiliations of him and of Yeltsin in the All-Union People's Congress sessions in 1989, Gorbachev himself would be so contemptuously and decisively evicted from power by Yeltsin in 1991? And that both the Communist Party and the Soviet Union would suddenly become history? My guess is that events in 1989 were now moving too swiftly even for Sakharov with his great wisdom to comprehend the fast-emerging possibilities in Russia for radical change. For so many years he had struggled heroically against a rock-solid immobile system: he can hardly be faulted for not seeing the widening cracks in the granite. All his political writings and speeches seemed to accept as given that the powerful Soviet Communist Party institutions and entrenched values were there to stay and could only be humanised gradually, step by step.

O'Clery writes powerfully on the political impact of Sakharov's death and burial:

On the evening of December 14, 1989, Andrey Sakharov, the intellectual force for change in Russia who complemented Yeltsin's crude political force, died from a heart attack. The former dissident was eulogised by a guilty nation that realised it had lost its moral compass. His body was laid out in the Academy of Sciences building, and tens of thousands of mourners queued in heavy snow to file past the bier. Gorbachev and other politburo members came and stood briefly to pay their respects to the honest scientist whom they had kept in internal exile as a dissident. Boris Yeltsin stood motionless for several minutes by his body, as if absorbing Sakharov's spirit and acknowledging his own new role as undisputed leader of the opposition in a fast-changing Russia. Yeltsin was now the most prominent member of a loose collection of elected radicals known as the Interregional Group of Deputies, which had held some chaotic, freewheeling sessions since it was formed in a Moscow hotel lobby during the summer to press for speedier reform.

Before Sakharov was interred in the Vostryakovskoye Cemetery, over 100,000 people attended a funeral rally in a slushy car park at which calls for the end of the Communist Party's monopoly predominated. Commuters in a passing train opened windows to shout and wave encouragement. The public mood was becoming more defiant of authority. Such displays boded ill for a party that relied on control of an apathetic people to remain in power.[6]

I talked to my taxi driver on the way to the train station to catch my train back to Moscow. He said Sakharov had been a decent man, and seemed quite proud of the connection to Nizhny Novgorod, but he said Yelena Bonner had been a CIA agent who had turned Sakharov away from his loyalty to Russia.

My taxi driver said life had been more secure for him under the Soviet system. True, there was more opportunity now for some individuals to do well, but he was just getting by with his own owner-driver taxi business. He had used to be a good athlete at college: he had competed in events in East Europe, in a Soviet Volga Region team. He thought the present government was keeping the country safe. He was sad about the conflict with Ukraine, saying, 'They are just like us – it should never have come to this'.

Chapter 8

Yekaterinburg and Boris Yeltsin

I flew to Yekaterinburg (former Soviet name Sverdlovsk), Russia's fourth-largest city, population 1.387 million in 2012, and 1422 kilometres and four hours' time-zone change east of Moscow, on the far side of the Urals, that separate European Russia from Siberia. Yekaterinburg is the same distance from Moscow as is Berlin. I wanted to see a major Russian heartland industrial city, far from Moscow; to get a glimpse of Siberia; to witness where the Tsar's family had been murdered; and to visit the very recently opened Boris Yeltsin Museum.

I arrived in Yekaterinburg on a clear, sunny but very cold day: minus 15 degrees Celsius, far colder than Moscow; real Siberian weather at last. Coming in to land, the snowy countryside looked refreshingly unspoiled – almost Australian. My taxi into the city passed tidy dacha communities scattered among the surrounding forests and open fields, all deeply buried in snow. As we entered the city, there was an interesting mix of old and new: modern zones of high-rise office and apartment buildings, scattered among older Soviet-style apartment housing, and heritage areas of Tsarist-era public buildings and old timber homes and communal dwellings.

From my mid-town hotel, the Tsentralnaya, I walked up a main street to the site where the deposed former Tsar Nicholas II and his family were executed by volunteer firing squad on 16 July 1918, at the height of the Civil War. White forces were advancing on Yekaterinburg. Moscow feared that if the Whites rescued the Tsar, he might become a rallying point of invigorated resistance. Unwilling to risk moving the royal family again, Moscow ordered all of them killed in their house of imprisonment. They were secretly shot overnight by volunteer firing squad in a cellar, their bodies smuggled out in carts and hidden in unmarked country pits.

And yes, I wept at the immediacy of the dreadful memory of this atrocity inflicted on innocent people. I wept for Tsar Nicholas and his young family. In no way did they deserve this cruelty.

I saw the imposing new cathedral built at President Boris Yeltsin's urging, grandly named the 'Church on Blood in Honour of All Saints Resplendent in the Russian Land'. Yeltsin supported the construction of this church partly in expiation of his own remorse: he had been the young local Communist Party chief in Yekaterinburg who in 1977 had dutifully carried out the order to bulldoze the Ipatiev House – the local merchant's house in whose cellar the royal family had been killed – because it was rapidly becoming a national shrine of pilgrimage.

Construction began in 2000 – the same year the Romanov family was canonised as saints and martyrs by the Russian Orthodox Church, nineteen years after they had been similarly canonised by the Russian Orthodox Church Abroad.

Next stop was the new Yeltsin Museum downtown, opened very recently by President Putin on 25 November 2015.[1] I had expected this museum would deepen my understanding of the profound changes in Russia between the late communist period and the present Putin period, but I had little idea how interesting and even moving it would be. I want to report on this museum in some detail, because it is impossible to make a fair evaluation of the Putin years since 2000 without some familiarity with the dramatic and painful preceding fifteen years of revolutionary upheaval and Western intervention: a story little known in the West outside specialist circles.

I had gone into Russia with some broad impressions of Gorbachev and Yeltsin. Roughly, I had believed that Gorbachev was a good man, a liberal at heart but held back from full achievement of his political ideals by the conservative Communist Party hierarchy and bureaucracy. From 1985 to 1991, he had gone as far and as fast as he prudently could in humanising and modernising the Communist Party. His greatest achievement was to end the Cold War and to achieve détente with the West, first with US President Reagan and then with President George H. W. Bush.

I had believed his successor Yeltsin (1991–99) was an unsophisticated, impulsive demagogue from Siberia, a Russian nationalist who abandoned communism and exploited Russian populism in order to advance his personal ambition for the top job; who irresponsibly engineered the dissolution of the Soviet Union, which was under no particular threat from the West at the time; who had bravely defended democracy in the Moscow streets against communist coup leaders' army tanks in 1991, but then turned the same tanks on the people in 1993; whose political judgement was impaired by alcoholism; who fecklessly presided over uncontrolled, almost random processes of privatisation that caused huge economic insecurity and hardship to millions of people in 1991–99; and whose one final useful act was to bequeath the leadership to a more competent and clear-headed Vladimir Putin in 2000.

This museum offers a more nuanced, generous view of Yeltsin. Sponsored by Yeltsin's widow and daughters, and supported by President Putin, it urges a more balanced appreciation of the immense challenges Yeltsin faced and how he addressed them. It is presented chronologically, as a narrative of key days of decision in the political life of this first president of post-communist Russia.

First we saw a graphic film in a panoramic 3-Max theatre, presenting highlights of Russian history since the time of the ninth century Varangian invasions and the founding of Kiev Rus' until now. Its message was the perennial conflict in Russia between natural popular strivings for democracy, and the repeated reimposition of autocratic rule from above: always justified by elites by the claimed need for a strong militarised centralised state to defend the nation against foreign invaders. Then, a large display room titled *Labyrinth* offered a mini-museum of highlights of twentieth-century Russian history and the story of Yeltsin's family origins.

Yeltsin was the same age as Gorbachev, born in 1931, but the two men could not have been more different. Yeltsin was a tall, strong country kid from a village near Sverdlovsk. His father was an independent peasant farmer who was arrested and sent to the Gulag for five years when he resisted the confiscation of the family grain harvest during Stalin's collectivisation. His mother, Klavdiya, supported the family in those hard years as a seamstress. Yeltsin went to a technical university and qualified in construction. Initially, he worked as a foreman on city building sites. A charismatic natural leader, he was invited to join the Communist Party where he advanced rapidly. In 1976, he was appointed party boss for the Sverdlovsk region. In 1985, looking for new blood to rejuvenate the tired and jaded party elite in Moscow, General Secretary Gorbachev, the new CPSU General Secretary, promoted Yeltsin to Moscow as First Secretary (party chief) for the capital city – though Gorbachev was warned that Yeltsin was a firebrand and might be hard to control. Yeltsin was now an ex officio candidate member of the politburo – effectively, a junior minister in Gorbachev's first perestroika Communist Party Cabinet.

The first display, *We are waiting for changes*, presents an animated 3-D holograph of Yeltsin's defiant 'secret speech', throwing down the gauntlet to the Party Central Committee meeting on 21 October 1987. We see and hear the actual speech Yeltsin made, as Gorbachev and politburo colleagues grimly stare down on him from the podium.

Gorbachev, the cautious master tactician steering the uneasy balance between conservative and reformist forces in the Soviet Communist Party, the man who decided how far and how fast his goals of glasnost (openness) and perestroika (reconstruction) could safely be implemented, had just made a major set-piece speech to the meeting. Unexpectedly, Yeltsin put up his hand to speak.

In Moscow as in Sverdlovsk, Yeltsin's populist style of governance – riding commuter buses, inspecting shops without notice, chasing down corruption scandals – had endeared him to the people. But his and Gorbachev's political styles were antipathetic. They had first openly clashed in a closed politburo meeting in February 1987. Now, Gorbachev had decided to give the upstart Yeltsin enough rope to hang himself. Which Yeltsin duly did.

Yeltsin criticised the lack of progress under perestroika: he said it was 'mostly words', there was too little real change. He accused Gorbachev of the beginnings of a personality cult. There was uproar. Yeltsin was ridiculed for his naivety by Gorbachev and every subsequent speaker. Despite his abject apologies, Gorbachev sacked Yeltsin from the Moscow-party-boss job and from the politburo candidate membership, and gave him a minor bureaucratic job as a consolation prize. It seemed the end of Yeltsin's political career. Yeltsin was only fifty-six.

But news of his speech got around Moscow, and the people admired his courage and rebellious spirit. They did not allow him to be forgotten. When in March 1989 Yeltsin decided to stand independently for election for the Moscow seat in the Soviet Congress of People's Deputies, a new directly elected all-Soviet parliament – and a Gorbachev perestroika initiative to decentralise Communist Party power and give more voice to the people – Yeltsin won brilliantly, receiving nine out of every ten votes cast in Moscow. This victory brought him firmly back into the political mainstream and cemented him in the affections of Muscovites.

His next opportunity came a year later in March 1990, when he stood for his old base of Sverdlovsk in the new Russian republican parliament, the Russian Congress of People's Deputies – another Gorbachev democratising initiative. Yeltsin's platform called for a multi-party system, a popularly elected president, and freedom for non-Russian republics to secede from the Soviet Union if they wished – all revolutionary ideas at the time. He won convincingly in a landslide, gaining 84 per cent of the vote. Conor O'Clery comments:

> He had drawn on a deep well of discontent with the failure of communism to feed and clothe its people adequately and on the perception that Russia was exploited by the other fourteen republics, where people lived better lives.[2]

Two months later in May 1990, building his platform of greater sovereignty for Russia, Yeltsin stood for election by the members of the Russian Republic Parliament as Chairman of its Presidium: in effect, as Russia's first elected head of government. Gorbachev, now feeling really threatened by Yeltsin's drive to power, visited the new parliament (which still contained many old communists accustomed to obeying the party leader) to campaign openly against its members electing Yeltsin as their chairman. In spite of this stern warning,

Yeltsin narrowly won by just four votes. The popularity of his Russia-first program continued to grow.

Yeltsin was riding the new public wave of Russian national pride and sense of grievance against the old Soviet and Communist Party straitjackets. Like a lover promising a new life with a more exciting partner to a wife stuck in a stale and joyless marriage, he was offering to the resentful Russian people the hope of a new political union with their real love – Russia.

And he believed this himself. A revelatory visit to an average supermarket during his first official US tour as Russia's president had convinced him that the Soviet Communist Party – of which he was still a card-carrying member – had over many decades cheated Russian people out of the welfare and comfort that was their right.

Gorbachev and Yeltsin had hated each other since their first clashes in 1987. They were like chalk and cheese – Gorbachev the crafty, risk-averse, cold and at times arrogant contingency planner, versus Yeltsin the romantic, impetuous, charismatic force of nature. Their personal feud was now being played out on an epic national battlefield of two competing visions: the old communist hierarchy-driven Soviet Union, versus Yeltsin's dream of a new democratic, populist Russia. Gorbachev had aroused public hopes and expectations for change, but had failed to deliver. Now Yeltsin was openly challenging him – though ironically, they shared many similar political values and long-term goals.

In this contest, Yeltsin and Russia would prevail: one and a half years later, on 25 December 1991, the Soviet Union and Gorbachev's job as its president would cease to exist. But in 1987, and even in May 1990, all that was still in the future, and I doubt if Yeltsin planned so far ahead. My sense is that Yeltsin, a big fuzzy bear of a man, a warm man of reckless emotion and impulse, took his political life one step at a time, seizing opportunities in reaction to events as they unfolded.

The next important challenge – what the museum calls the Second Day – came two months later in July 1990, at the 28th Congress of the Soviet Communist Party. Communist conservatives – still in the numerical majority, but increasingly despised and ignored by progressives who were dominating debate and driving the public agenda – were by now highly apprehensive about the whole perestroika program and Gorbachev's leadership of it. Following an unenthusiastically received speech by Gorbachev, a succession of senior conservative communist speakers rose to speak. They included the defence minister and the head of the KGB, who would be leaders of the attempted communist rising against Gorbachev a year later. They openly denounced 'antisocialist elements' in the party, implicitly criticising Gorbachev himself for his weakness in not suppressing these elements.

Yeltsin seized his moment. Impetuously, he strode to the podium and declared that as Chairman of the Russian Parliament he preferred to 'bow to the will of all the people', rather than follow party instructions. He was therefore resigning his Communist Party membership. Handing in his card, he dramatically walked out of the Party Congress. He was followed out by several radicals. It was a turning point in history.

Gorbachev was urged by his more progressive advisers to follow Yeltsin's lead. But – and this is typical of the man – he chose proudly and cautiously to remain as Soviet Communist Party leader, and not to risk civil war by triggering an open split within the party. He still hoped to carry the conservative party membership forward with him step by step, and he still believed in the Soviet Union as the best hope for all of its intermingled peoples. He thought Yeltsin's Russian nationalism and extremist style was highly dangerous. Gorbachev memorably warned the media after this historic Congress: 'We are knee deep in kerosene...and we are tossing matches'.[3]

Gorbachev hoped the public would finally see through Yeltsin's showmanship. But in the eyes of the increasingly politically discerning Moscow public, Gorbachev had chosen the security of the old Communist Party and Soviet institutions over democracy. Contempt was building for his cautious gradualism.

Meanwhile, the economy was sinking fast, with old central-command economic relationships confused and destabilised by perestroika. Gorbachev, though still greatly admired in the West as the architect of glasnost, perestroika and détente, was now seen in Russia as an indecisive, failed leader. The Baltic States spoke with increasing militancy of secession. There was an armed attack on Soviet border guards.

Yeltsin, buoyed by public enthusiasm, pressed on with his separatist agenda. In June 1991 – eleven months after his resignation from the party – took place the first direct mass election for the post of President of the Russian Republic, a position Yeltsin already occupied de facto as Chairman of the Presidium of the Russian Parliament, but only at the pleasure of that parliament. Yeltsin now secured by public referendum approval to hold a direct popular vote for the new post of 'President of Russia'. Yeltsin won this election decisively – 46 million votes against 22 million for the other three candidates combined. His position in Russia was now politically unassailable.

In a grandiose ceremony, Yeltsin was inaugurated as 'the first freely elected leader in Russia's thousand-year history'.[4] He was blessed by Patriarch Alexy II of Moscow and all Russia, as a choir sang the triumphal *Slava* ('glory') hymn from Glinka's nineteenth-century national opera *A Life for the Tsar*.

Yeltsin declared euphorically: 'Great Russia is rising from its knees. We shall surely transform it into a prosperous, law-based, democratic, peaceful and sovereign state'.[5]

Two months later came the communist hardliners' botched coup of 18–22 August 1991. The museum has a life-size 3-D display of democrats manning hastily erected street barricades with Yeltsin leading them in defence of the White House, the seat of Russia's new parliament, against encircling Red Army tanks still obeying orders from the Soviet Minister for Defence.

In this summer of 1991, I was halfway through my first year as Australian Ambassador to Poland, and reporting to Canberra that the Poles were genuinely apprehensive that the Soviet Union might try to reimpose the Warsaw Pact by force, if Gorbachev were to be toppled by communist hardliners. While an exhausted and despondent Gorbachev was on holiday with his wife, Raisa, at their official Black Sea mansion, the most senior members of his Cabinet, including the KGB Head, the Defence Minister and the Minister for the Interior, made their long-feared bid for power. They flew to the Black Sea and demanded that Gorbachev declare a state of emergency and martial law. If he refused, they would 'invite' him to resign and set up an emergency committee to run the country themselves. Troops loyal to the plotters would take control of the White House, the new Russian Parliament building, and arrest anyone who resisted. Gorbachev by his own account told the traitors to go to hell. He was put under KGB house arrest. The plotters returned to Moscow.

Yeltsin first heard about the coup on Monday 19 August, as it was already being announced on Russian news media as an accomplished fact. The strong and popular mayors of Moscow and Saint Petersburg, Yuri Luzhkov and Anatoly Sobchak, who happened to be visiting Moscow at the time, came straight to Yeltsin's home. They urged him to resist the coup in his capacity as Russia's president, and they promised to organise popular resistance in both cities. Emboldened by their support, Yeltsin drove straight to the White House in an armoured car flanked by bodyguards. Unarmed, he stood in the street facing the irresolute army-tank crews outside the building, and told them to go home. Over the next two crucial days, the coup plotters' nerve broke and their military support melted away. By Wednesday, the coup had collapsed in ignominy and its leaders were arrested.

O'Clery tells an important story about parallel events in Saint Petersburg. When Mayor Sobchak confronted troop commanders there and persuaded them not to enter the city, standing by his side was his Special Assistant, former KGB officer Vladimir Putin. As Putin later told the story:

> Sobchak and I practically moved into the city council. We drove to the Kirov factory and to other plants to speak to the workers. But we were nervous. We even passed out pistols, though I left my service revolver in the safe. People everywhere supported us.[6]

In the middle of this turmoil, Sobchak at Putin's request telephoned the head of the KGB, Kryuchkov, to advise him that Putin had today resigned his KGB commission. Putin was prudently concerned that if the plotters won, his support as a serving KGB officer for Sobchak could be considered by Kryuchkov as a 'crime of office', i.e. treason.

The failed coup sealed Yeltsin's political victory over Gorbachev. Yeltsin was now the undisputed master of Russia and Gorbachev a spent political force. The Communist Party had been fatally discredited by its own top politburo leaders' anti-democratic attempted coup and their irresolution in pursuing it. Gorbachev, protected physically by President Bush's urgent plea to Yeltsin that he not be harmed or humiliated, would nominally preside for just four more months over a fading Soviet Union. Yeltsin already ruled the real new nation of Russia.

Gorbachev was criticised later for placing his trust in his most senior communist national-security ministers in the politburo, and not seeing their disloyal coup coming. There was even a suspicion, shared by Yeltsin but which Gorbachev hotly denies, that Gorbachev may have had advance knowledge of the coup and was waiting it out in the safety of his Black Sea house to see which side won. Gorbachev's version was that he had wanted to keep his enemies close to him.

The museum confronts without flinching the next epochal event a few months later – the December 1991 Belavezha meeting when Yeltsin and his fellow Ukrainian and Byelorussian presidents agreed on a fast-track timetable to terminate the Soviet Union. I watched a film clip of a history professor saying confidently:

> The Soviet Union was already dead, Yeltsin [and the two other republic presidents at Belavezha] just signed the death certificate. The Soviet Union was beyond saving, it had lost all credibility by this point.

There is a huge audiovisual wall map showing how the Soviet Union split into fifteen independent nations during the last months of 1991, as one country after another declared sovereign independence, starting with the Baltic States. The process is presented positively, as a happy democratic transition, with national anthems playing and new flags popping up as each new nation's borders appear on the screen map and the Soviet Union's territory correspondingly diminishes. Finally, Russia claims its own independence as the Russian Federation: the tricolour Russian flag is raised to proudly fly over the large space that had formerly been the Russian Republic within the Soviet Union.

Russia still fills a very large area on the new map, but it is oddly misshapen now. If one visualises the old Soviet Union as a large rectangular slice of bread, it is no longer: it is as if hungry rats have nibbled giant mouthfuls out of the slice, leaving ragged holes and gaps around its edges. Seeing this powerful map it is easy to empathise with Putin's lament to the Russian Federal Assembly in April 2005: 'Above all, we should acknowledge that the collapse of the Soviet Union was the major geopolitical disaster of the [twentieth] century'.[7]

Putin listed his reasons: the tens of millions of Russians who suddenly found themselves living outside Russian territory, the depreciation of individual savings, the destruction of old ideals, the disbanding of institutions, the mass poverty that became the norm, and the emergence of the oligarchs. Putin concluded poignantly: 'Who could have imagined that it would simply collapse? No one saw this coming – even in their worst nightmares'.

Though only 25 per cent of the former Soviet Union's territory was lost in the transition to Russia, it was easy to see on this map how some of the best had been lost: most of the warm Black Sea coast, major ports and military bases like Odessa and Sevastopol, the breadbasket of Ukraine, Byelorussia, most of the Baltic coastline, Kazakhstan, Russia's Tsarist conquests in the Caucasus and Asia. The list of losses goes on and on...

So much of the huge multicultural experiment, first under the Tsarist Empire, and then under seventy-four years of the Soviet Union, had now ingloriously ended. And I thought especially of the 26 million Russians left outside the new Russia's national boundaries, as stranded minorities with uncertain futures in their new non-Russian nations. Also, that Russia had not really solved its own multinational problems, but merely exchanged them for different ones. If Muslim Azerbaijan could be an independent new nation, why not Muslim Chechnya or Daghestan or Ingushetia within Russia? The Russian Federation was still a complex multicultural nation, obliged to balance national unity with protections for minority rights and religious freedoms within its new borders. It was just that much smaller now. Would it not have been better to hold onto what it had held before?

I was not the only spectator to linger thoughtfully over this map. I would guess that others were saddened or troubled by it, despite the joyful message of self-determination it sought to project.

The 'Third Day', labelled *Unpopular Measures* by the museum, depicts the extreme economic hardships under the crash privatisation program pursued by Yeltsin from January 1992 onwards. These reforms, strongly encouraged by the United States, led to huge public poverty and distress, and to another armed confrontation in Moscow in September–October 1993 between the executive president and the now communist-dominated elected Russian Parliament, in what is nowadays blandly described as the '1993 Russian constitutional crisis'.[8] This political face-off ended finally on 3–4 October 1993 in a bloody imposed military solution. History is written by winners. But this was clearly a very ugly armed clash.

The Russian people's honeymoon with Yeltsin had worn off quickly under the extreme economic hardship of the forced transition to a market economy, imposed by Yeltsin's first prime minister and architect of 'shock therapy', liberal economist Yegor Gaidar. Yeltsin and Gaidar believed that gradual economic reform would only prolong the nation's agony. Russia's national income had already fallen 22.5 per cent between 1990 and 1992 and would actually be reduced by half over the next few years. Many factories had closed down or stopped paying wages. The shops were empty of the most basic foodstuffs, as corrupt higher-priced sales of necessities took place on the black market, sometimes literally from delivery trucks parked outside the back doors of the empty shops. The museum shows a typical grocery shop at the time, with empty shelves apart from a few out-of-date cans of fish. It is clear that everybody had to get on the take in order to survive: Russian mafia power and open criminality grew explosively in these years.

Russia was undergoing a fundamental revolution in property ownership and capital–labour relationships, as huge in reverse as had been the communist collectivisation revolution after 1917. Property was now being transferred from collective state ownership back into individual ownership of assets, under paper shareholding-coupon systems wide open to abuse by those with money, prestige, and financial and management acumen. Vulnerable people were being swindled as former communist factory executives rapidly reinvented themselves as shareholders and factory owners. Runaway inflation destroyed savings. A rich new oligarchy took shape, while ordinary people starved and froze and scrambled for disappearing paid jobs. Nobody seemed to be in charge.

The communists, with their reproachful message of 'we warned you', experienced a surge of renewed popularity. Yeltsin's vice-president, Alexander Rutskoy, a well-respected Afghanistan war hero who had been Yeltsin's running mate in the June 1991 presidential election, denounced Yeltsin's privatisation program as 'economic genocide'.

Yeltsin became more autocratic as the parliament increasingly ignored and defied him. He put forward a new Constitution with weakened parliamentary powers and strengthened presidential powers. Parliament rejected it. He abolished parliament. They ignored him. It was a political stalemate which could not last. On 21 September 1993, parliament impeached Yeltsin and proclaimed Rutskoy to be Russia's acting president. Yeltsin ignored this attempt to shame him into resigning. He surrounded the White House with police cordons. On 3 October hundreds of pro-parliament demonstrators forcibly removed these cordons and defensively barricaded themselves in the White House – just as Yeltsin and his democracy supporters had done two years before. They also occupied the mayor's office and attempted to seize the strategic Ostankino television tower, the national media centre. Sixty-two people were killed in a pitched battle against Special Forces and other troops loyal to Yeltsin who had surrounded and defended the tower's transmission studios. Pro-Yeltsin broadcasting was resumed from Ostankino late that evening. The armed forces then finally, after days of apparent irresolution, swung behind the president as the ultimate state authority.

On 4 October, state censorship of radio and television broadcast media began. On Yeltsin's orders on that day, army tanks shelled the White House upper floors and soldiers then forcibly took the building, floor by floor. Police said 187 died in the fighting and 437 were wounded. But communist sources claimed much higher numbers of defenders killed, up to 2000.

The media, now under firm presidential control, was quick to condemn the Russian Parliament's defiance of the president as 'a pre-planned fascist-communist armed rebellion'. This was the version of events immediately endorsed by the West, which had invested all its hopes in the Yeltsin–Gaidar shock-therapy privatisation program, and was deeply suspicious of Rutskoy and the old communist parliamentarians who had challenged it.

In the aftermath of the crisis, Yeltsin removed from positions of power all the people who had sided with Rutskoy's group. The main leaders were imprisoned for several months but all were amnestied and released in 1994, when Yeltsin felt his position was sufficiently secure. Rutskoy is still alive, but no longer active in politics.

Yeltsin put through the now tamed parliament a new Constitution, with even stronger presidential powers than he had previously proposed. This remains Russia's constitution today. Although Russia is still a dual presidential-parliamentary system in theory, the real power now rests in the president's hands. A prime minister heads a Cabinet and directs the state administration. But this prime minister is appointed by, and can be freely dismissed by, the president. In effect, this resembles the French system with its strong presidential powers.

This still does not fully explain how Putin in 2008, at the end of his first two allowed terms as president, swapped the presidency with Prime Minister Medvedev (known by analogy with chess as his 'castling' move), yet was still able over his next four years as prime minister to retain the real de facto executive power in Russia, and to ensure his legal re-election as president in 2012, potentially for a second eight-year double term to 2020. This still-unclear history suggests that in the amenable personality of Medvedev, Putin had found a safe temporary pair of presidential hands for four years – within the rules of the Yeltsin Constitution.

Subsequent exhibits portray further key challenges faced by Yeltsin: first, his humiliatingly unsuccessful 1994–96 war against the Chechen Muslim nationalist insurgency, which would remain a running sore for years, with terrible human rights abuses on both sides, only finally settled by Putin's pragmatic peace deal in 2004 after the Second Chechen War, when Putin made a tough local warlord Ramzan Kadyrov his ally and Head of the Chechen Republic.

In 1996, under his new Constitution, Yeltsin ran for a second term as president, this time facing another formidable and respected opponent, the new Communist Party leader Gennady Zyuganov, who campaigned legally under a potent nationalist platform (as O'Clery paints it): 'to revive the socialist motherland, lumping Yeltsin and Gorbachev together with a world oligarchy as the destroyers of Russia'.[9]

Even Gorbachev – finally publicly abandoning communism, seven years too late – now ran against Yeltsin as head of a miniscule Social Democratic Party: he got a humiliating 0.5 per cent of the vote.

Yeltsin, blamed by many voters for the continuing economic hardships of the seemingly endless transition to a functioning market economy, looked set to lose the election to an increasingly confident Zyuganov.[10] He was urged by fearful advisers to violate his own Constitution by illegally delaying the election for two years. But his family warned him that this could provoke a new civil war. They persuaded him to sack his old election team and recruit a new, youth-oriented one. O'Clery again:

> The sixty-five-year-old Yeltsin stops drinking, loses weight, and manages to summon up one more great burst of energy to campaign for re-election. American and European leaders troop to Moscow to boost their free market champion. Yeltsin's campaign is helped by financial donations from the oligarchs, a timely announcement of a $10 billion loan from the IMF, the anti-communist bias of the television networks, and television advertisements produced with the expert advice of the American PR firm of Ogilvy and Mather. The Russian president wins re-election by 54% to 40%.[11]

This election was criticised by the disappointed communists as having involved widespread vote rigging. Zyuganov had come very close to victory in the first all-candidate round, but sagged badly in the second two-candidate run-off. It was to be the communists' last credible bid for power in Russia. From now on, changing demographics and economic growth would increasingly marginalise them as an ageing-voter, regressive party of the past.

Zyuganov became a respected elder statesman in politics, retaining the shrinking communist vote. In the most recent presidential election in 2012, he came in second after Putin, gaining just 17 per cent of the vote. Here is how Zyuganov bitterly summed up Russia's situation in 2008, eight years into Putin's presidency, speaking at the 13th Party Congress:

> Objectively, Russia's position remains complicated, not to say dismal. The population is dying out. Thanks to the 'heroic efforts' of the Yeltsinites the country has lost 5 out of the 22 million square kilometers of its historical territory. Russia has lost half of its production capacity and has yet to reach the 1990 level of output. Our country is facing three mortal dangers: de-industrialization, de-population and mental debilitation. The ruling group has neither notable successes to boast of, nor a clear plan of action. All its activities are geared to a single goal: to stay in power at all costs. Until recently it has been able to keep in power due to the 'windfall' high world prices for energy. Its social support rests on the notorious 'vertical power structure' which is another way of saying intimidation and blackmail of the broad social strata, and the handouts that power chips off the oil and gas pie and throws out to the population in crumbs, especially on the eve of elections.[12]

While all this was true enough in 2000, it was becoming less true in 2008, by which time the economy had at last stabilised as a market system and begun to grow again. Zyuganov, however, was now a revered voice of nationalist-populist conscience, a sort of 'holy fool' whose views Putin had to consider seriously.

I believe that Putin has taken deeply to heart Zyuganov's uncompromising message: that the Russian people must never again be humiliated and outsmarted by their own corrupt politicians and oligarchs, and by a manipulative and exploitative West.

The last exhibit, Seventh Day, *Farewell to the Kremlin*, is of particular interest and pathos. It presents Yeltsin in 1999, sixty-eight and ailing, knowing he must retire soon or risk dying in office, and considering a shortlist of five good potential successors, including Vladimir Putin and the promising young democratic politician later to be assassinated on the Kremlin bridge in 2015, Boris Nemtsov. After interviewing them all, Yeltsin endorses Putin.

We finally see and hear, again in unnervingly realistic 3-D holographic representation and using the real news tape, Yeltsin's surprise resignation speech televised to the nation on 31 December 1999 from his actual office desk in the Kremlin, and announcing Putin as his recommended successor. He spoke poignantly and with great dignity:

> I want to ask for your forgiveness, that many of our dreams didn't come true. That what seemed to us to be simple turned out painfully difficult. I ask forgiveness for the fact that I didn't justify some of the hopes of those people who believed that with one stroke, one burst, one sign we could jump from the grey, stagnant, totalitarian past to a bright, rich, civilised future. I myself believed this. One burst was not enough…but I want you to know – I've never said this, today it's important for me to tell you: the pain of every one of you, I feel in myself, in my heart…in saying farewell, I want to say to every one of you: be happy. You deserve happiness. You deserve happiness, and peace.[13]

The Yeltsin Museum shows him as a strong, well-meaning man. While it pays lip service to the principle of 'you should make up your own mind about him', it really presents him as an only slightly flawed hero. It glosses over his serious alcoholism – saying he was profoundly distressed by his mother's death in 1993 at the height of the challenge from Rutskoy's communists. It presents his rivalry with Gorbachev not as a clash of personal ambitions, but as Yeltsin trying to protect democratic gains in Russia that Gorbachev – still a communist – was not clear-headed enough to protect. There may be some truth in that. The disturbing contradiction between Yeltsin defending the Russian White House against Soviet tanks in 1991, and then himself ordering army tanks to shell civilian demonstrators in the building just two years later, is glossed over here.

Yeltsin was easily influenced by his family, his advisers, and by the Western leaders he came to trust. He was irresolute until he had made up his mind. An improviser, he sometimes had no clear picture of where he wanted to go. He came very close to cancelling the cliffhanger 1996 election against Zyuganov.

Though the museum emphasises the nastiness of some of the revanchist fascist-communist elements supporting Rutskoy in 1993, it also shows the people's real desperation and dislocation as their old frugal but secure Soviet economy dissolved under Yeltsin's and Gaidar's shock therapy. Shock therapy was not just about economic reform – it was about dissolving the power of the Communist Party which had set the rules for life in Russia for seventy years. We cannot begin to imagine how hard it was for Russians to have to live through these terrifying years of reform.

Things were not all bad: oligarchs and their privileged workforces in wealthy cities like Moscow benefited from trickle-down prosperity, and these were exciting years politically and culturally for the urban elite. But they were dismal and dangerous for most ordinary Russian people, especially in the countryside and small industrial towns which were cast adrift by the economic reformers, effectively told to sink or swim. Many sank. Alcoholism and suicide were rife. The birthrate plunged.

Putin, with his KGB-trained skills in social observation, watched sadly and quietly, witnessing the scope and limits on effective Russian presidential power. He saw how Gorbachev, and Yeltsin after him, had progressively lost autonomy and agency, each coming in turn to depend on Western goodwill, expertise and resources for their very political survival. He saw how this political dependency left Russia open to Western advantage-taking and exploitation. And he saw how readily elements of the Russian people could be tempted into dangerous flirtations with proto-fascist nationalist tendencies, if subjected to too much deprivation, stress and national humiliation: if the spring was compressed too tightly.

The Gorbachev–Yeltsin years were Putin's university in how to lead Russia after 2000.

In the museum cloakroom, I saw a larger-than-life bronze statue of Yeltsin sitting quietly on one of the public benches where people put on their street shoes. People were having their photo taken sitting next to him. And yes, I had my photo taken with him, too. Because after a few hours in this brilliant museum, I couldn't help liking and respecting the man. He was a real human being, a natural and within limits decent political leader. And I found myself liking Gorbachev a little less than I had before I visited this museum. I still sympathised with his predicament, in those difficult early years of glasnost and perestroika; in football parlance, Gorbachev had to do the hardest yards. Yeltsin kicked the goals.

Another impression I took away was that despite everything, Russian politics was steadily becoming more humane, more civil, during these turbulent fifteen years of transition. It starts with Gorbachev in 1986 releasing Sakharov and the Jewish refuseniks, and introducing new non-party democratic political institutions at all Soviet and republic levels. We see Gorbachev never resorting to his latent powers as supreme Soviet leader in 1987–89 physically to purge Yeltsin. We see Yeltsin peacefully resolving the attempted communist coup in 1991, and protecting the now very vulnerable Gorbachev thereafter. Then, after he ruthlessly suppressed the very serious popular challenge to his power in 1993, amnestying all the challengers a year later. We see Yeltsin accepting tactical defeat in Chechnya, when he could have just bombed the daylights out of the rebellious province. We see Yeltsin accepting the risk of losing in 1996 to Zyuganov. We see him conscientiously trying to choose the best next leader for Russia – and choosing Putin. And at the end we see him saying sorry.

There is really much to admire here: an acceptance of a growing civility and sense of proper limits in Russian political life. Most of this story is still unknown in the West, which is why I have told it in some detail here: and because it is so relevant to a balanced evaluation of what has followed in Russia under Putin.

This museum actually endorses Putin's own claim to legitimacy in Russia, as Yeltsin's anointed presidential successor. For Putin, there was no choice but to welcome and bless the museum: though he disagrees with its claim that Yeltsin had no alternative but to break up the Soviet Union.

Reading the journalists' assessments,[14] I found myself leaning towards Anna Nemtsova's view – she is the daughter of the murdered politician Boris Nemtsov – that this museum is Putin's respectful homage to Yeltsin. I don't see the museum's message as Yeltsin 'taking on' Putin.

Time will tell: Yeltsin only died in 2007 and it is too early to know how history will finally judge him. This museum is a creditable interim assessment.

Back at my hotel, a big Saturday-night wedding reception was in full swing. It had taken over the main restaurant, so I ate in the front bar. Everyone was dressed in party best: men awkward in dark suits and ties, women zipped into tight party dresses and high heels, primping their hair and makeup in lobby mirrors before gliding regally into the hall. There was something sweetly old-fashioned and country townish about it all: a real Russian knees-up. I listened happily to the familiar dance tunes being belted out by the dance band, like *Ochyi Chorniye* ('Black Eyes') and *Kalinka*. The old Russia again, forty-five years later, but still alive and well in peoples' hearts.

After a sleep-in the next day, I caught a random tram out to the suburbs, where I found dilapidated factories and sagging old wooden nineteenth-century houses that looked just like Lara's house in Pasternak's imagined Urals town of Yuryatin. I had already identified what I thought was the City Library building where Zhivago ran into Lara again during the Civil War, working as a librarian. Only later did I read that the nearby Urals city of Perm where Pasternak had worked during World War I, and not Yekaterinburg, had been his model for Yuryatin. But old Yekaterinburg is of the same era architecturally, and it was in the thick of the same fierce Red–White battles about which Pasternak wrote in *Doctor Zhivago*.

On the icy pedestrian main street, Baumanskaya Ulitsa, mums and dads were on Sunday strolls, contentedly herding their toddlers and pushing babies in prams. I had *pelmeny* (Siberian meat dumplings) and soup for lunch in a pleasant cafe, where I met an interested older local man, incredulous at how and why an Australian traveller had turned up in midwinter in his backwoods Yekaterinburg. '*Molodetz!* Fine fellow!' he kept repeating. I dropped into the Scotch Bar on the walk back to my hotel for a farewell whisky, and got talking with Max the bartender, a friendly young man. He told me that few Westerners came to Yekaterinburg these days, apart from Czechs curious about the Czech Legion's major role on the White side in the Civil War hereabouts, and who enjoyed the region's extensive nature and sporting tourism offerings (cross-country skiing, cycling, kayaking, hunting etc). Yekaterinburg is still off the beaten track for international visitors. It should not be: I found it a delightful and welcoming city full of genuine friendly people, with good direct international air links to Europe and China. I was sad to have to leave it so soon.

Chapter 9

Yasnaya Polyana and Leo Tolstoy

We have at home in Canberra a handsome, traditional Russian silver-plated brass samovar, on a high wooden pedestal stand. Because it is a charcoal-burning samovar, we don't use it. Were it to be lit, the smoke would soon blacken the white ceiling of our dining room. It is there for sentiment and for its beauty: a symbol of Russian hospitality and comfort, with its warm feminine shape on its four-legged raised base, and its decorative silverplate and bone wrought tap and handles. There is a central cylindrical coal-burning furnace, whose heat would have been regulated by air controls at the top and bottom. Surrounding this fire chamber is a five-litre water tank, which would have been regularly topped up with water and kept at near boiling point. There is a tap near the base on the front side, to pour hot water safely into tall Russian tea glasses or teapots. A small matching silver-plated brass teapot (long since lost) would have stood on an open grate above the fire chamber, containing hot strong concentrated tea, to be mixed like a cordial with hot water from the tap according to taste.

Samovars (a conjoined Russian word meaning 'self-boiler') became an essential home appliance in nineteenth-century upper- and middle-class Russian homes, where tea was the most popular social drink at all times of day, and guests were always welcome. 'To sit by the samovar' was to have a leisurely talk over glasses of tea with family or friends. Samovars were made not just as domestic appliances but as things of beauty and prestige, bought to be enjoyed in the family for a lifetime and more. Production, originally by hand, became more mechanised in the nineteenth century, but samovars were always finished and maintained thereafter by hand. Today they are still being made in specialist factories in Tula. To see a samovar is to be reminded of Russia's love affair with its past.

Tea itself is an interesting Russian story. The Mongols first brought Chinese tea to Russia in 1638 as a luxury goodwill gift to the first Romanov Tsar, Michael. A thriving overland exchange trade by camel caravan soon developed – trading Chinese tea for Russian furs. In 1689 a well-policed merchant Tea Road was set up from China through Russia's new territory of Siberia. By 1796, Russia was importing over 3 million pounds of Chinese tea per year by this land route, enough to lower the price so that middle-class Russians began to afford tea. By the mid-nineteenth century, tea had become the national drink in Russian households, as in Britain, and was enjoyed by all classes. It still came overland from China, or was imported by sea to Black Sea ports like Odessa. Tea now began to be grown within the Russian Empire: first in subtropical Georgia and Azerbaijan, but then further north, in Krasnodar Province in Russia, in the temperate hills behind Sochi on the Black Sea coast. In 1901 a Jewish Ukrainian called Judas Koshman, who had worked most of his life managing a tea plantation in Georgia, had saved enough money to retire and buy a suitable plot of land in the hills near Sochi. He began to grow there a winter-resistant hybrid tea he had bred, which he called Koshman House Krasnodar Blend. The family business grew rich. This same brand of fine tea is still being grown and sold in Russia.[1]

I bought my samovar at a flea market in Warsaw twenty-five years ago. I can just make out the stampings on the lid, almost polished away by diligent previous owners. It was made in Tula, in Russia, around the end of the nineteenth century, by a metalworking family firm, B. G. Teile and Sons.[2] My samovar's lovely rounded shape is characteristic of Teile samovars.[3] The brothers Reingold and Emil Teile (Reingold was a retired Russian-German army general) started a factory to make samovars in Tula in 1870, and their brand soon became well known across Russia for reliability and innovation. The firm went on to make kerosene-fuelled and electric-powered samovars.

Tula was famous for its samovars. The first samovar factory was founded there in 1778 and a huge Russia-wide and export industry to Eastern Europe, the Middle East and India developed. The Russian saying, 'Carrying your own samovar to Tula', is exactly equivalent to the British saying, 'Carrying your own coal to Newcastle'.[4]

Surrounded by rich metallic ore deposits, and a convenient 180 kilometres south of Moscow, Tula had for hundreds of years been Russia's leading centre of gun-smithing and cannon-making. Tsar Peter the Great ordered the first modern armaments factory in Russia to be built there. Tula soon became the premier metalworking centre in Eastern Europe, specialising in weapons and cannon. A sort of Russian Sheffield.

Tula grew rapidly in the late nineteenth and twentieth century. After the shock of Russia's military reverses in the Crimean War of 1853–56, the empire realised it urgently had to modernise and mechanise its armed forces if it were to keep up with the Western European powers. The resulting industrial revolution across European Russia in the years 1861–1917, after the abolition of serfdom in 1861, was staggering in speed and scale. Tula was at the heart of this.

In the twentieth century, Tula was still an important armaments-manufacturing centre. Tula-made weaponry was used in the 1905 Russo–Japanese War, in World War I, and in the Russian Civil War. In the 1941–45 war, Tula found itself on the frontline facing Hitler's offensive. The German Army tried very hard to take the city in their initial 1941 blitzkrieg. They captured Orel, the nearest city to the south. But Tula held out, and thereby secured Moscow's southern flank during the Battle of Moscow and subsequent Russian counter-offensive, for which Tula was awarded the prized title of Hero-City.[5] It is home today to the Tula Arms Plant and has a population of around 500,000. It is an average sort of Russian medium-sized industrial city, a mixture of beauty and ugliness, middle-class wealth and working-class austerity.

Yasnaya Polyana – the country home of famed Russian writer Leo Tolstoy (in the West, he is Leo – in Russian, *Lev*) – is not buried in deep bucolic countryside, as I had romantically imagined it. It is only 12 kilometres south of Tula, just outside the city limits. With a northerly wind blowing, the smoke and fumes from Tula's metal factories would reach Yasnaya Polyana.

My friend Julian Oliver had arrived in Moscow on Monday night, as I returned from Yekaterinburg. Wednesday dawned bright and clear, a pleasant minus 2 degrees – a perfect day for a trip to the country. We took a fast train to Tula and a local taxi from there to drop us at the Yasnaya Polyana Estate Museum gates, on a quiet rural road a few minutes' drive out of town. Walking up the long driveway past forests and frozen ponds towards two nineteenth-century country houses set well back on a slight rise, we entered another world.

Tolstoy is incontestably the most significant figure in Russian literature.[6] His two great novels *War and Peace* and *Anna Karenina* have been translated and read for pleasure in every major world language. There have been many fine film versions, in Russian and in English. Most recently in 2015, the BBC made a new six-part English-language television series of *War and Peace*, acclaimed in the West and Russia alike for its authenticity. And one can still see an unusual recent broadcast: 1300 Russian actors reading on stage and in appropriate real settings (and even by a cosmonaut in space) the whole of *War and Peace*, a marathon sixty-hour dramatised reading in Russian.[7]

Tolstoy never dates. He spans space and time, and he remains today a strong cultural bridge between Russia and the West, and between his own late-nineteenth-century imperial Russia, Soviet Russia, and Russia today. What was the source of his genius, of his storytelling power and deep insights about human nature?

Essentially, his source was his own remarkable life, lived through years of enormous challenge and change in Russia.[8] Tolstoy was never a bookish intellectual. He was the quintessential nineteenth-century Russian, actively engaged in many public pursuits, while agonising about the moral meaning and purpose of his own life, about Russian identity and the nation's destiny. He never resolved those conflicts – indeed, they became more fevered as he grew older.

The consensus is that he was not a very likeable man, either in his younger bachelor years as a callous young libertine, gambler and army officer (and there are many such characters represented in both novels), or as an increasingly irascible, domineering patriarch as he grew older at Yasnaya Polyana – a sort of Prince Nikolai Bolkonsky, Prince Andrey's lovable but hard-to-live-with father.

Born into an aristocratic family at Yasnaya Polyana in 1828, the fourth of five children of Count Nikolai Tolstoy, a veteran of the Napoleonic Wars, Leo's younger years were conventional enough. A mediocre student, he never completed a university degree. He ran up heavy gambling debts. In 1851 he joined the army. His first three years of service were spent in war against Chechen Muslim rebels (some things never change): harsh counter-insurgency campaigns on Russia's mountainous and troubled southern frontier in the Caucasus. He then fought for two years in the Crimean War (1854–55).[9] When peace returned in 1856, he resigned his military commission. He was twenty-eight, and already enjoying a growing reputation as a writer. He travelled through Europe in 1857 and 1860–61, when he met Victor Hugo in Paris. He returned in 1861 to Yasnaya Polyana – the year serfdom was abolished in Russia – determined to make writing and farming his full-time career. He married in 1862, aged thirty-four, to a very pretty much younger bride from a similar aristocratic family, Sophia (Sonya) Behrs, aged eighteen. She was a virgin: he was nothing of the kind, notorious for his depredations in the Caucasus, and even now with local serf-girls on the estate. They had thirteen children of whom eight survived childhood.

Tolstoy began to write while still in the army. He was a natural writer, brilliant in depicting a wide range of situations and characters, both male and female, from different points of view. His first writings were three short autobiographical novels – *Childhood*, *Boyhood* and *Youth* – written between 1852 and 1856. His *Sevastopol Sketches* (1855) were essentially war-correspondent dispatches, relating his experiences and observations fighting as a Russian officer in the Crimean War, in particular, during the harrowing year-long siege of Sevastopol by British, French and Turkish forces. These works brought home to Russia's literary public the horrors of this first modern mechanised war. His major novels *War and Peace* and *Anna Karenina* – both written after he had returned to settle at Yasnaya Polyana – were published in 1869 and 1877 respectively, when Tolstoy was forty-one and forty-nine. Both novels drew heavily on his first-hand and recent memories of Russian imperial army life and war – which is what makes them so vivid and convincing.

Tolstoy lived on for many more years, dying in 1910 aged 82. Based on the success of his two major novels, Yasnaya Polyana already many years before his death had become a centre of reverent literary pilgrimage. By the 1870s, Tolstoy had retreated from Russia's nineteenth-century modernity and industrialisation, becoming a sort of mystic prophet of the people, and an internal émigré into an idealised Russian past. He was now a non-conformist Christian, and a fervent pacifist and non-violent anarchist. We see the striking transition in his photographs: from a neatly dressed army officer in his twenties, to a straggly-bearded wild-eyed prophet in peasant garb in later life.

These tendencies were already latent in him earlier, but the horrors of the siege of Sevastopol were life-changing. According to one recent commentator, Tolstoy's entire six-year military career had pushed him towards pacifism:

> By this stage [1856], Tolstoy was on the other side of his journey of disillusionment, one that had begun in the forests of Chechnya and ended on the Black Sea coast. He was nursing the ideas that would define his work as a mature writer: that battles were a form of deliberate folly, that the only enduring nation was humanity, that ordinary Russians were always better than the rulers whom history seemed to give them.[10]

Like many intellectuals of his period and place, Tolstoy was deeply conflicted about the impact on Russian identity of industrialisation and material progress. He worried that Russians could lose their essential national values as a people, succumbing to European cosmo-politanism and material progress. Yet he knew Russia aspired to be a strong world power. These conflicts are represented throughout *War and Peace* with its Napoleonic Wars setting sixty years earlier, and *Anna Karenina* with its contemporary late-nineteenth-century setting. Both Pierre Bezukhov and Count Andrei Bolkonsky in *War and Peace*, and Konstantin Levin and Count Alexei Vronsky in *Anna Karenina*, are chronic worriers about Russian society.

Pierre and Levin are never happier than when they are in contact with the common people – for Pierre, getting to know them while fleeing French-occupied Moscow and seeking refuge and food in the deep countryside, or out walking in the forests; and for Levin, spending a joyful day hand-scything a grain harvest with his family's recently emancipated former serfs. Is agricultural productivity all that matters? Sometimes Levin thinks so, but then he asks, what is Russia losing of its soul in its mad rush towards mechanisation and efficiency?

Tolstoy experienced these anxieties at first hand, as Russia – and his local city Tula – were changing quickly around him. The emancipation of the serfs in 1861 created, as it was intended to, a large surplus labour force in the countryside that could no longer live off the land, and began to stream into low-paid industrial jobs in the cities. Pay and living conditions were very bad, and trade unionism was suppressed. The Russian *intyelligyentsiya* looked on, aghast at the hardships the working people endured both in the countryside and cities, in what quickly became a ruthless oligarchy-ruled capitalist economy. Seeing the indifference of the ruling class – to which most of the intelligentsia belonged – to the people's poverty and suffering, the Russian intelligentsia became increasingly radicalised politically, but they also looked back sentimentally to an imagined past Russian Golden Age, in art, architecture, music and literature. To be a Russian *intyelligyent* was not just to be well educated, cultured and well off – it was also to have a strong social conscience.[11]

Tolstoy was a leading inspirational figure in this movement. He actively farmed his estate, working with the local peasants in traditional and selectively modern ways. He opened, and himself taught in, free schools for poor village children. He (as a younger son) and his large family lived in a fairly modest-sized house not far from the main estate house. Tolstoy – who also owned a townhouse in Moscow where the family spent their winters – had exchanged his former professional military and civil-service circle of acquaintance for a new more literary-artistic-musical circle, including the painter Leonid Pasternak and his pianist wife, Rosa.

It was not so easy for me to get a sense of Tolstoy's character or life from the home-museum tour. The guides were excessively reverential – the house was presented not as a home but as a shrine to the great man. We were warily shepherded through small rooms crammed with photographs, paintings, curio display cases and furniture, all behind thick intimidating guard ropes. I tried to imagine how this might have once been a crowded, noisy and jolly family home, with the many Tolstoy children running around, being chased outside by their mother or nannies so as not to disturb the great man at his work, and with lots of busy country summer pursuits on the large, warm, covered verandah or indoors in cold weather, like cooking, jam-making, pickling, weaving, knitting and sewing.

Was Tolstoy, the reformed-libertine-become-pacifist-prophet, a good father? Did he play with his children, read to them, take them for walks and pony rides? I suspect he was more often moody, hierarchical and remote, wrapped up in his writing and his causes, retreating to his study while Sophia was left to bring up the children.

I was told by one of our museum guides that until near the end of his life, Tolstoy was 'happy in his marriage and family' in this rural intelligentsia lifestyle he had created for himself. I suspect this is improbable hagiography: he was known to treat his wife most inconsiderately from the beginning, exploiting her and becoming increasingly estranged from her as he became absorbed in his religious beliefs, in running his schools, in corresponding with his admirers and conversing with his literary and artistic guests.[12] But even if they were a mismatched couple, Sophia loyally stuck it out, bearing their numerous children, copying his manuscripts, and managing the business side of the estate and his literary accounts as he grew older.

People came from all over the world to meet the great man. His later work is less approachable than the popular early works, but still of value and interest. It greatly influenced Gandhi's pacifism and successful civil disobedience campaigns in India.

At the end of Tolstoy's life, he panicked and lost the plot. He was increasingly distressed – what had it all been for, what had he really achieved in his life? He spoke wildly of disinheriting his family and giving everything to the poor. At this, Sophia rightly drew the line. One midwinter night, probably after a quarrel, he packed a few things and in the dead of night fled his home and family, accompanied by his beloved youngest daughter (and secretary) Alexandra Tolstaya aged twenty-four, and by his personal doctor. They caught a train from a nearby country station, travelling south. They were later found in a country station a day's journey away, where he had collapsed with pneumonia. For a week, he refused Sophia's pleadings to come home: he refused even to see her. She did not know what to do, she could not force him to return. He died in this cold little station, a sad, undignified – and possibly deranged – end to a rich productive life. Sophia lived on another nine years to 1919, at last free to be herself. The communists respectfully left her in peace. Most of the children emigrated as soon as they could.

Tolstoy lived through the great changes of mid- to late nineteenth-century Russia. The ruling class knew that Russia's victory over Napoleon in 1812 had been a close-run thing and that Russia might not be so lucky next time. This view was confirmed by Russia's near-defeat in the 1854–55 Crimean War.

It is hard now in the West to visualise what a major war this was. We have domesticated it in British legend to cosy-heroic symbols like the Charge of the Light Brigade and nursing reformer Florence Nightingale, memorialising it as a minor colonial-type engagement in the smooth spread of British imperial power around the globe. For Russians, it was much more significant than that. It was a serious unprovoked Western invasion: it was the war that did not follow the defeat of Napoleon, when Russian armies were at the gates of Paris and British Foreign Secretary Lord Castlereagh was grimly wondering whether Britain would soon again be at war, with Russia this time. Thanks to the 1815 Congress of Vienna peace accords, it did not happen for around forty years. But finally it came.

In 1854, 1.6 million men in arms from four European major powers engaged in a year and a half of war around the world. The immediate casus belli was Russian zeal to protect the human rights of their South Slav brethren against oppression in Turkey's decaying Balkan Empire. Russia declared war on Turkey and Western Alliance obligations to Turkey were engaged. British, French and Turkish forces attacked Russian land and naval forces and bases in the Balkans, the Caucasus, the Black Sea, the Baltic and White Seas, and even the North Pacific. Britain enthusiastically went to war, determined to use this opportunity to bloody Russia's nose at last – and to halt Russian naval and territorial expansion into Europe and Central Asia. France and Turkey followed Britain's lead and mobilised.

It was the first modern mechanised war, fought with accurate long-range naval artillery bombardments of Russian coastal fortifications (and return fire at allied ships), military use of railways and telegraphs, and Florence Nightingale's revolutionary new approach to the medical care of sick and wounded soldiers. Russia was technically outclassed by its European opponents, yet casualties on both sides were huge. The invaders frittered away their superiority in numbers of armed men, and their technical superiority, in a war fought mostly on Russian ground. As always, the Russians fought a resolute defensive war, which over time wore down the invaders' morale and superior armament.

It was a huge war for its time. Russia had 700,000 men at arms, the British, French and Turks 900,000. Deaths on the Russian side were 143,000, on the allied side at the minimum 213,000. The defining final engagement in the war was the year-long siege of Sevastopol, the main city of Russian Crimea and her major Black Sea naval base. The siege took 102,000 Russian lives as they desperately defended the stronghold city, encircled by the allies on sea and land. Sevastopol finally fell in September 1855, but the cost to both sides had been huge. It is a battle honoured in Russian memory.[13]

The war ended in March 1856. Most Western historians write that Russia 'lost' the war, but it seems to me rather that it ended in a negotiated peace between exhausted adversaries who had lost the taste for more combat. Russia did not lose any of its sovereign territory in Crimea, but the peace treaty demanded destruction of its naval docks and fortifications in Sevastopol and forbade it from having a Black Sea naval fleet. Fifteen years later, with German diplomatic support, Russia renounced these disarmament clauses, rebuilding its Black Sea fleet and re-fortifying its Sevastopol naval base. It was back to the status quo ante bellum.

The Crimean War left a legacy of British hostility and suspicion of Russia. No great imperial power on a roll, as Britain then was, likes to be challenged and fought almost to a stalemate. Anti-Russian stereotypes came to dominate late Victorian popular literature: Kipling's *Kim*, steeped in the trope of the 'Great Game' of Russo–British imperial rivalry in the Middle East and northern approaches to India through Afghanistan; Joseph Conrad's malevolently portrayed Russian officials and secret police in his novels *The Secret Agent* and *Under Western Eyes*; John Buchan's Russian as well as German villains. Long before communism, the British Empire nurtured a rich tradition of Russophobia. Even in faraway Australia, naval fortifications were being built in Sydney Harbour against the imagined Russian naval threat from Vladivostok.

The lesson the Russian ruling class drew from these military tensions with the West was that Russia had to industrialise to levels matching the most advanced European nations – Germany, Britain and France.[14] Tsar Alexander's decision in 1861 to emancipate Russia's serfs had several aims: social reform; encouragement of a more efficient, cash-motivated and more productive agricultural labour force, producing enough marketable surplus to feed and clothe Russia's growing cities and to grow food exports to earn foreign exchange for machinery imports; and creation of a large landless workforce to man the new factories and to build the huge transport infrastructure – roads, railways, canals, riverine and maritime steamer fleets – that Russia now realised it needed, if it was to have an economy strong and resilient enough to deter enemies and defend itself in future wars.

It all worked, up to a point. Landless workers poured into the cities seeking work and food. Agriculture necessarily became more efficient. National transport infrastructure grew at incredible speed. Export earnings from mines, timber and primary produce supported purchases abroad of capital goods, and immigration of entrepreneurial talent. Russia needed more capital and capitalists, and encouraged the import of technology, skills and money. Moscow and Saint Petersburg became cosmopolitan commercial cities: places for ambitious Europeans to immigrate, settle and make money. It was a new frontier, as exciting in its own way as the American New World frontier.

Russia's breakneck industrialisation did not happen in a liberal market economy. It was mostly done through state-protected monopolies or oligopolies. The Crown gave licences or franchises to favoured groups of oligarchs or family firms to develop particular key industries and infrastructure assets. The strong state thus participated directly in Russian capitalism. In 1899 the state itself bought two-thirds of Russian metallurgical production. By the early twentieth century the state controlled 70 per cent of the railways.

The results of this strong state-led capitalist model of development were spectacularly successful. Between 1890 and 1900, railway trackage virtually doubled and coal production increased by 266 per cent. By 1900, the Russian Empire was the world's fourth-largest producer of steel and second-largest source of petroleum. In what economic historian Alexander Gerschenkron called Russia's 'great spurt', Russia's industrial economy had grown more in this one decade than it had over the whole previous century.

By 1900, Russia, with its thriving modern Baltic Sea capital at Saint Petersburg, was poised for economic take-off – set to rival major Western economies and even the United States. The Russian Empire now covered one-sixth of the earth's landmass. It was by now the world's fourth- or fifth-largest industrial power, and the largest agricultural producer in Europe.

However, it was at a huge human cost: its per capita GDP had reached only 20 per cent of the United Kingdom's, and 40 per cent of Germany's; average life expectancy at birth was just thirty years, far below the United Kingdom (fifty-two), Japan (fifty-one) and Germany (forty-nine); Russian literacy remained below 33 per cent – lower than Britain had been a hundred years earlier.[15] It was a grossly unequal and illiberal society by the European standards of the time.

Growth was achieved through a regime-protected oligarchy, tightly linked to the ruling class. The existing aristocracy were offered privileged shares in new commercial ventures, often in partnership with favoured immigrant entrepreneurial families – Balts, Germans, Scots, East European Jews – who settled and quickly became Russianised. With protected market franchises and low worker wages and conditions enforced by the state, it was not hard to make money and plough the profits back into rapid capital expansion. One had to be really stupid not to share in this remarkable wealth creation, if one came from the right class, had the right capital and business connections, and employed trustworthy banks and accountants.

Very little of this wealth trickled down to the people. As a new professional and managerial middle class grew and prospered, the deprived and exploited working class simmered in angry discontent in city slums.

The creative intelligentsia – people like Tolstoy and Anton Chekhov – in the second half of the nineteenth century reacted indignantly against the lack of compassion and social values in Russia's frantic industrialisation and capital accumulation. The Russian intelligentsia were searching for better ways to express their shared Russian identity with the people. The intelligentsia were radicalising themselves, artistically, economically and increasingly politically. They were rejecting Russia's industrial superpower present, idealising its past, and dreaming of a more ethical future. As they sat around their cosy stoves and samovars, drinking tea or something stronger, they argued over their fiercely contesting visions. It is all there, in the writingsof Dostoyevsky, Turgenev, Chekhov and Tolstoy. As the century drew to its close, more and more of the intelligentsia turned to radical socialism or communism.

As the compelling statistics of industrial growth kept piling up, Russia failed to pull off the British, German and American trick – to unite dynamic elite entrepreneurship and affluence with enough civility and social conscience to keep the workers calm and the creative intelligentsia safely lodged within the middle class. Russia's fatal tendency to political polarisation, to adopting extreme solutions to social ills, led the country – which was doing remarkably well economically, if one looked only at wealth creation and not at its distribution – inexorably towards the revolutions of 1905 and 1917. One cannot forget, even now, the terrible images in *Doctor Zhivago* of mounted Cossack troops, swinging sabres, riding down and trampling peaceful protesters – which was what happened. The intelligentsia rushed willingly and headlong towards the national tragedy of communism. Ivan Bunin's haunting questions again – Why did we Russians do this to ourselves, when we were doing so well? Could not we have avoided this tragic revolution?

Tolstoy began his adult life as a Bolkonsky or Vronsky; he ended it more as a Bezhukov or Levin. He saw the emotive power of pan-Slavism to impassion Russians, when they saw their kindred peoples being treated unjustly by foreigners. In Bolkonsky and Vronsky he portrays the ruthless side of the Russian character, the determination to exploit workers to the limit, to defend one's interests at whatever cost when challenged, to fight wars to the end. In Vronsky's army-officer values, he shows us the glamour and excitement of the proud, expanding late-nineteenth-century Russian imperial state. And after Anna's despairing suicide, Vronsky assuages his guilt by going off to fight for the South Slavs' rights in the Balkans.

Yet Tolstoy himself, remarkably, transcends these values, becoming a lifetime pacifist, rejecting his whole professional mindset as a young army officer of the expanding Empire. Had he not died in 1910, what would have been his stance on the war against Germany? We will never know. We do know that his favourite youngest daughter, Alexandra Tolstaya, who although sharing her father's doctrine of non-violence enlisted in World War I, was awarded three Saint George medals and attained the rank of colonel.[16]

Yasnaya Polyana, the hero cities of Tula and Sevastopol, the Crimean War, Tolstoy's flawed character and his genius, Tula's metalworking industries and my graceful samovar at home – for me they all illuminate facets of the awe-inspiring saga of nineteenth-century Russia, this rich in potential, rapidly industrialising but morally conflicted imperial state. This is no longer a remote past. It is now again as close to today's Russia as our own nineteenth-century histories are to countries like Britain or the United States or Australia. Russians today are again free to reclaim and celebrate honestly their real nineteenth-century past, its achievements and its inner dilemmas of values and identity.

Chapter 10

The Gulag Museum

Vergangenheitsbewältigung – *a composite German word with individual and collective significance that describes processes of coming to terms with the past.* Vergangenheit *means 'past';* Bewältigung *means 'overcome' [negative, repressed and incriminating, mental injuries and guilt]). The composite word is best rendered in English as 'struggle to overcome the negatives of the past'. It is a key term in the study of post-1945 German literature and culture.*[1]

Traditional national museums are there to celebrate and glorify a proud past: the treasures and artefacts of past cultures, including one's own, or what one's collectors have brought home from around the world; scientific collections and exhibits of technical achievements; displays commemorating great events or great persons in national history. Julian Oliver and I visited two modern, post-perestroika museums in Moscow, which differ greatly in their approaches to Russia's past: the Gulag Museum and the Jewish Museum. Each in its own way is an exercise in *Vergangenheitsbewältigung*. Both are attempts to come to terms with troubled histories, to unlock repressed Russian memories and to expose suppressed feelings of injury or guilt. Both, in my view, substantially succeed in this, though both seem to me to be works in progress.

These were not easy museums to visit. It was with some trepidation that I entered them, wondering – will this Gulag Museum be yet another recycling of familiar Stalin-era horrors? And will this Jewish

Museum be another harrowing journey through the Holocaust? I was pleasantly surprised by both. These were not joyous outings by any means, but the courage and triumph of the human spirit through incredible adversity that each museum memorialises and yes, even celebrates, was inspirational and uplifting. And I admired those activists, political leaders and generous donor organisations and individuals, both in Russia and the West, who pressed for, facilitated and helped to fund these two brave, honourably motivated, nationally supported new museums. These are good places, profoundly educational in a country where much of the public remembers too little of such adverse things, with many people wanting to suppress memory of them. They are museums worthy of admiration and attention by international visitors, as well as by the Russian citizens at whose enlightenment they are primarily aimed. They are also outstanding examples of genuine East–West cultural and funding cooperation in common endeavours that are, sadly, becoming harder to achieve in the current circumstances of political point-scoring and narrowing opportunities for genuine cultural exchange between the West and Russia.

When does memory qualify as history? Can there be history without memory? Can memory be successfully suppressed? British writer Jenny Diski (who died in 2016) addressed such questions in her 2009 memoir of growing up in London, *The Sixties*:

> Now that it has gone, the twentieth century has become an idea. The past is always an idea which people have about it after the event. Those whose job it is to tell the story of the past in their own present call it history. To generations born later, receiving the recollections of their parents or grandparents, or reading the historians, the past is a story, a myth handily packaged into an era, bounded by a particular event – a war, a financial crisis, a reign, a decade, a century – anything that conveniently breaks the ongoing tick of time into a manageable narrative. Those people who were alive during the period in question, looking back, call it memory – memory being just another instance of the many ways in which we make stories.[2]

I am trying to get my soft Western mind around how it must be for Russians to 'remember' in Diski's sense the most terrible time in Russia's communist history: Stalin's thirty years of cruel and despotic rule, from Lenin's death in 1924 to his own undeservedly peaceful deathbed in 1953. This period – a nadir of tyranny and terror – is characterised by the forbidding term *Gulag* – an acronym of *Glavnoye Upravleniye Ispravitelno-Trudovykh Lagerei*, i.e., 'Chief Administration of Corrective Labour Camps', the Soviet Government's national penal network of labour, detention and transit camps.

The Soviet Union made remarkable industrial, infrastructural and military progress in these years of Stalin's cruel autocracy – it defeated Hitler and went from a poor, civil-war-ravaged country to a nuclear-armed world superpower – but at what human cost? The best introductions for Western readers to how bad life was in these deeply oppressive years are three great imaginative works of fiction: Arthur Koestler's 1940 novelisation of the 1936–38 Moscow 'show trials' of top communists, *Darkness at Noon*,[3] and George Orwell's subsequent brilliant pair of novels inspired in part by reading Koestler, the allegorical novella *Animal Farm* (1945) and the dystopian novel *Nineteen Eighty-Four* (1949).

The culture of the Gulag raises acute questions of Russian collective memory, because the Gulag system defined the whole society of the Soviet Union in such dreadful ways and for so many years, without any hope of relief. Cambodia experienced the horror of Pol Pot's rule, but for just three and a half years. Russia underwent a comparable horror of Stalin's whimsical tyranny for thirty years, and there seemed no end in sight as Stalin lay dying – just more of the same under his anticipated hardline successor, his trusted secret police chief, Lavrentiy Beria.

One could interpret the subsequent 38-year history of the Soviet Union since 1953 – and even of post-communist Russia since 1991 – as a long drawn-out rehabilitation of an entire nation suffering from post-traumatic stress disorder. True, life had gone on under Stalin – people fell in love, got married, had families, tried to be happy in prudently inconspicuous and circumspect ways: it was not a time to be a tall poppy. The Moscow metro lines and massive Soviet hydro-electric schemes and dams and canals got built (much of it using

Gulag slave labour). Moscow was modernised and beautified. But all the while, Russians lived in a society that was actually a cruel and dangerous madhouse. And they had to think of this as 'normal', if they were mentally to survive these years.

How does the human spirit cope with this? How does it recover afterwards? I do not think these questions have yet been properly explored. Though a highly commended new novel by English novelist Julian Barnes about the composer Shostakovich's years of living and composing under Stalin's terror, *The Noise of Silence* (2016), offers important clues to Western understanding.[4] This is why I call the Moscow Gulag Museum a work in progress. These questions have not yet been answered. Perhaps they never will be now, except through fiction.

First we went to the former Gulag Museum site, on Petrovka 16 in downtown Moscow, and found locked gates.[5] We were told by a brusquely unhelpful guard, 'No, it's closed – no museum here'. No word on where the museum had gone, or even if it still existed. But with the help of the internet, we soon found the new Gulag Museum address, in the bleak northern suburbs, near Dostoyevskaya metro station. On the station walls were murals of Dostoyevsky's haunted face, and of *Crime and Punishment* motifs: how appropriate, we thought. And as we approached the museum on foot – a large, grim three-storey brick-and-steel rectangular building of the Stalin era, or older – our apprehensions deepened.

I thought I knew a fair bit about the Gulag system already: that it was a massive nation-wide penal system of brutal forced labour camps, greatly expanded by Stalin especially after he gained supreme power in 1928, and reined in by his successor Khrushchev as soon as possible after Stalin's death in 1953. Since then, the Gulag system has been immortalised by Russian writers Alexander Solzhenitsyn (his novel *One Day in the Life of Ivan Denisovich* was first published in the Russian literary magazine *Novy Mir* in 1962, during the years of the 'Khrushchev Thaw'),[6] and by Anatoly Rybakov in his less well-known in the West tetralogy of novels, *Children of the Arbat* (written in 1966–83, but only published from 1987 onwards).[7] Poet Yevgenia

Ginzburg's (1904–77) Gulag memoir *Journey into the Whirlwind* (first published in the West in 1967, first published in Russia in 1990) was a powerful account of her life as a woman prisoner in the Gulag and in exile following her eighteen-year sentence in 1937 for counter-revolutionary Trotskyite activities. She steadfastly protested her innocence of all charges. She was released from post-Gulag Siberian exile in 1953, and rehabilitated in 1955.

The numbers of prisoners kept growing and, according to Anne Applebaum, the eminent American historian of the Gulag, peaked as late as the early 1950s.[8]

There had existed in Tsarist times for over a century the practice of penal labour colonies and long sentences of forced exile in Siberia – including for political crimes – as far away as Sakhalin Island, which penal colony Chekhov visited and wrote about. As in Britain, transportation of convicted criminals to forced labour in remote parts of the empire was the norm: as to America or to Australia, so to Siberia. Lenin continued the practice. And after 1928, the now all-powerful Stalin decided to use prison forced labour in massive numbers to speed up Soviet industrialisation and to speed development of the Arctic North and Siberia.

Over the next twenty-four years, Applebaum estimates that 18 million people passed through the Gulag system as sentenced prisoners. A further 6–7 million people were administratively exiled to similar remote areas. Applebaum estimates the number of prisoners in the camps at any one time was usually around two million. The Wikipedia article on the Gulag cites an estimate of 2.4 million people in camps in 1953 – of whom roughly one-fifth, more than 465,000 persons, were political prisoners. The Soviet Union's population was then 190 million, making on my calculation an imprisonment rate of 1.26 per cent.

These rates were horrendously high, though historically both the United States and Soviet Union, and now Russia, have continued to maintain the world's highest incarceration rates. As recently as 2008, the United States had around 750 prisoners per 100,000 population, and Russia was not far behind at around 620.[9]

Nevertheless, the Soviet Union's incarceration rates from 1934 to 1953 were historically the world's highest for any modern-day country.

Around one in ten Soviet citizens would have been imprisoned in the
Gulag system or exiled at some time during these thirty years of mass
arrest, sentencing and exile. This means that almost every Russian
family, from every class, would have had close relatives or friends in
the Gulag at some time in this era. For example, both Gorbachev's
grandfathers were sent to the Gulag; so was Yeltsin's father; Pasternak's
lover Olga Ivinskaya; the mother of Sakharov's wife, Elena Bonner
(and Elena's father was executed). The ferocious Gulag spared few
Russian families.

The Gulag was Russia's entire criminal detention system. Anyone
who fell foul of the Soviet Penal Code for whatever reason, whether
criminal or political – it made no difference – would be sentenced
to death or to long terms in the Gulag: common criminals, high-
profile political offenders, or innocent law-abiding ordinary people
who were deemed for trivial or imaginary reasons to have violated
the notoriously open-ended Article 58 of the Russian Federation
Penal Code.[10]

Article 58 listed offences and punishments in a wide range of
'counter-revolutionary' actions, defined as 'any action aimed at over-
throwing, undermining or weakening of the power of workers' and
peasants' soviets...or at the undermining or weakening of the external
security of the USSR and main economical, political and national
achievements of the proletarial revolution'. Such alleged serious
offences descended from more obvious ones like deliberate or accidental acts of sabotage, down to minor 'thought-crimes', like contacts
with foreigners 'with counter-revolutionary purposes', or 'propaganda
and agitation that called to overturn or undermining of the Soviet
regime'. As applied in Stalin's time, such a phrase in practice could
mean virtually anything that a state security interrogator or informant
wanted it to mean.[11] For the slightest deviation from public postures
of cheerful enthusiasm for the government, people could come under
suspicion. Life came to be about falsification – about always pretending
in public to be happy. Orwell's '1984' was no exaggeration.

Worse, one section of Article 58 allowed for third parties to be
prosecuted for not reporting instances of 'propaganda and agitation'.
In effect, this section empowered – indeed, obligated – the secret
police to arrest and incriminate anyone doing anything they

deemed suspicious: for making or even laughing at a Stalin joke, for complaining or even listening to complaints about some government action or omission, for having foreign friends. Article 58 terrorised and traumatised an entire nation, and created a national culture of informers.

This politicised criminal justice system – already broadly in place in Lenin's day –grew monstrously under Stalin, due to his suspicious nature bordering on paranoia, his belief in the Gulag's efficacy as a deterrent, and his belief in the productivity of unpaid forced labour. But Stalin could not have put the Gulag in place alone. The whole higher Communist Party leadership and rank and file were complicit in the rapid expansion of this brutal system. Senior politburo members like secret police head Yezhov, Defence Minister Voroshilov, members Mikoyan and Kaganovich co-signed key decrees on the Gulag. Hundreds of thousands of officials implemented the system. Many officials were themselves devoured by it.

The Gulag also imprisoned peasants who opposed forced collectivisation, especially in the Ukraine Black Earth region, but actually everywhere – even in Siberia itself as happened to Yeltsin's father; minority nationalities who resisted forced national-security deportations, like the Crimean Tatars; 'enemy' prisoners of war captured or surrendered in the war, including large numbers of former Polish Army soldiers de-commissioned and arrested after the Stalin–Hitler partitioning of Poland in September 1939; even repatriated Russian prisoners-of-war after war ended in 1945, who were considered guilty of treason for not having fought to the death but having surrendered to German forces.

Stalin's Great Purges of the Communist Party and the Moscow and Leningrad intelligentsia began in 1934. In 1936–38 took place the Moscow Show Trials of senior Communist Party members (the most famous was Bukharin) accused of conspiring to assassinate Stalin and his close associates, to dismember the Soviet Union and to restore capitalism. These trials were staged pseudo-judicial events in which tortured, starved, sleep-deprived former top communists usually broke down and confessed to whatever they were instructed to confess to. Few ever pleaded not guilty – most sooner or later succumbed. Unimportant people were convicted by rapid, simplified administrative procedures – usually, by three-man NKVD (security police) tribunals.

The Gulag was a world of its own with its own rewards and punishments, recreations, even its own slang dialects. Model prisoners could be promoted on the spot to guards, and inefficient guards demoted to prisoner. Huge mortality was routine. Prisoners often had to build their own camps from scratch in the snow, and were worked and starved to near death in them. Over the period 1929–53, independent estimates of deaths in the camps or of prisoners who died very soon after release – record-keeping was unreliable – range between 1.6 million and 10 million. Having said that, these were not deliberate extermination camps – they were just utterly indifferent to human life.

This museum's focus is different from most previous Western-published or online academic work on the Gulag system: for example, it differs from the earlier-established online American *Gulag Museum on Communism*, which describes itself as:

> An exhibit of the Museum on Communism – a project of the non-profit, non-partisan Victims of Communism Memorial Foundation, established by an Act of Congress on December 17, 1993 and signed into law by President Bill Clinton.[12]

During the continuing Cold War after Stalin's death – i.e. for at least thirty-two years between 1953 and 1985 – the memory of the Gulag was used by the West as an ideological weapon to discredit Stalin's more moderate successors and the Soviet communist system as a whole, which was to remain in place until 1991.

By way of comparison, here is how the official website of the Gulag Museum in Moscow describes (in the English version) its purposes:

> The State Museum of Gulag History was founded in 2001; the exhibition was opened in 2004. The Museum's founder, Anton Antonov-Ovseenko, a well-known historian, writer and public figure,

was himself a prisoner of Stalin's labor camps. The museum collection comprises a documentary archive, letters and memoirs by former Gulag prisoners, their personal belongings and a collection of artworks by former Gulag inmates and contemporary artists offering their own vision of the subject. The exhibition is dedicated to the history of the rise, development and decline of the Soviet labour camp system, an instrumental and integral part of the Soviet state machinery in the 1930s–50s, and its political, administrative and economic role. The exhibition room also displays personal cases of various people who fell victims of the Soviet repressive policy and were sentenced to labour camp imprisonment.

The 'Our Projects' part of the Museum website contains these significant words on the Museum's concept:

> The demand for an open space dedicated to the study, discussion and public presentation of the era of Stalinist repression can be felt especially keenly now. The history of 20th century Russia is tragic and complex from a moral and humanistic standpoint; to this day, there is no distinct, commonly accepted interpretation. At the same time, without a thoughtful and dispassionate analysis of the past, it is impossible to build a contemporary society with a conflict-free national identity.

To my mind, the museum's greatest strengths lie in its authentic Russian agency, its national ownership and language; its personal accounts of ordinary people caught up in the Gulag system; its accumulation of detail through small artefacts and keepsakes; and its in-your-face immediacy. It does not dwell on gross atrocities in particular camps, nor does it compare camps. It does not go in much for statistical metrics. Its real focus is on bringing home how life was for the little people caught up in the Gulag's arrest, sentencing and punishment system.

The museum shows how this system was in no sense a civilised or rational system of justice: it shows how it was a militarised secret police arrest and punishment mechanism, not bound by account-ability or the rule of law. The first holding prison after arrest was a place from which people were not expected to return to normal life. There would be no hearings and no impartial court decision: a summary guilty verdict, decided beforehand from above before arrest orders were made, was followed by a sentence to the Gulag or summary execution.

The museum explores in depth – through real-time newsreel films and feature movies, through contemporary newspapers and posters, through video interviews – the paranoia and hysteria of the era, the random nature of arrests, and the casual brutality of the subsequent processes of interrogation and sentencing. And the museum looks at the return home of survivors after the camps were closed, and the difficulties they and their families had in trying to rehabilitate their damaged bodies and minds and public reputations.

An important part of the museum display, the *My Gulag* Project, aims 'to create an archive of reminiscences and interviews tied to the Gulag theme'. It shows frankly how the system devoured innocent ordinary people, as well the 'Children of the October Revolution', a privileged elite who might have thought themselves safe: intellectuals, professionals, secular Jews, party members, people who lived in middle-class districts like Arbat and Kropotkinskaya. The museum website comments that this section aims 'to bring to the forefront memories of things that were at one time purposely squeezed from the mental space of our fellow citizens and, as a result, remained unacknowledged and impersonal'. Museum staff recorded lengthy video interviews with former camp prisoners, their family members who were also affected by the repressions, and staff workers in the Gulag system. By this means, they are bringing home to visitors the stark message, 'This was about you, your parents or your grandparents'.

I watched video interviews with now elderly people who had been arrested as young adults as late as the early 1950s. Beautiful and hopeful young women, idealistic and happy young men, loyal communists, children of important people, writers, artists – it made no difference. The best years of their lives were destroyed, even if they survived the rigours of the Gulag. I watched in horror these brave and calm testimonies by warm, credible, articulate witnesses to what they went through, people now in late middle age or elderly, arrested as young people in the later years of the system.

I can't forget one particular video of an elderly lady – obviously educated, and of intelligentsia background – telling her story. As a young woman, I would guess in around 1950, she had been denounced by an informer for making the mistake of innocently attending a wedding while abroad in the West as part of some official delegation. She was picked up by secret police in Kropotkinskaya Street in Moscow and taken to her nearby home to pack a few clothes. She kept protesting her innocence of any crime, as her parents, knowing what was in store for her, went white. Her weeping mother brought out her warmest winter coat and gave it to her. But the young woman still believed she would be cleared, that it was all a silly mistake. Later, during her interrogation by three policemen after a sleepless night alone in a cold cell, she got upset and angry when the police started to swear crude obscenities at her. She protested at this unlawful violation of her civil rights. They then kicked her chair from under her and sent her sprawling on the stone floor. She said these were the tactics of breaking down innocent people and securing signed confessions: food and sleep deprivation, cold cells, casual brutality, abusive language rather than studied acts of torture. It was just as effective in breaking down pride and the will to resist, she said.

It was so brave of these people to revisit these dreadful memories in interviews. Or maybe it was finally a relief to them to be able to talk freely about the memories and know they would be listened to at last, after so many years of repressed memories and of their families telling them not to talk about it.

The museum finally asks visitors the question, on a big billboard towards the end of the tour path – *What would you do to help prevent this from ever happening again in our country?*

Still emotionally overwhelmed, I met some friendly young school students in the foyer afterwards. They asked me what I thought and I tried to reply in my halting Russian. I also wrote in the Visitors' Book:

> Such a moving and sad museum. So important that people can come here and see the facts of what happened and how it ended. Credit to the Russian Government and everyone involved for facing up to this awful history so honestly.

Months after my visit, I came across an article about the opening of this Gulag Museum on 30 October 2015, in the independent English-language internet weekly *Moscow Times*, by a young British journalist working in Moscow, Howard Amos.[13] Much of what he writes amplifies my own impressions. Amos comments that this state-owned 'museum with a mission' opens at a time 'when many Muscovites remain unwilling to talk about political repression, and as the country remains polarised by the legacy of its brutal system of Soviet-era prison camps'. He quotes Gulag Museum director Roman Romanov, saying that this history is 'still painful and unrecognised in our country', and that 'even successful, well-educated people believe repression shouldn't be talked about, without ever wondering why'. Romanov said the new museum is 'a space where people – visitors – can meet themselves, meet with their personal history, or with themselves in this history. It is a moment of contact'. He adds: 'People are repelled by the memory [of the Gulag] because it burns and brings them pain…(but) we cannot turn away from ourselves'. Asked what he wants the new museum to evoke in visitors, Romanov replied that this museum 'is not to frighten people, it is not about death. It is to understand and feel that humans did this to other humans'.

Amos reports Natalya Solzhenitsyna, the widow of Alexander Solzhenitsyn, telling city officials, historians and human rights activists who attended the museum's opening ceremony: 'There are lots of people, particularly the young, who do not know they are walking on bones'.

In a survey conducted by independent pollster Levada Center in March 2015, 45 per cent of Russians said they thought the sacrifices of the Stalin period were 'justified'. This opinion seems to be gaining ground. And here, of course, is the real difficulty. As Russia rebuilds confidence in itself after the Gorbachev and Yeltsin years of self-criticism, and in the face of Western superiority and condescension, some Russians – around half, it seems – want to remember the Stalin years proudly as years of great industrial progress leading to victory in World War II and nuclear superpower status.

Amos again:

> Discussion of twentieth-century political terror burst into the open in
> Russia after the fall of communism [in 1991] and remains a controversial
> topic...critics say Putin's ideological narrative of a resurgent Russia has
> seen a creeping rehabilitation of Stalin and helped marginalize [sic] the
> Gulag in official histories, which tend to focus instead on industrial
> progress and victory in World War II.[14]

Thus, a BBC news item of 30 October 2015 on the opening of this
Gulag Museum comments: 'Under President Vladimir Putin's rule,
Russian officials have tended to downplay Stalin's crimes focusing
more on Stalin's role in the World War II victory over Nazi Germany'.

This seems to me to be a misunderstanding. It is entirely possible for
Russians to take pride in Stalin's industrialisation of Russia and defeat
of Nazi Germany, while being ashamed of the Gulag. There is a
question still of how Russia is to deal with its Gulag history. Germans
after 1945 were left time and space to process their own memories of
Nazism. Russians since the death of Stalin have not had that freedom.
Debate about the Stalin era and the Gulag has morphed into debate
about the faults of Soviet communism, or even of post-communist
Russia. Some Western commentators seek to use the horrors of the
Gulag years in order to discredit both the Soviet Union's subsequent
history as a communist state in 1953–1991, and even present-day post-
communist Russia since 1991 or since 2000. And this naturally evokes
defensive Russian nationalist responses, even from quite reasonable
Russians like Foreign Minister Sergey Lavrov.

Perhaps we should now in the West begin to give more credit to
the huge liberalisation in Soviet life that began soon after the death
of Stalin in 1953, a theme which comes through clearly in this Gulag
Museum. It was Stalin's politburo member Nikita Khrushchev, aided
by a few key allies, most importantly, World War II hero Marshal
Georgy Zhukov, who in the tense first days after Stalin's death, and
at great risk to their own lives, arrested and had quickly tried and
executed the powerful secret police chief Lavrenty Beria.

Khrushchev then started as fast as he could to pardon or amnesty large numbers of Gulag political prisoners and petty criminals, to close down most of the camps, and to cancel orders for compulsory exile. In his 'Secret Speech' to the 20th Party Congress in February 1956, he denounced the damage done to the Soviet Union by Stalin's cult of personality and his repressive purges. He initiated a wave of legal rehabilitations that officially restored the reputations of many millions of innocent victims who had been killed or imprisoned under Stalin. He made tentative moves to relax restrictions on freedom of expression held over from the rule of Stalin. Khrushchev introduced and oversaw a cultural 'thaw' that humanised Soviet life in many important ways.

Khrushchev, like Gorbachev thirty-two years later, was trying to humanise communism, while keeping it communist. Cold War tensions eventually discredited and defeated him, but the Soviet Union never returned to the harsh horrors of Stalinism. Brezhnev, Andropov, Chernenko, Gorbachev – all ran regimes under which people felt it safe at last to criticise Kremlin leaders.

I see no basis for doubting the sincerity of Putin's condemnation of the Gulag system. He has fully supported the establishment of this museum and other similar sites of human rights remembrance across the country. The Moscow Gulag Museum is owned by the Department of Culture of the City of Moscow. Although generously financially assisted by the US-based *Forbes Magazine*, it is not connected with any foreign-based NGO and so does not fall under the 'foreign agent' law. The museum opened on a 30 October – the officially endorsed annual Russian Day of Remembrance for Victims of Political Repression. Amos again:

> In 2015, the Russian Government approved a new policy that unequivocally condemned attempts to justify Soviet repression and mapped steps to be taken ahead of the upcoming centenary of the 1917 Revolution. A monument to victims of political repression ordered by President Vladimir Putin is due to be unveiled in Moscow next year [2016].[15]

Gulag remembrance will continue to raise difficult questions of historical interpretation in the present contested East–West information warfare arena. Western historians like Robert Conquest and later Anne Applebaum were the first to open up this highly sensitive history: history which most Russians under late communism feared for a long time to tackle because the archives were closed, because the still-communist regime was incapable of a full accounting, and because the human wounds were still so raw. Their work, while highly professional, was framed by anti-Soviet and anti-communist values. The Washington online Gulag Museum on Communism set up by President Clinton in 1993 – though it has great educational merits – is similarly framed, and lacks Russian ownership or agency.

We should also, it seems to me, acknowledge that there was no Western assistance in Russia's post-Stalin dismantling of the Gulag system from 1953 onwards. Khrushchev and his co-conspirators against Beria bravely did this for themselves. What courage this must have taken after so many decades of learned habits of prudent submission, in a one-party state built around the unchallengeable power of Communist Party dictators, whether Lenin or Stalin.

But there was important Western agency in supporting persecuted late-era Soviet dissidents like Pasternak, Solzhenitsyn, Sakharov and the Jewish refuseniks, right up to Gorbachev's relaxation of Jewish emigration restrictions in 1987: through international pressure at bilateral (US–Soviet and UK–Soviet) diplomatic levels, and in the monitoring of human rights abuses under the Helsinki CSCE 'Third Basket' machinery.

Now that post-communist Russia is itself exploring and trying to come to terms with the cruel underside of the Soviet Stalinist past, might it not be time for the West to give Russia (and Vladimir Putin) more credit for sincerity and good faith in this unfinished endeavour? Otherwise, the hundredth anniversary of the Bolshevik Revolution in 2017 risks becoming yet another East–West battlefront in 'history as propaganda'.

Finally I understood better, after spending a day in this museum, why Moscow was still such a strange, frightened city when I lived there as a diplomat in 1969. Why older people were so obviously afraid to speak with or even meet the eye of foreigners at concerts or in cafes, but clung to small protective groups of trusted relatives or friends. The fear of being informed against under Penal Code Article 58, and memories of the Gulag, must have bitten very deeply to be still influencing public behaviour sixteen years after the death of Stalin. This was a society still in 1969 in post-traumatic stress disorder. No wonder so many people were glum and wary. They had had every reason to be.

Chapter 11

The Jewish Museum

For our last day in Moscow, Julian and I tackled the Yevreiski Muzei i Centr Tolerantnosti (Jewish Museum and Centre of Tolerance). From the start I wondered: why the name? I needed to unpick this title, which rings oddly to Western ears. What exactly are museum visitors being invited to 'tolerate'? There are so many other words that might have been used in a subtitle, if one were needed at all – centre of mutual respect, or understanding, or acceptance, or friendship...so why this freighted word 'tolerance'? Were there buried meanings here, known only to Russians and Russian Jews?

After I got home to Australia, I researched this a little. The Russian dictionary offers two translations for the English word 'tolerance': the first, *terpimost*, from an old Slavonic root; the second, *tolerantnost*, a borrowing in modern times from Western-language words based on the Latin root *tolerantia*.[1] *Terpimost* is an abstraction from the Slavonic word *terpenie* – which translates directly into English as 'patience' or 'forbearance'. *Terpimost* may be understood as a willingness to 'tolerate' something, in the sense of putting up with something which one might not like, or might believe to be harmful or in error. This is 'negative' tolerance – i.e., 'we should let them do their own thing, as long as they do not trouble us'.

Tolerantnost conveys Western human-rights-based notions of 'positive' tolerance or toleration, characterised by genuine mutual respect and willingness to share the public space with individuals and groups who hold values different from one's own. This 'positive tolerance' concept did not penetrate very far in nineteenth-century

Russia beyond the Westernising elite, perhaps because Russia did not directly experience the lessons Western Europeans had to learn painfully from the Reformation and subsequent religious wars about the necessity of true toleration of value differences within an open, plural society.

Russia never experienced, outside the law-making Westernised elite in Saint Petersburg and Moscow, the separation of church and state and the triumph in society of essentially agnostic, tolerant Enlightenment values. In important ways, Russia's national experience was different. Since the ninth century it has always been firmly a majority Orthodox Christian nation (as the other meaning of 'orthodox' signifies – normal, standard, accepted by the majority). Under the tsars, Orthodoxy was the established state religion, and other faith-based communities were always regarded as 'heterodox' minorities in imperial Russia as a whole, though they might be numerical majorities in some specific provinces or towns. Examples of this were Catholics in Poland, Lutherans in Finland, Muslims in southern and eastern provinces, Jews in some locations in the Jewish Pale of Settlement in Lithuania, Byelorussia, Ukraine and Galicia, and Buddhists or animists in parts of Siberia. Separation of church and state was neither desired nor achieved in Russia before communist rule. Then came the communists, who as atheists disdained and barely tolerated all religions, which they saw as moribund superstitious relics of the past.

Now under Yeltsin and Putin, Russian Orthodox Christianity has regained its traditional respected status in Russian culture: the state spends lavishly on church rebuilding, restoration and maintenance, and Russian political leaders defer to the church hierarchy and make a point of attending churches on major religious days. But Russia remains formally a secular, multinational state. The new Constitution introduced by Yeltsin in 1993 is quite clear in Article 14:

> The Russian Federation is a secular state. No religion may be established as a state or obligatory one. Religious associations shall be separated from the State and shall be equal before the law.

So how do Russians of majority Orthodox cultural background, of religious faith or secular, really regard the other religious traditions in today's Russia? I suspect that many of the contradictions of the nineteenth century have returned: while Russia's Constitution and legal system at least in words guarantee freedom of religion and religious equality, many Russians' understanding of religious toler-ance is still *terpimost or veroterpimost* (religious tolerance) rather than *tolerantnost*, the museum's preferred word.

Under the framework of *veroterpimost*, the tsars gave generously from imperial state revenue not only to the majority Orthodox Church, but also to minority faiths to help them build their major places of worship. But the tsars also turned a blind eye to, even at times found it politically convenient to encourage, violent pogroms against Russia's Jewish citizens. I concluded that the museum's inclusion of the word *tolerantnost* in its title sends a deliberate freighted message, acknowledging head on the fact that Russia has had a troubled history of Christian–Jewish relations: that this country has always had a problem of 'tolerance'.

And it still does. One only has to look at Russian online political website reader comments pages to see the extent of vicious anti-Semitic, anti-Muslim, homophobic, male supremacist, anti-Western attitudes still prevalent in parts of Russian society. There are many angry, prejudiced older white men out there on the fringe, as in Western countries. Fortunately, this anger has not been politically focussed through a powerful, fascist-leaning political party. Putin's balanced policy towards minorities has sucked the air out of any potential mass Russian fascist party.

We walked to the Jewish Museum from Maryina Roshcha metro station. As we walked towards the museum building, we passed a kosher grocery where we met an Orthodox Jewish teacher, escorting a group of lively Jewish primary schoolchildren in his care.

First, a few important facts and figures. According to Wikipedia's entry *History of the Jews in Russia*,[2] the latest Russian census reported that perhaps 200,000 to 500,000 Russian Jews lived in Russia in 2010, of whom between 157,763 and 194,000 people self-identified as Jews, making up around 0.1 per cent of the total population of Russia of around 200 million. This compares with 900,000 Russian-born Jewish emigrants living in 2010 in Israel and 350,000 Russian-born Jews living in the United States. Germany comes fourth, with 119,000 Russian-born Jews. Clearly there has been a huge emigration of Jews from Russia during my lifetime. Yet Russia's Jewish population in 2010 was still said to be the third-largest Jewish population in Europe, after France and Britain. The figures today would be not far from in 2010, as Russian Jewish emigration virtually ceased after 2006.

In the nineteenth century, it was very different. The Russian Empire then hosted the largest population of Jews in the world, primarily of Ashkenazi origin. Under the reign of Catherine the Great (1762–96), the Russian Empire conquered vast territories and new non-Orthodox populations from the former Polish–Lithuanian Kingdom, in which many Yiddish-speaking Jews had lived peacefully for centuries in their own *shtetl* (village) communities alongside adjoining Christian communities, in the tradition of *terpimost*. Empress Catherine ruled that Jews were required by Russian law to remain in this area, defined as the Jewish Pale of Settlement – twenty-four provinces comprising a very large region in the western part of the extended empire, through Lithuania, Russian Poland, Belarus, Galicia and Ukraine. The old way of life here is accurately and sympathetically depicted in the stories of Sholem Aleichem and in the musical *Fiddler on the Roof*.[3] This museum similarly displays *shtetl* life in the Pale positively, as I read on this explanatory placard:

> A Jewish town: even when Jews were a minority in the *shtetl*, its Jewish character gave them the feeling of dominance. Never through their long history of wandering had Jews felt as comfortable as they did in the *shtetl*...made up of dwellings and workplaces of different standards from sheds to mansions, and centred upon the synagogue and schools.

From 1827, Jews living in the Pale were allowed to claim Russian citizenship. Modernity began to break down *shtetl* culture, as better-educated, more ambitious Jews chose to leave the sheltered *shtetl* life and to become more assimilated into contemporary Russian urban culture, either in the growing cities within the Pale (like Vilnius, Warsaw, Minsk, Berdichev, Kiev and Odessa) or further east in old Russia. They were now being conscripted to serve in the army, spoke Russian, and many became secular Jews. Pasternak's parents in Odessa are an example. So with Isaac Babel, Vasily Grossman, and Ilya Ehrenburg. Intermarriage and abandonment of religious practice became common.

Beginning in the 1880s, waves of anti-Jewish pogroms swept through the Pale of Settlement areas, especially in Ukraine, recurring over the next four politically unsettled decades. Jews made convenient scapegoats for social unrest. Nevertheless, according to the 1897 Russian census, the Russian Empire still had the largest Jewish population in the world: 5.2 million (4.13 per cent of the total population); 94 per cent still lived in the twenty-four provinces of the Pale of Settlement, where Jews comprised 11.5 per cent of the population.

Over the next century, Russia's Jewish population was to shrink dramatically and also change its social character. More than two million Jews emigrated from Russia between 1880 and 1920, mostly to the United States but also to popular destinations like Australia and Canada. Some 150,000 Jews were killed in pogroms during the Polish–Russian War and Civil War in 1918–22, mostly in Ukraine (125,000), and in areas controlled by anti-communist White Army or nationalist Ukrainian or Polish forces. Generally, though not always, the Red Army defended Jews from its enemies' pogroms.[4]

Secular urban Jewish culture flourished in the early years of the Soviet Union which professed non-discrimination and gave equal educational and employment opportunities to Jews. At the beginning of the 1930s, Jews were (according to this Wikipedia article) still 1.8 per cent of the Soviet population – and a remarkable 12–15 per cent of university students, studying for professions like medicine, science, engineering, journalism and music. The majority was still living in the old Pale of Settlement areas, but many had moved into the growing cities within the Pale.

During the Great Patriotic War, according to this article, an estimated 500,000 Red Army soldiers were Jewish: about 200,000 were killed in battle. About 160,000 were decorated, and over one hundred became generals. Over 150 were honoured as Heroes of the Soviet

Union, the highest possible military award. More than two million Soviet Jews are believed to have perished during the Nazi Holocaust, victims of warfare and of genocide in German-occupied territories. Both *shtetl* life and urban Jewish life in the Pale of Settlement were destroyed by the mass killings and cultural genocide under the Nazi occupation. On the other hand, a large number of Jews from these areas were able to survive the Nazi invasion by fleeing early enough in the war to areas of Russia beyond the Russian–German frontline, where they resettled and worked to support the war effort as soldiers or in war industry.

In 1959, the first postwar Soviet census showed 875,000 Jews, but it is estimated the number of assimilated secular Jews who did not declare themselves in the census as Jewish would have been considerably higher at this time. There then followed years of large-scale Jewish emigration, beginning around 1970 and tailing off in the 1990s. The census in 2002 showed only 233,000 declared Jews in Russia, most living around Moscow and Saint Petersburg.[5] Some believed that Russia's Jewish population would fade away, as more and more Russian Jews entered mixed marriages and their children ceased to identify themselves as Jews. But others said that Russian Jews' pride in their Jewish roots was recovering, and that the demographic tide would turn. It is perhaps too early to say.

The museum is organised chronologically, making ingenious use of state-of-the-art interactive technology. It starts with an impressive 3-Max wraparound movie depicting Jewish religious beliefs and values from the Biblical Creation story through the Exodus, the glorious reigns of Kings David and Solomon, the Roman destruction of the Temple and the resulting Jewish diaspora across the Roman Empire and beyond.

Fast-forward through medieval Europe, to the Polish–Lithuanian Kingdom, in which from the sixteenth century onwards, Jews had come to live peacefully and securely in Yiddish-speaking *shtetl* villages, as market gardeners, dairymen, innkeepers, small traders, tradesmen etcetera, filling intermediary roles between the Polish–Lithuanian aristocracy and the rural peasantry; a system Russia inherited and maintained till late in the nineteenth century, as *Fiddler on the Roof* accurately depicts. Life was precarious but generally not bad in these years. Russian-speaking community leaders like Tevye the dairyman functioned as go-betweens between the Jewish *shtetl* and adjacent Christian communities, and everybody usually got along. But there was an edginess, an existential insecurity, as the introductory scenes in *Fiddler* symbolise so clearly.

The next major display area shows the next phase: Jewish urbanisation, acculturation in Russian society, and the growing Jewish role in Russia's intellectual and cultural life and rapid industrialisation during the nineteenth century. The explanatory plaque says:

> At the turn of the 20th century, Russia was experiencing dramatic change, which directly affected the lives of its five million Jews. In this period, hundreds of thousands of Jews migrated from the *shtetls* to the cities in search of a better life, hoping to find work and educational opportunities, seeking to become a part of the modern world and its achievements...The primary setting of Jewish life shifted from the *shtetl* to such cultural and industrial centres as Kiev, Minsk, Odessa and Vilna [Vilnius]. Here, new generations identified themselves as 'Russian Jews': they spoke Russian, were attuned to Russian culture, and aspired to integrate into the social life of these urban centres. The face of Russia's cities was changing with the influx of large numbers of Jews, who made up as much as a third of the population in some places. During this period, large cities became breeding grounds for pogroms, but they also gave birth to such new expressions of Jewish identity as Zionism.

We see displays showing benign periods of official toleration, punctuated by periods of violent pogroms, and the difficult choices now facing educated Jews in Russia – whether to fight for their political rights as Russian citizens – as members of the Bund, the Jewish workers' socialist trade union, which worked with other trade unions to better the lot of the working poor; or to emigrate; or to assimilate and try to keep a low profile, as secular citizens of undisclosed Jewish background. The museum asks visitors in a walk-in display depicting an urban cafe with some famous Jews of the time sitting at tables where you can join them and converse interactively with them – what option would you have chosen?

Then we see displays showing the Jewish role in the early Bolshevik movement and in the February and October 1917 revolutions (Trotsky being only the most famous of many Jewish social democrats and communists). We see the early, relatively stable years for Russian secular Jews under communism until 1941. We see the major contributions of Russian secular Jews in the arts and sciences. Jews like all religion-based communities in Soviet Russia came under strong party and state ideological pressures to abandon their religious practices and values. Jews suffered under Stalin's purges as everyone else did. And Jews were also part of the party hierarchy, security police and Gulag apparatus that implemented the purges.

The extensive Great Patriotic War display offers a stunning, distressing blown-up 3-Max scene, using Nazi newsreel footage and soundtracks, memorialising the massacre of Jews in Ukraine at Babi Yar. Russian poet Yevgeny Yevtushenko recites his famous poem.[6] This display is deeply affecting. We then see Jewish soldiers fighting heroically in the Red Army, battling to reverse the Nazi onslaught and push the invaders all the way back to Berlin, where finally we see the Red flag raised over the Reichstag in victory. I photographed and translated a highlighted plaque here quoting Ilya Ehrenburg, a famous Jewish writer and war reporter:

> I grew up in a Russian city. My native language is Russian. I am a Russian writer. Now, like all Russians, I am defending my motherland. But the Nazis have reminded me of something else: my mother's name was Hannah. I am a Jew. I say this with pride. Hitler hates us with all his strength. And that does us honour.[7]

Ehrenburg (1891–1967) was a prolific and much-loved Soviet writer, born in Kiev in a secular Lithuanian Jewish family, who had a complex and adventurous life. A contradictory and outspoken figure, he somehow survived Stalin's purges while keeping the respect of his colleagues. He became Russia's top war reporter. In 1954 he wrote an influential short novel called *The Thaw*, portraying the liberalisation of Soviet life after Stalin's death. First published in a literary journal, it sold all 45,000 copies of its first book edition in a single day. His memoir *People, Years and Life* (1965), a long book, is full of insightful reflections on the Stalin years.

I photographed another plaque, a quotation from Vasily Grossman's great wartime novel *Life and Fate*:

> Human history is not the battle of good struggling to overcome evil. It is a battle fought by a great evil, struggling to crush a small kernel of human kindness. But if what is human in human beings has not been destroyed even now, then evil will never conquer.

Grossman (1905–64), was born in Berdichev, now in Ukraine. He was a correspondent for the Soviet military newspaper *Krasnaya Zvezda* throughout World War II. He spent around 1000 days on the frontlines. *Life and Fate* was his defining achievement as a writer. Grossman lived by his philosophy – that if good can only stay alive even against huge odds, it will prevail – both in the struggle against Nazism and against Stalinism. *Life and Fate*, written after Stalin's death and submitted for publication in 1960, was rejected by the party on grounds that if published, it could inflict even more harm on the Soviet Union than *Doctor Zhivago*. It was smuggled out to the West in 1974 with the help of Andrei Sakharov, where it was published in 1980. Grossman died in 1964, never having seen his book published. It was published in Russia in 1988 under Gorbachev. Some critics compare its cultural importance in Russian literature to that of *War and Peace*.[8]

We then see exhibits using contemporary newsreels of the time when Stalin in the early postwar period came to suspect an alleged Jewish doctors' plot to poison him; and the first ominous warning signs of a possible new upsurge of officially sponsored Soviet anti-Semitism. And how this paranoid old dictator's fantasy engendered a renewed great despair among Russian Jews that, even after the Holocaust, things would never get better for them in Russia; that anti-Semitism would always be endemic and unchallenged in this country.

Next I saw a really absorbing and moving display devoted to the Jewish refusenik movement which developed in the 1970s Soviet Union. The story is told through video interviews with its main leaders, Nathan Scharansky and Vladimir Slepak, and their family members. The name *refusenik* derives from its Russian equivalent word *otkaznik*, based on the *otkaz* ('refusal') stamp put on Russian Jews' applications to emigrate. We see the enormous courage of the refuseniks, in asserting over many years their human right to be Jews, to have a Jewish-based religious and community life in Russia if they wished, and to be free to emigrate to Israel if they wished – all in accordance with the Helsinki Final Act of 1975. We see the subtle and unsubtle pressures put on this group of defiant Russian Jews to give up, to conform. We see how their struggle was from its beginning in 1970 an important part of the general human rights struggle in Russia, testing the boundaries of human rights under Brezhnev, Andropov, Chernenko and finally Gorbachev. The refusenik movement acquired increased momentum and unstoppability after 1975, as Western governments became increasingly engaged in supporting Soviet Jews' rights to emigrate freely.[9] I remember from personal experience how both Malcolm Fraser and Bob Hawke, Australian prime ministers for whom I worked on foreign policy in the years 1976–85, were deeply emotionally engaged in this issue. It was the hinge on which Australian–Soviet relations came to turn, even more so than in US–Soviet relations, which also had the wider strategic arms-control agenda to manage. But every American president after Nixon cared about the refusenik issue: they had to.

Like the Gulag Museum, the Jewish Museum makes its points impressionistically and in human terms rather than statistically. We see from extended interviews in the Russian language with Vladimir and his wife, Maria Slepak, both engaging, sympathetic and very Russian characters, recorded when they were at last living safely in Israel with their children and grandchildren, just what it had cost them to lead the fight for their community's human rights in the late Soviet period, which though softer than the Stalin period, could still be brutally harsh on those individuals it singled out to be made deterrent examples of (for Vladimir and Maria, as for Olga Ivinskaya and the Sakharovs).

Vladimir had been a radio engineer and a member of the Moscow Helsinki human rights group. Like all refuseniks, he automatically lost his job at age forty-three when he applied to emigrate, but was told he could not leave the country because he had gained important national-security information in his former state job. He thus became officially a jobless parasite. We see Vladimir's and Maria's heroism in persisting year after year with their struggle despite poverty, relentless official harassment and finally punitive imprisonment: after eight years of demonstrating in 1970–78, Slepak was sentenced to five years' exile in Siberia and Maria to four. He was finally allowed to join his children in Israel in 1987 – seventeen years after he had begun his campaign. He died a happy and proud man in 2015.

One particularly moving large photograph I saw in this room was of a Jewish community picnic in a public forest near Moscow (such picnics were routinely officially harassed, but the community bravely persisted with them). The children are learning a traditional Jewish line dance as their parents look on, clapping and smiling. The joy on the children's and mothers' faces is so inspiring and so heartbreaking at the same time. These people were such heroes.

Finally, there is a display called *Perestroika to the present*. This room conveys how life finally improved for all Russians, including Russian Jews, under Gorbachev and then, after the fall of communism in 1991, in the Yeltsin and Putin eras. The takeaway message is that Russian Jews are rightly free nowadays to emigrate, and to return to Russia as and when they wish. Or, they can go on living in Russia as Russians, and practise their religion freely; that their contribution to Russian life is valued and respected however they choose to live. In other words, as in the West.

The museum does not dwell on the extent of Jewish emigration: its message is about Russia today – that it is now a multicultural society that respects equally all its citizens of whatever background. The final plaque, *Prosperity through Tolerance (tolerantnost)* makes this message crystal clear:

> In the Russian Federation, people of many different religious and cultural groups, social and ideological associations, hundreds of ethnicities and nationalities, live side by side. We are diverse, and this is our strength. Respect for other people's cultures, histories, and traditions, is an essential prerequisite for peace, harmony and prosperity. In the Tolerance Centre [a discussion room attached to the

museum], you will have the opportunity to join in a discussion about the importance of inclusiveness to our social and cultural enrichment.

We saw in the foyer pictures of the museum being jointly opened in 2012 by President Putin, by the mayor of Moscow, and by Israel's late President Shimon Peres, with major donor Ronald Lauder of the US-based Estee Lauder family cosmetics corporation looking on. It was a very happy ending to an emotionally full-on museum tour.

I want to share some afterthoughts and subsequent research.

The refusenik issue deeply influenced Russia–Western relations in the Soviet period as no other domestic Russian issue had. It engaged Western governments directly in issues of human rights in Soviet and early post-Soviet Russia, even more so than did the fates of Pasternak or Solzhenitsyn or Sakharov. No longer could the Kremlin say to Western governments – these are matters of our national sovereignty, and none of your business. The Helsinki Accords provided the legal basis for Western leverage, and the near-universality of sympathy in the West for the refusenik cause provided the political impetus. In this way, the West developed a propensity to become deeply engaged in Soviet and subsequently Russian internal affairs, on questions like democracy, press freedom, corruption, gay rights, and so on. Western governments began to support the setting up of numerous democracy-based foundations, institutes and non-governmental organisations in Moscow, operating outside normal state-to-state diplomatic channels and protocols, and openly aimed at influencing Russian values and behaviour in a liberal democratic or free-market-economy direction. Post-Soviet Russia for some years through the 1990s accepted this unusually high degree of Western intervention in internal affairs as the new normal. Russia was broke, poorly governed, and had lost confidence in its own values and systems. It welcomed any help of any kind from the outside world.

But eventually, in the Putin era, the inevitable reaction came. Russia got up off its knees and reasserted its sovereignty. A hurt and angry West still asks, why? But of course it is easy to see why, if one studies Russian history: Russian pride always finally reasserts itself, after times of national weakness.

Secondly, it is interesting that in all these years of disruptive political and social changes, the normalisation of the situation of Russian Jews, including their rights freely to emigrate and to return, continued steadily. The emigration figures tell the story.[10] From 1970 to 1988, the years of *refusenik* challenges to harsh Soviet emigration laws, 291,000 Jews emigrated from the Soviet Union: 165,000 of these went to Israel and 126,000 went to the United States. In these years, the United States was accepting any Soviet Jews as refugees.

In 1989, after Gorbachev lifted all restrictions on emigration, the US Government stopped treating Soviet Jewish emigrants as refugees. Israel continued to welcome them and assist their resettlement after 1989, both those meeting Orthodox religious definitions of Jewishness (i.e., having a Jewish mother), and those applying under the State of Israel's more liberal Law of Return (i.e., anyone who has a Jewish grandparent or is married to a Jew). In 1988, 58 per cent of married Soviet Jewish men and 47 per cent of married Soviet Jewish women had non-Jewish spouses. Increasingly, as Russian Jewish emigration to Israel swelled after 1989, it was made up of such mixed-marriage secular part-Jewish families.

From 1989 to 2006, 1,607,000 Jews as thus defined left the former Soviet Union. Of these, 979,000 went to Israel, 325,000 went to the United States, and 219,000 went to Germany. Finally by 2006, the outflow had ceased. Everyone who wanted to emigrate to Israel or elsewhere by claiming a Jewish family history had already done so: and those who remained in Russia knew they could leave if they wanted to in the future.

The scale of this emigration from 1970 to 2006 – nearly two million people – was a massive brain drain from Russia and a massive brain gain to Israel, the United States and Germany. Many – perhaps most – of these emigrants were highly educated middle-class professionals – doctors, scientists, engineers, artists and musicians – from Russia's cities. Their arrival as settlers in Israel has enriched Israel's intellectual and cultural life in many obvious ways, including in classical music, medicine, engineering, military science, IT and universities. Israel has become culturally more Russian in character – a mixed blessing in the view of some Israelis, because Russian-background politicians in Israel tend to join the harder-line right-wing parties. Today, Russian is widely spoken in Israel: there are Russian-language newspapers and television programs, and well-filled daily direct flights between Israel and major Russian cities, catering to family reunion visits and tourism. Russians feel safe and welcome holidaying at Israeli beach resorts and there are plenty of Russian-background hotels and restaurants. Russia has sent teams to the Maccabiah Games, the international Jewish Games, for the past twenty-four years. One in four teachers at Israeli universities is of Russian background.

This normalisation of Russian–Israeli relations since perestroika has pretty much gone unnoticed in the West, but it seems to me important, and a gain to both sides and indeed to the world. It might have helped Russia feel more confident to play a larger peacemaking role in religiously wracked Syria, where it has historically been the main protector of the Christian communities. Relations between Putin and Netanyahu seem to have stabilised. Putin's inner circle of friends includes prominent Russian businessmen of Jewish background. The presence of the late Israeli President Shimon Peres at the Jewish Museum opening in 2012 was symbolic of a warmer, more confident state-to-state relationship.

I believe Russia hopes that relations with Israel will continue to strengthen at people-to-people and interstate levels, as Russia seeks to demonstrate to former Russian Jews and to their children and grandchildren, now a significant part of Israel's demographic, its growing civility and respect for human rights since 1989.

I look back warmly on this unique Jewish Museum as a hopeful place. I believe the tragic history of official Russian anti-Semitism is over. As with Germany, Russia has left that history behind. The numbers of Russian Jews are greatly reduced, sadly, but they continue to exercise beneficial influence in many fields, and the future looks brighter for them. Of course there remain significant pools of ignorant anti-Semitic pathology in Russia – as in Western countries. But it seems to me that the bigger problem areas now are not in Russia, but in Eastern Europe – especially in Ukraine, which is wrestling with major unacknowledged demons of anti-Semitism.

Chapter 12

City of the Tsars

The end of my Russian journey was just four days away now: Saint Petersburg was to be the last hurrah. I felt sad to leave Moscow and my cosy hostel home-away-from-home. The staff ladies were sorry to see me leave too. We said goodbye with some shared Irish whiskey.

Julian and I had splurged on tickets for the best train to Saint Petersburg, the Grand Express. Boarding the train around midnight was spectacular: at every carriage door stood ramrod-straight lady cabin attendants in smartly tailored red woollen overcoats and matching caps, courteously checking in every listed passenger by name. We made straight for the warm dining car. Upholstered red velvet banquettes, friendly and prompt service…finally, we were on the Russian train of my dreams. We settled in with a flask or two of Armenian cognac and some smoked salmon on ryebread, as the train silently glided away from Moscow…I was in heaven.

In Saint Petersburg the next morning, we arrived at our hotel, the Astoria Forte, on Saint Isaac's Square near the landmark Saint Isaac's Cathedral, the 'Bronze Horseman' statue of Tsar Peter the Great, and the Winter Palace and Hermitage Art Museum. The hotel – the city's best in Soviet times, and where my ambassador used to stay on official visits to Leningrad while I stayed in the cheaper Evropeiskaya Hotel – was built in 1912 at the zenith of the empire, and completely refurbished by the Rocco Forte Group as a five-star luxury hotel in 2002. I cannot speak too highly of this hotel and its courteous, obliging staff. I am embarrassed to reveal how inexpensive our off-season room was, for a hotel of this quality.

The hotel had a good dining room, lobby lounge for high teas, and an elegant cocktail bar: the Lichfield Bar, named after the famous photographer and Queen's cousin Patrick Lichfield (The Earl of Lichfield, 1939–2005) who had been an iconic figure of London's Swinging Sixties and a regular visitor to Russia. Around its polished dark timber walls hung blow-ups of some of his most famous photographs. Julian and I began our Saturday evening there propped on bar stools, remembering the period – we had missed most of the excitement, being hard at work studying economics in Trinity College Dublin. We drank generous martinis, and then went out to meet friends for dinner at a nearby vodka museum-restaurant.

Such unabashed lazy hedonism in my last Russian days in Saint Petersburg was a relief after so much high-impact travel, so many serious museums, so much emotionally wrenching history. With my marathon air journey home to Australia fast approaching, I relaxed in the hotel steam bath, drank tea from their samovar, and drifted aimlessly around the city.

Saint Petersburg – the historic old central part – is a breathtaking human construct. Peter the Great – proud, ambitious imperialist that he was – was determined to impress all of Europe, and above all, Sweden the rival Baltic power at the time, with Russia's wealth and power and civilisation, to prove that he could build a 'Venice of the North' on this swampy flat Baltic foreshore, that would rival any European city in scale and architectural magnificence and liveability. He brought in hundreds of European architects, artists and craftsmen, and tens of thousands of Russian serf labourers, many of whom suffered and died in the building of his imperial dream. This city of granite built on sand was completed over many decades, under Peter and his successors, the empresses Elizabeth and Catherine the Great. It was the administrative and military capital of Russia's great nineteenth-century empire, and it looks the part. I have never seen such perfect cityscapes, in such profusion – palaces, terraces, frozen white canals, gently arched stone and ironwork bridges – the whole place is amazingly beautiful and speaks of a grand Russian vision of its destiny as a great European power.

Like Moscow, the city was freshly painted in pastel colours, and clean: its Soviet-era poverty and shabbiness a dim memory. But the streets seemed unnaturally quiet as we walked around. Maybe things get livelier in summer? There were only small crowds of visitors in front of the main Winter Palace and Hermitage Museums. Things were livelier along the main thoroughfare, Nevsky Prospect, which runs around five kilometres from the Admiralty to the Moscow Railway Station and beyond: the grandest shopping boulevard in all Russia, and a wonderful street for just promenading of an evening, lined with palaces, churches, gracious apartment buildings, shops and department stores, restaurants and shopping arcades.

But we saw hardly any Western tourists, in our hotel or around the city. This surprised me, as I was expecting to see many people who had come in on weekend ferries from Stockholm or Helsinki. I remembered from 1969–71 that, even in winter, the Evropeiskaya Hotel had its dining rooms and bars crammed with merrily carousing Finns and Swedes, taking advantage of Leningrad's cheap alcohol and no anti-drinking laws. Those days seem long gone, and I wondered why; is it just that we all live in more abstemious health-conscious times now, or was there something more behind the absence of Westerners here?

There was quite a lot of domestic upscale weekend tourism from Moscow. Saint Petersburg has become a favoured winter weekend destination for busy corporate Muscovites to come and unwind with their families. Road, rail and air connections are good, the city is full of good hotels and restaurants, and no doubt many people have their own holiday apartments. Tickets to Moscow-standard operas, ballets and concerts are easier to come by and very much cheaper than in the capital. Moscow-based tourism might be Saint Petersburg's mainstay for some years to come if politics continues to put a damper on Western-sourced tourism.

We were lucky with the weather: it kept on snowing gently the whole time we were there and never thawed. Crisp snow underfoot kept the streets safe and pleasant to walk in. *The Bronze Horseman* looked better than ever in his snowy overcoat and wig. This huge equestrian statue of Peter the Great is iconic of the city. Commissioned by Empress Catherine the Great, it was completed in 1782. The statue exudes strength and imperial power and is rightly one of the city's top sights. Peter sits easily in the saddle on a rearing stallion, on a granite redoubt, his right hand raised as if signalling his army forward into battle. He is dressed in a Roman-style military cloak. From every angle, the energy and authority of the statue are overwhelming.

It certainly impressed Pushkin, who wrote an epic narrative poem completed in 1833, *The Bronze Horseman*, about this statue and about the terrible flood which took place in 1824 when the River Neva burst its banks, causing great destruction and loss of life in the city.[1] His poem begins with these famous lines (Professor Walter Arndt's excellent 1972 free translation gets closest to its sonorous, pounding rhythm):

> *Na beregu pustynnykh VOLN*
> *Stoyal ON, dym velikikh POLN*[2]

> Upon a shore of desolate waves,
> Stood *he*, with lofty musings grave,
> And gazed afar. Before him spreading
> Rolled the broad river, empty save
> For one lone skiff stream-downward heading...

> ...He thought;
> 'Here, Swede, beware – soon by our labour
> Here a new city shall be wrought,
> Defiance to the haughty neighbour.
> Here we at Nature's own behest
> Shall break a window to the West,
> Stand planted on the ocean level;
> Here flags of foreign nations all
> By waters new to them will call,
> And unencumbered we shall revel'.[3]

Pushkin sings the praises of the city, its beauty, its sophisticated and exciting society life, in these lovely lines:

> I love thy winter's fierce embraces
> That leave the air all chilled and hushed,
> The sleighs by broad Nevá, girls' faces
> More brightly than the roses flushed,

> The ballroom's sparkle, noise, and chatter,
> And at the bachelor rendezvous
> The foaming beakers' hiss and spatter,
> The flaming punch's flickering blue.

This was Pushkin's world: it is the world Tolstoy again portrayed fifty years later in *War and Peace*, when unhappily married nobleman Pierre Bezukhov parties recklessly with the bachelor military officers, and on a dare risks his life drinking a bottle of vodka while balanced precariously on his toes, looking inwards in a third-floor window opening. It is a scene I have never forgotten.

Then Pushkin's poem changes tone completely, telling the tragic story of a struggling penniless clerk, in love with an equally poor girl who lives in a hut on the riverbank on the other side of the Neva: they are too poor to marry. When the great flood comes, he nearly drowns and is only saved by clinging to a bronze lion on a palace's steps. After it recedes, he goes in search of his sweetheart, but her hut has been swept away and she is gone forever. He goes mad over losing her, and roams the city homeless. One day he curses the statue of Peter – 'the Idol' – for ruining his life. The statue comes to life, and pursues him through the city to his death, in punishment for his insolence.

It is an enigmatic fairytale which has provided fertile ground for critics in nineteenth-century Russia and in the Soviet period, to speculate about what Pushkin was really saying here. Was he protesting against Tsarist autocracy's ruthless lack of concern for the welfare of all those ordinary Russian people whose lives had been sacrificed to build the grandiose Saint Petersburg project? Was he saying the imperial decision to build Saint Petersburg here in this dangerously flood-prone estuary, in defiance of Mother Nature, had been a huge and arrogant mistake with tragic consequences for ordinary people? Or was he dutifully warning his readers to respect the Tsar, of the dreadful consequences of disrespect?

Like much in Pushkin, many interpretations are possible. Every educated Russian has learned and loved the poem, and formed their own views on its inner meanings.

The other high points of Saint Petersburg for me were two first-rate musical performances, of Prokofiev's *Romeo and Juliet* ballet by the Mikhailovsky Ballet Troupe, and of Tchaikovsky's opera *Evgeny Onegin* by the Mariinsky Opera.

Evgeny Onegin is the quintessential Russian opera. Again, it has a strong Pushkin connection. It started life as a long narrative poem by Pushkin, completed in 1825.[4] (Spoiler alert – do not read the next two pages if you don't know the story and think you might sometime want to see it live or on film.)

Evgeny is an archetypal Russian character – a *lishniy chelovyek*, or 'superfluous man': a young, rich, bored and restless nobleman, with no idea of his function in society. Russian nineteenth-century literature is full of such self-absorbed, troubled characters: Pushkin's Evgeny was the first such, followed by many others: Lermontov's *Hero of Our Time*, several Turgenev characters, and even Tolstoy's Vronsky.

Tchaikovsky wrote the opera in 1879, fifty-four years after the Pushkin poem, and he sentimentalised Pushkin's story. In Tchaikovsky's hands, Pushkin's ironic tale of obsessive love becomes softer, more wistful. As it begins, Evgeny, bored in his newly pur-chased estate in the deep countryside, idly chats with a neighbouring landowner's naive and serious young daughter Tatyana. He thought-lessly arouses her affections and then coldly rebuffs her when she declares her love for him in a secret overnight letter. He then treats his friend Lensky outrageously, openly flirting at a country house dance with Lensky's frivolous fiancée, Olga, Tatyana's sister, resulting in Lensky being forced to challenge Onegin to a duel or risk becoming the laughing stock of local society (a moment of high drama in the opera). Without meaning to, Onegin kills his friend. Shame-stricken, he flees abroad for a few years. Returning to Saint Petersburg, he attends a society ball where the host – a rich, powerful older prince and retired army general – proudly introduces his wife whom, as he has earlier told Evgeny, he loves dearly and she him despite the difference in their ages (not unusual in this time and society). Evgeny with a shock recognises Tatyana and realises that he has only ever loved her. They meet privately the next day at his urgent request. He begs her to run away with him to Europe, but she refuses, saying she has sworn loyalty to her husband and is honour-bound to keep her promise. The opera ends quietly with Evgeny left alone and broken-hearted.

It's a more complex story than it sounds here. It is about trust, respect, commitment and the Russian sense of honour. Tatyana does not decide to stay with her powerful older husband in preference to the passionate younger Evgeny out of conventionality or fear or greed – Evgeny would be rich enough to take her back to Europe and live there with her safely in rich émigré style – but because she knows it is the right thing to do. She admits frankly to Evgeny that she is still attracted to him, but she is not going to act on it. This is a very Russian ending, sad and noble.

The opera starts quietly but builds in intensity towards its remarkable tables-turned ending. It is an amazing collaboration of two, very different, Russian geniuses – the writer and the composer.

The opera is insightful and moving about much else besides: the class relations, sometimes warm, sometimes distant, between rich landowners and their household servants and estate serfs, marked by customary exchanges on feast days of gifts, festive songs and hospitality (the story takes place in the 1820s, before serf emancipation); the compromises women were forced to make in this male-dominated world; the tragic consequences of duelling, but its inevitability if men were not to be shamed in this harshly competitive society where women were little more than objects of ownership and desire; the rollicking boisterousness of the country house dance and the icy formality of the Saint Petersburg society ball.

The drama of the former friends' tragic duel is the occasion of a lovely aria *Lensky's Farewell*, in which Tchaikovsky sets directly to music some of Pushkin's loveliest lines. Lensky knows he will probably die, because Evgeny is a much better marksman than he. He mourns his coming, pointless death. The aria begins:

Kuda, kuda, kuda vi udalilis, vesni moyei zlatiye dni?...
O where, O where, O where have you fled away, golden spring days of my youth?...

Part of its emotional force is that we know – as Tchaikovsky knew – that Pushkin himself was killed in an eerily similar duel in 1837, twelve years after writing this poem. There had been scandalous rumours that Pushkin's wife, Natalya, had begun a love affair with her sister's husband, the disreputable Georges d'Anthes. In defence of his wife's honour, Pushkin was forced to challenge her alleged lover to a duel, in which d'Anthes killed Pushkin. Lensky's Aria is so powerful because it is actually Tchaikovsky's, and Russia's, lamentation for the untimely loss of its greatest poet. Pushkin was only thirty-seven.

What makes Pushkin so important and unique in Russian literature? His sheer versatility of genre – epic poetry, short-form and love poetry, short stories, novels, plays, fairytales. The way he used and expanded vernacular Russian in what was still an aspirational French-speaking elite society: he proudly created the modern Russian literary language still in use today. His archetypal Russian themes, emulated by other Russian writers after him: the arrogant indifference of the powerful, and the helplessness of the weak; the tension between individual self-fulfilment and the conventional rules and protocols of a class-stratified society; the hard choices under the social code between honour and personal happiness; his love of life and of women; his courage in pushing his work to the limits of Tsarist censorship; and his fierce Russian patriotic pride.

Pushkin was full of contradictions. Part of the bragging, male-chauvinist culture of the Saint Petersburg elite military caste, tenderness vied in him with the keen pursuit of available women. He wrote a famously subtle love poem to a married woman: it tells of a poet's grief over a great unrequited love that was not returned. He speaks politely, using the plural pronouns *Vas* and *Vam* (like 'vous' in French), which makes the poet's pain at his rejection even more clear – and there is a subtle sting in the tail:

Ya Vas lyubil: lyubov isho, byt mozhet, V dushe mayei ugasla ne sovsem;...
I loved you: and the feeling, why deceive you,
May not be quite extinct within me yet:
But do not let it any longer grieve you;
I would not ever have you grieve or fret.
I loved you not with words or hope, but merely
By turns with bashful and with jealous pain;
I loved you as devotedly, as dearly
As may God grant you to be loved again.[5]

He was at most times a democrat – known for his sympathy for the 1825 Decembrist rising, involving many of his military fellow officers, who aspired to a constitutional monarchy, and which was savagely put down by the Tsarist autocracy. He was for years a friend of the Polish national poet Adam Mickiewicz. Yet he could also be an arrogant, proudly nationalist, imperialist Russian. In 1831, stung by West European criticisms of Russia's harsh suppression of a Polish uprising in that year, he wrote a scathing political poem, *To the slanderers of Russia*, which makes interesting reading in today's climate of tense Russian–Polish relations.[6] Pushkin's theme here is that Russian–Polish conflicts are family quarrels, with a centuries-long history, which Western Europeans can never understand, and in which they should not take sides. He reproaches Europeans for their short memories of how Russia saved them all from Napoleon's tyranny, and – like Alexander Blok ninety years later – warns that Russia is big and strong enough and ready again to defend itself against all invaders:

> Leave us alone: you have not read
> Those bloody tablets;
> To you is unintelligible, to you is alien
> This family feud;
> Mute to you are the Kremlin and Praga;
> Unthinkingly you are beguiled
> By the valor of a desperate struggle –
> And you hate us…
> And for what? Reply: is it because
> On the ruins of blazing Moscow
> We did not acknowledge the insolent will
> Of him under whom you quaked?
> Because we hurled into the abyss
> The idol heavy-looming over kingdoms,
> And with our blood redeemed
> Europe's freedom, honour, and peace?

On our last evening in Saint Petersburg, Julian and I went out for dinner to a remarkable little restaurant in Malaya Morskaya Street, one block from our hotel – the Gogol. The decor of the restaurant – the ground floor of a former townhouse, with several smallish rooms each decorated differently in authentic period style – evokes the famous nineteenth-century Saint Petersburg writer (1809–52). It was a warm hospitable place, decorated with memorabilia of Gogol. The initially aloof young waiter warmed to us when I spoke Russian with him, and looked after us well. A highlight of the evening was when a lady pianist in a light-grey Orenburg shawl quietly slipped into the room, sat down at the piano, and began to play the most accomplished classical medley of well-known piano pieces and her improvisations on other classical themes. I recognised Chopin, Tchaikovsky, Mozart, Beethoven and Mendelssohn. She played without sheet music and segued flawlessly from one piece or key to another.

During her break I chatted a little with her, asking where she had learned to play the piano so well. She replied smilingly, in the school of music in her home city of Voronezh. I knew nothing about Voronezh so I looked it up later. It is a medium-sized city of about a million people in the Black Earth region near the Don River, about 500 kilometres south of Moscow, and close to the Ukrainian border and the city of Kharkiv (Kharkov). When the Russian Army halted the initial Nazi advance on Moscow, Hitler redirected the main German army attack to the south-east, towards the Caucasian oilfields. Voronezh was on their line of march. The Germans took the city in bitterly contested fighting in July 1942, during their advance on Stalingrad (now Volgograd), 500 kilometres further south-east. They occupied Voronezh for eight months, until they were driven back by returning Soviet forces; 92 per cent of Voronezh was destroyed in the war. The city was completely rebuilt in the 1950s as a city of heavy industry. It again fell on hard times during the post-Soviet period.

Some famous people come from Voronezh: including writer Ivan Bunin, the poets Andrei Platonov, Osip and Nadezhda Mandelstam, and the ex-KGB agent turned Western agent and later mysteriously murdered by his former colleagues in London, Alexander Litvinenko.

Somehow, this average little Soviet Russian city that I had never previously heard of – I did not even know where it was, until I looked it up on the map – had been touched or scarred by so much of what I had been trying to understand during my return visit to

Russia: the bitter-sweetness of life in the late Tsarist Empire, as fondly remembered by Ivan Bunin; the 1917 Revolution and Civil War, which raged in the Don River region all around this city; Stalin's forced collectivisation of the kulak peasants in the surrounding rich Black Earth region, and his purges of Russian artists and intellectuals like Osip and Nadezhda Mandelstam; the unimaginable suffering and destruction of the Nazi invasion and occupation; Khrushchev's thaw and his efforts to rehabilitate Stalin's victims; Gorbachev's perestroika and the economic disaster it brought upon rust-belt Soviet heavy industrial cities like Voronezh; and now the new Cold War, as symbolised by the nearby tense border with a hostile Ukrainian state; and the 'honour' poisoning of a turned KGB agent in London.

Most of all, I will remember Voronezh for another reason: the beautiful piano music played on my last night in Russia, by my nameless but talented and charming classical pianist in the Gogol Restaurant in Saint Petersburg.

PART THREE

...AND BACK AGAIN

A journey does not need reasons. Before long, it proves to be reason enough in itself. One thinks that one is going to make a journey, yet soon it is the journey that makes or unmakes you.[1]

Chapter 13

An Alternative Reality

I had planned this book simply as a personal travel account, comparing impressions of Russia today with the Soviet Union of my memories forty-five years ago. But somehow the book has grown into something more as well: a personal appeal against current locked-in hostile Western misreadings of contemporary Russian reality, and against the insensate Western drive to a new Cold War with Russia.

There is the reality that I saw, of the civilised country in which I enjoyed living for a month; nor too different, I surmise, from the way many educated Russians see their own country today. And there is the alternative dark reality of 'Putin's Russia', as presented across multiple Anglo-American media, in today's massive information war against Russia. Of these two sharply opposed 'realities', it is the latter which has firmly colonised most Western minds – to the point that most of us no longer know that it has done so.[2]

I could have ended my book with the charming pianist in the Gogol Restaurant in Saint Petersburg. But I felt I needed to try to draw these musings together in a slightly more analytical way, even though I never intended this to be a rigorous academic book. I found a convenient hook for these final chapters in Professor Stephen Cohen's latest work. In a new 2011 Epilogue to his 2009 scholarly work *Soviet Fates and Lost Alternatives*, Cohen (on pp. 200 and 218) lists and challenges some current Western 'axioms' about today's Russia – in Euclidian geometry, axioms are statements said to require no proof because they are self-evidently true:

America won the Cold War.

It was Putin, not the US-backed Yeltsin, who began dismantling Russian democracy.

The US–Russian relationship soured after 1991, largely because of policies made in Moscow, not Washington.

Present-day Russia is as brutally anti-democratic as its Soviet predecessor.

Russia's nature makes it a growing threat abroad, especially to former Soviet republics, as demonstrated by its invasion and occupation of Georgia in 2008 (and now of Crimea and Eastern Ukraine in 2014).

More NATO expansion is necessary to protect both Georgia and Ukraine.

I believe every one of these axioms to be factually wrong, and a dangerously misleading guide to Western policy towards Russia.

The Russia I went to, enjoyed living in for a month, and tried to comprehend in as much depth as I could during that short time, is a reasonably decent political society, which is trying to move forward with dignity and civility, and in conditions of peace and security, to repair the damage of an unimaginably traumatic past hundred years, and to contribute positively as a major Eurasian regional power and United Nations Security Council Permanent Member to a stable and improving world order of sovereign states, in accordance with the UN Charter.

The other Russia is a corrupt, kleptocratic, often brutally malevolent and vengeful, sometimes incompetent and ridiculous, kind of Mordor:[3] a sham democracy, a mafia state that spends much of its time and energy scheming to gain strategic advantage over the civilised world upon which it borders, and which it threatens. This Russia literally cheats and poisons its way to prevail over its enemies. According to Timothy Snyder in the *New York Review of Books*, Russia in 2016 offers to the West only: 'faked elections, institutionalised oligarchy, national populism, and European disintegration'.[4]

The gulf between the Russia I lived in and this comic-book caricature that is now broadly accepted by many in the West, including some of my friends and colleagues, is disturbing. I need to address this dissonance to round off the story of my journey 'there and back again'.

The issue of opposed Russian realities is not about the West needing more 'research' or 'knowledge' about Russia – though it would certainly be nice to see more funding for serious Russian studies, as one of the world's major source civilisations. I would suggest, however, that to take an informed position on what is today's Russian reality, all the necessary knowledge is out there now on the internet with a few mouse clicks: much of it will be readily accessible via the Endnotes sources in this book. It is a question of how we as individuals choose to frame Russian reality, and the trust we choose to place in alternative sources of information and assessment. Of course many of us do not have time to check for bias: we rely on the filters of our quality media and our traditional assumptions of Western media objectivity. Sadly, much of our quality Western media can no longer be relied on for truth and objectivity where Russia is concerned.

Just during the year I was engaged on this modest book project, the momentum and intensity of the Anglo-American information war on 'Putin's Russia' has grown, to the point that it is now difficult for readers to keep up with the white noise of adverse news stories and commentaries that fill Western media. There is no end to it.

Let me try first to situate this in a familiar framework. We have agreed, since the illegal and now widely condemned Anglo-American invasion of Iraq in 2002, which did huge and still unfolding damage to human life, human rights, and peace and stability in the Middle Eastern world which we now have essentially destroyed, on this: that a strong world empire – in this case, let's call it the 'Anglo-American' empire, because Tony Blair's Britain was such an important part of the public legitimisation of George W. Bush's invasion and occupation of a sovereign country at peace with its neighbours – was able to create and sustain a false alternative reality regarding Iraq, which for a long time overwhelmed the reality of observed and reported facts.

Here is journalist Ron Suskind's now famous 2004 account in the *New York Times Magazine* of the disturbing conversation he had in 2002 about Iraq, months before the invasion, with an unnamed senior adviser to President Bush:

> The aide said that guys like me 'were in what we call the reality-based community', which he defined as people who 'believe that solutions emerge from your judicious study of discernible reality.' I nodded and murmured something about enlightenment principles and empiricism. He cut me off. 'That's not the way the world really works anymore,' he continued. 'We're an empire now, and when we act, we create our own reality. And while you're studying that reality – judiciously, as you will – we'll act again, creating other new realities, which you can study too, and that's how things will sort out. We're history's actors... and you, all of you, will be left to just study what we do.'[5]

Post-modern novelist Don DeLillo in his 2010 novel *Point Omega* expanded on that historic discussion of the allegations even then known by Western intelligence agencies to be false, but which George W. Bush was determined to act upon, of hidden Iraqi weapons of mass destruction.[6] A US defence intellectual is sparring with DeLillo's narrator, a filmmaker, who is trying to extract from him some Robert McNamara–style contrition for a US Government international action that went wrong:

> 'There were times when no map existed to match the reality we were trying to create.'
> 'What reality?'
> 'This is something we do with every eye-blink. Human perception is a saga of created reality. But we were devising entities beyond the agreed-upon limits of recognition or interpretation. Lying is necessary. The state has to lie. There is no lie in war or in preparation for war that can't be defended. We went beyond this. We tried to create new realities overnight, careful sets of words that resemble advertising slogans in memorability and repeatability. These were words that would yield pictures and then become three-dimensional. The reality stands, it walks, it squats...'

The creation of false alternative realities and of artful tropes by which to represent them in arresting and memorable images, did not end with George W. Bush and Tony Blair. It is alive and well in the way official Washington, London and NATO headquarters in Brussels today, and their attendant compliant media, seek to frame 'Putin's Russia' in the public mind. In scale, persistence and audience reach, the now dominant alternative reality image of Putin's Russia goes far beyond propaganda in the old US–Soviet Cold War sense. President Reagan's 'evil empire' trope was a primitive metaphor by comparison with today's armoury of powerful anti-Russian words and visual imagery.

I cannot see this ending anytime soon. This rock-solid carapace of prejudice, preconditioned thinking and hostile phraseology is an impregnable creation from which facts slide off like drops of water sliding off a turtle's hard shell.

Even to work in Russia today as a foreign expatriate or diplomat does not guarantee that reality will break through. As I found living in Moscow as a diplomat in 1969–71, strong expatriate communities sustain their own reality. A few of the people – not all – whom I met on my recent visit to Moscow were like this. Perhaps people who spend most of their professional time talking with one another, or with dissident Russians, or with expatriate former dissident Russians, or with anti-Russian East Europeans, absorb a negative view of Russian reality, conditioned by their interlocutors' bitter personal or family memories. Entire careers and media cultures can become invested in such perceptions. False beliefs become locked into a solidifying consensus: for example, that Putin's Russia habitually eliminates its enemies by poisoning them.[7]

Tourists are not left untouched. Some good friends of mine, a couple of inveterate travellers around my own age, spent a week last summer (by their choice, but I encouraged them) travelling on the Trans-Siberian Railway. They had no Russian. This of itself might not have mattered – smiles can go a long way – but they found to their disappointment what I would now surmise they might have expected to find from their preconceived mental picture of Russia: that they were surrounded by mostly hostile, cold, suspicious and rude people. Their week on the Siberian train was lonely and alienating. Maybe their own unease was felt and reflected back to them by Russian fellow passengers? I think now that perhaps if I had been there with them to break the ice with a few smiles and words of Russian, an offered whisky shot or two, some exchanges of family photos and information, things might have gone better, as they did for me on my Russian train journeys. And I do not blame my friends. It is simply an example of the problems we face in the way our views of Russian reality are now being framed by powerful forces. These problems go to the heart of the widening East–West political and cultural divergence.

The other day I went to a public meeting of the Australian Institute of International Affairs in Canberra. The speaker – an eminently respectable and articulate visiting foreign policy wonk from a major Western European country – was answering my question in Q&A, 'Is the case for a better Western relationship with Russia as a European neighbour and potential strategic partner getting a fair hearing in the West today?'

I recalled in my question his several negative remarks about Putin – who, he claimed, is now waging 'hybrid warfare' on Europe, but, as he joked, with little prospect of Russian tanks coming over the border 'anytime soon'. He had said that Russia, along with Daesh in Syria, is 'a major external strategic challenge' to Europe. I suggested that there are respectable policy circles in Western Europe still invested in the idea of Russia as a good neighbour and strategic partner – such as in Germany, France, Spain and Italy. But there was another growing group of governments in the European Union, whom I called rather provocatively the 'war party' (in Professor Stephen Cohen's well-known Washington-based usage[8]), who see Russia primarily as a threat: comprising Poland, most of the Scandinavians, the ex-Soviet Baltic nations, and increasingly it seems led by Britain. I asked him, were any more positive views about relations with Russia getting a hearing in Western policy community discussions?

He clearly had a well-prepared brief. He suggested that German thinking had soured greatly on Russia recently. If I wanted to refer to a 'war party' in the European Union, Germany was now an increasingly firm part of it. Putin's style of governance – the false democracy, the kleptocracy and corruption, the organised criminality of the Sochi

Olympics, the sports doping, Russian military aggression in Crimea and Ukraine, the controlled mass media, the killings of journalists, the KGB-style spy assassinations abroad – all meant that Europe could not trust 'Putin's Russia'. Everything Putin did was about asserting and trying to expand Russian sovereignty, and threatening the hard-won sovereignties of its smaller neighbours. Fortunately, Putin's circle of support at home was narrowing. The bottom line as the speakers saw it is: trade with Russia and engage diplomatically with her, yes – but do not become dependent on the Russians, because they cannot be trusted not to exploit any trade or other advantage. In other words, the standard British Government and NATO doctrine on Russia: when you sup with the Russian devil, use a long spoon.

My question went unanswered. I suspect the answer would have been, 'No, such pro-Russian views are now beyond the pale of respectable debate in NATO countries.'

My interlocutor was polite about Russia, but others are not so well mannered. I have an abiding memory of a European think-tank public discussion in Riga, Latvia, in April 2015 that I watched on YouTube a few weeks after I came home, on the theme *The World According to Putin, Putin According to the World*.[9] The general audience mood was disdainful and derisory towards Russia. The panel was one-sided, comprising two Westerners (a Finnish policy wonk, and Michael McFaul, a well-known American democracy studies academic who had been a popular Western-NGO human rights activist in Moscow in the early perestroika years, and who went back not so successfully as Obama's US ambassador in 2012–14), and two Russian émigré dissidents (a former Kremlin official, and a former liberal journalist in Russia). There was nobody there to represent views from or close to Russia's government: Russia was definitely an object, not a subject, in this talkfest of 'world opinion'. I noted a few highlights from opening statements:

> Former Kremlin official: Putin is an able gamer and gambler with a long-term planning horizon. He can play on many chessboards at the same time. His methods include terrorism and disinformation. He asks for equality of nations, but actually he seeks 'a sphere of privileged interest around Russia', ignoring the sovereignty of smaller neighbours.

Early in Obama's term, Putin offered Obama a 'grand bargain' to re-divide the world: to give Russia a free hand in the former Soviet lands, and the United States a free hand in the rest of the world. Obama had properly rejected this.

Former Russian journalist: Putin likes to be number one. His political mentality, formed by his KGB career, starts with the premise that the United States is Russia's main enemy. He has a strategically antagonistic view of the world. He admires Western modernity, style and market economy, but he thinks that he is stronger, smarter, and more popular than any Western leader. He comes from a non-intellectual family and is uninterested in the views of dissidents. He thinks he will lead Russia for ever. His ideal is, 'A powerful state as we enjoyed it before 1991, but with fast cars, good highways, and being able to buy vodka at any hour or day or time of the year.'

McFaul: Many contradictions in Putin. He thinks he can buy the cooperation of Western big business corporations as long as the price is right. His main goal is to stay in power: foreign policy goals are secondary. The December 2011 protests in Moscow after the last presidential election which returned him to the presidency (vacated by Medvedev) infuriated and frightened him. Now he sees himself as fighting against local Nazis in Ukraine and against an evil United States. He needs perpetual struggle against the United States – no war, no peace, no settlement. He is a prince, not an engineer; he is not interested in solving problems. He thinks he is leading a fight for Russia's survival. He needs Ukraine to fail, in order to show that his model is the right one. If the Ukrainian market economy and democracy succeed, that would be failure for him. He is a revisionist – he has to keep revising and updating his policies in order to stay in power.

Finnish policy wonk: Many of us find today's Russia is just too nasty to contemplate: we just wish it would go away. There is no shared analysis in the West of the gravity of this situation. There has been too much simplistic analysis and wishful thinking in the West over the past fifteen years. We are so disunited that Putin no longer takes the West seriously.

From the ensuing discussion, more random jottings:

The émigrés: For Putin, Britain, the Scandinavians and Baltic States are frontline opponents with whom compromise is impossible. He sees France and Germany as friends who could one day become allies. In the correlation of forces and wills, the West is losing to Putin. Ideology is more important to him than money in his bid to hold power. His values are socially conservative and anti-liberal. Over 50 per cent, maybe 80 per cent, of Russians think as he does. He will keep the Ukrainian crisis simmering through until the next presidential election in March 2018. Worsening Western sanctions will not bother him, indeed they will make him stronger electorally.

McFaul: Putin is sure of his own judgement and few people around him are prepared to challenge him. He is becoming more religious, withdrawn, less connected with ordinary people. He thinks he has a mission to protect Russia. Our counter-Putin strategy must be to accept that we are fighting an existential struggle, and that we need a stronger strategy to sustain our side. We must strengthen NATO; push Putin hard; don't let Ukraine fail; convince Putin of the rising cost for Russia of its aggressive policy in Ukraine; and engage in ideological struggle with him.

This conference in Riga for all its manifest disdain towards Putin was a reminder of the intensity of anti-Russian attitudes openly declared in NATO policy circles today. Forget public manners: the gloves are off now, in ways unprecedented during the Soviet Cold War period, when Soviet heads of state or government were accorded some residual protocol courtesies in Western public discourse. No longer, clearly − it is now all very personal, about the West's 'existential struggle' against Putin and his cronies.

It also reminded me of old-fashioned semi-secret NATO-based policy-planning conferences I used to attend in Britain or Canada as an Australian diplomat in the 1980s: the anti-Soviet or anti-Russian biases vigorously on show, and the constant calls for a more united and resolute European–US policy front against the Soviet (or now Russian) adversary. I noted a similar emphasis then as now on the policy goal of isolating Russia: on framing the conflict as the civilised

Euro-Atlantic world against Russia, always portrayed as the odd country out: the wolf at the gates.

To check this was not an untypical event, I scanned the news calendar over the past year. It was not hard to find such stories as these:

On 9 July 2015, the incoming Chair of the US Joint Chiefs of Staff, General Joseph Dunsford, testified that Russia poses 'the greatest security threat to the United States', and that it is reasonable to send to Ukraine heavy weapons 'to defend itself against Russian aggression'. He advocated updating the way the Pentagon plans for Russian 'hybrid warfare', in which conventional military actions are combined with secretive operations such as arming separatists from another country.

> If you want to talk about a nation that could pose an existential threat to the United States, I'd have to point to Russia. If you look at their behaviour, it's nothing short of alarming.[10]

On 25 February 2016, testifying in US Congressional committees, NATO Supreme Commander General Philip Breedlove was on the same page as Dunsford: Russia, having decided to become an adversary of the West, now presents 'an existential threat' to the United States and its allies.[11]

The Moscow Times – a liberal Moscow-based English online news website – reported on 16 May 2016 an interview on BBC Radio 4 with the just retired NATO Deputy Supreme Allied Commander in Europe, British General Sir Richard Shirreff. He claimed that in any period of tension, a Russian attack on the post-Soviet Baltic States is 'entirely plausible' under less than twelve months' preparation time. Promoting his new book, which features an imminent nuclear war scenario in the Baltic States, he said:

> We need to judge President Putin by his deeds not his words. He has invaded Georgia, he has invaded Crimea, he has invaded Ukraine. He has used force and got away with it. The chilling fact is that because Russia hardwires nuclear thinking and capability, to every aspect of their defence capability [if Russia did attack the Baltic States] this

would be nuclear war. NATO needs to raise the bar sufficiently high for any aggressor to say it is not worth the risk.[12]

A May 2016 background article by Matthew Bodner in the *Moscow Times* gives numerical data on the growing semi-permanent rotating presence of NATO forces along Russia's western borders, and on Russia's decisions to build up its own forces there in response.[12] American, Polish and German NATO forces now exercise regularly in Latvia and Estonia with tanks together with local Baltic States' armies, within sight of Russia's borders. In March an American tank squadron drove in well-publicised convoy along highways from its base in Germany through the Czech Republic and Poland, to the frontline Baltic States. In June over 31,000 troops from twenty-four NATO countries, headed by US Army Europe, took part in 'Anaconda-2016' war drills in Poland – the largest NATO war games since the Cold War.[14] In the coming year 2017, several hundred troops from NATO countries will be stationed in the Baltic states, 'as a tripwire' against Russian aggression. This is all said to be about deterrence of Russian aggression.

In April, a Russian unarmed fighter aircraft without warning flew risky aerobatic manoeuvres metres away from armed American warships on patrol in the Baltic. A fatal accident or misjudgement by either side seems only a matter of time. The drumbeats of war are beating louder, and it is definitely not a game. Brinkmanship prevails.

East–West relations have worsened seriously since Russia 'got up off its knees' during Putin's first presidency in the early 2000s.[15] The policy markers were:

- Russia's Abkhazian war with Georgia in 2008, when Russia militarily intervened to defend non-Georgian minorities suffering human rights abuses under centralising 'Georgianisation' campaigns;
- the death of human rights lawyer Serge Magnitsky after abusive treatment in prison in Moscow in 2009, and the subsequent imposition by US Congress of the first wave of anti-Russian selective sanctions against 'friends of Putin' in 2012;

- US-encouraged Western governments' and NGOs' interventions in Ukrainian domestic politics over many years, culminating in support for the Maidan armed uprising in Kiev in February 2014 which ousted elected President Yanukovich and brought to power a violently anti-Russian nationalist government;

- the subsequent unification of Crimea with Russia after a Russia-backed voter referendum in Crimea in March 2014;

- the new Kiev Government's launch in April 2014 of a full-scale military offensive using aircraft, tanks and long-range artillery on the self-declared separatist Donetsk and Luhansk region in East Ukraine, causing huge destruction of these cities and surrounds, with up to a million refugees fleeing to Russia or other parts of Ukraine and over 6000 local civilian deaths as estimated by OSCE[16];

- the unexplained MH17 shoot-down in July 2014; and

- expanding reciprocal US–Russia and EU–Russia economic sanctions since 2014.

The vicious, unresolved – now perhaps unresolvable – Ukraine–Russia conflict has been at the centre of most of the growing NATO–Russia estrangement in recent years. It has become a major threat to world peace.

On each of these issues, there is a Western version of facts using its preferred language and imagery, and an opposed Russian counter-version of facts using its preferred language and imagery. Thus we read of US State Department senior official Victoria Nuland handing out trays of American Embassy homemade cookies to the 'heroes' of the 'Euro-Maidan' popular uprising in Kiev (the Maidan Square having been thus renamed), and of Russia 'invading' or 'annexing' defenceless Crimea and Eastern Ukraine. Alternatively, if we look for them on the internet, we can readily find accounts of an ultra-nationalist Fascist-inspired violent anti-democratic coup d'état in Maidan, of assassination squads pursuing a fleeing President Yanukovich out of Ukraine until he found safe refuge in Russia, and an atrocity of subsequent burnings to death of forty-six anti-Maidan pro-Russian protesters trapped in a besieged trade union building in Odessa; of Crimea's democratic act of national self-determination in which frightened Crimeans voted overwhelmingly to seek reunification with their preferred homeland, Russia; and of East Ukrainians' continuing heroic armed defence of their human rights against the harsh centralising authority of Kiev determined to reoccupy and 'Ukrainise' (ethnically cleanse) these separatist provinces at whatever the human cost to the people living there.[17]

There are deep historical undercurrents to the present widening East–West estrangement. Most importantly, Russia is angered by the West having broken the unwritten Gorbachev–Bush Sr. agreement in Malta in 1991 that Russia would accept reunification of Germany as a NATO member, if the West undertook not to expand NATO beyond East Germany towards Russia. That promise was set aside by NATO under successive US presidents Clinton, George W. Bush and Obama. NATO now, twenty-five years later, stations battle-ready troops and missile-defense systems, and regularly exercises its forces, in its new Baltic member countries on Russia's borders, and does not rule out inviting Ukraine and Georgia to join NATO at some future time.

Second is the widespread sense in Russia that Western powers used her 'time of troubles' in 1985–2000 to become heavily interventionist in Russian internal affairs: that the West exploited these years when Russia was 'on its knees', to make itself a powerful player, even arbitrator, on issues of Russian domestic politics, economic policy and social values, and that the United States and its allies resent the fact that Russia has now 'stood up' against such cultural colonisation by Western agencies and NGOs, reasserting its own sovereignty and right to choose how it runs its own society.

Third – an independent factor with a virulent life of its own – is the historic anti-Russian sentiment or Russophobia in the West, which goes back centuries and is now again resurgent. In the novels of Kipling, Conrad, Buchan, Ian Fleming and a host of others, Russians often made handy bad guys. Twenty-five years after Soviet communism ended, when Hollywood needs global villains, they are often again Russian. Much of this Russophobia dates back to the time of the Napoleonic Wars and even earlier, in the divergent paths taken by post-Enlightenment and multi-confessional Europe and by Tsarist Orthodox Russia. Russia's land victory over Napoleon's united European *Grande Armee* terrified Western Europe and alerted Britain's maritime-based world empire to a new dangerous rival. The hard-fought Crimean War reinforced European Russophobia. Later, British strategist Sir Halford Mackinder's influential 1904 work *The Geographical Pivot of History* cemented in Western minds (and, it must be admitted, some Russian minds) a simplistic strategic doctrine of eternal systemic tension between a sea-based 'World-Island' dominated by Britain and the United States, and a land-based Eurasian 'Heartland', most likely to be led by Russia.[18] On anti-Russian sentiment in various countries, past and present, a general historical review article in Wikipedia contains interesting polling data: the figures for public mistrust of Russia in Western countries are strikingly high.[19]

A leading Russian studies scholar working in the United States, Andrei P. Tsygankov, published in 2008 an important commentary article titled, *The Russophobia Card*.[20] Writing during the Obama–McCain presidential campaign, at a time when Putin's Russia was early in its post-Troubles economic recovery and still at the margins of world affairs, Tsygankov analysed the sources of Western Russophobia and correctly predicted it would grow as Russia recovered its strength:

> Russophobia's revival is indicative of the fear shared by some US and European politicians that their grand plans to control the world's most precious resources and geostrategic sites may not succeed if Russia's economic and political recovery continues. One Russophobic group, exemplified by McCain, includes military hawks or advocates of US hegemony who fought the Cold War, not with the aim to contain the Soviet enemy but to destroy it by all means available. The second group [Democrats supporting Obama] is made up of 'liberal hawks' who had gotten comfortable with the weakened and submissive Russia of the 1990s. They have an agenda of promoting US-style democracy and market economy. The fact that the Soviet threat no longer exists has only strengthened their sense of superiority. Finally, there are lobbyists representing East European nationalists who have worked in concert with ruling elites of East and Central European nations to oppose Russia's state consolidation of power as well as promote NATO

expansion, deployment of elements of a US missile-defence system in Poland and Czech Republic, and energy pipelines circumventing Russia. These groups have diverse but compatible objectives of isolating Russia from European and US institutions. Because of a lack of commitment to a strong relationship with Russia in the White House, a largely uninformed public and the absence of a Russian lobby within the United States, the influence that these groups exert on policymaking has been notable.

Tsygankov's prescient 2008 analysis of groups with 'diverse but compatible objectives of isolating Russia from European and US institutions' is hard to refute. As I write this, official relations between the West and Russia have seriously deteriorated, still mainly over the frozen conflict in Ukraine. Russia is, it would seem permanently, now excluded from the G8 group of major advanced economies' discussion club – now renamed the G7. Russia had been an invited member of the group since 1988, but was expelled from it in March 2014 following Russia's 'annexation' of Crimea.

There was a brief flicker of warmth between US Secretary of State John Kerry and Russian Foreign Minister Sergey Lavrov, after Russia stepped up its diplomatic and military involvement in the Syrian War in late 2015 and offered to work with the West politically and militarily to defeat Islamic State there, but this quickly faded in 2016. Kerry was criticised by 'liberal hawks' and Russophobes at home for going soft on the Russians, and weakening in the United States commitment to topple Syrian President Assad, 'the real enemy'.

Hillary Clinton is strongly identified with the liberal hawks in Washington who since the 1990s have supported confrontational US policies towards Russia. Obama's Vice-President Joe Biden, and US State Department senior figures like Victoria Nuland, implemented assertively anti-Putin and pro-Kiev government policies while Clinton was Secretary of State in 2009–13. Would she have been any different as president after 2016? It is hard to see how she would. One could have expected Michael McFaul, an implacable opponent of Putin, to be influential in US policy towards Russia again.

Russia sees itself as being forced by years of US strategic provocations around its borders to respond defensively, in what it says are 'asymmetrical' ways, designed to take the United States by surprise and leave it scrambling for a response. The successful 'little green men' hybrid warfare tactics in Crimea and Eastern Ukraine were one example: the Russian air force 'barrel roll' aerobatic wars of nerves, metres away from heavily armed US warships in the Baltic Sea, were another. Now, there is the surprise Russian–Turkish rapprochement following the failed anti-Erdogan coup, which Russian intelligence helped him to outsmart. Russia will continue to come up with surprises in this new asymmetrical Cold War, and will find new friends within NATO Europe and beyond it. We can expect a stronger Russia-China strategic relationship and a stronger BRICS economic association (Brazil, Russia, India, China, South Africa). Russia is unlikely to succumb to NATO pressure, however heavy-handed it becomes.

Chapter 14

The West's Information War on Russia

Information warfare has itself become a major new arena of East–West tension. Vladimir Putin and his Foreign Minister Sergey Lavrov are both keen to explain Russian Government world views to Western public opinion. But they are rarely offered media opportunities in Western journals to do so; and when they do, quickly framed rebuttals by an army of 'Russia experts' follow. On 11 September 2013, Putin was given an unusual opportunity by the *New York Times*: his signed opinion essay calling for East–West cooperation on Syria, *Plea for Caution from Russia*, appeared on its Op-Ed Page.[1] His essay, a significant public and moderately worded message to the US Government and people, was at once rejected by a White House spokesperson and mocked in print by a parade of anti-Russian US pundits.

Two years later, on 7 June 2015, Luciano Fontana of the *Corriere Della Sera* interviewed Putin extensively over two hours in the Kremlin. The full text was published the next day by the newspaper.[2] Just two days later came a rebuttal piece by one Andrew Rettman in an EU media site, wittily titled *Corriere della Putin: Interview raises questions*.[3] According to Rettman and the four or five 'Russia experts' he consulted, Putin 'made false claim after false claim about Ukraine and Russia'. Fontana, he complained, did not 'confront' Putin and did not 'insert factual context': he had given Putin a 'platform for Russian propaganda', and this was a 'breach of good journalism'. The interview was 'naive' and 'boring', 'lame and sycophantic', and it offered 'nothing new to those who follow Russian developments from close range'. Another expert, Ulrich Speck of the Carnegie Europe think tank, said Putin had used the interview to attack EU sanctions (true), and suggested that 'journalists can trust Western sources [on Russia] because they're part of a free and competitive information environment driven by the idea of objectivity'. If only this were true.

The fact is that Anglo–American media – even quality outlets like the UK-based *Guardian* – now habitually blend together their news and editorial comment about Russia, framing every Russia news story within familiar anti-Putin themes. Good news and bad news stories about Russia remorselessly ram home anti-Putin messages, even when there is no connection or very little connection with him.

When the Panama Papers story broke in early April 2016, a story that was centrally about massive tax avoidance in tax havens by thousands of mostly Western, rich corporations and individuals, the Western media for the first four days ran it almost entirely as an anti-Putin story, focusing on a few Mossack Fonseca Panama account holders named and shamed in a narrow selection from the leaked papers: rich Russians said to be personal friends of Putin. A suitably sinister *Godfather*-style photograph of Putin, as an implied indirect account beneficiary, for several days graced every newspaper front page and internet story on the Panama Papers, with no clear reason for doing so, except the Western media assumption that somehow Putin as Russian mafia boss must surely be taking a cut from his friends' Panama accounts. It was not until two months later that the *New York Times* reported in detail how Mossack Fonseca had set up at least 2800 companies in the British Virgin Islands, Panama and other jurisdictions that specialise in hiding wealth, on behalf of at least 2400 US-based clients.[4] It belatedly put the Panama Papers Russia story in a little more factual perspective.

Putin is the bogeyman at Europe's gates: in any argument, he will be enlisted as the bad guy. He was front and centre in the 2016 US Presidential campaign. Hillary Clinton, in a much-vaunted national-security-focused campaign speech on 2 June 2016, suggested that Donald Trump was 'not someone who should ever have the nuclear codes'.[5] She said that if Trump were elected president, 'they'll be celebrating in the Kremlin'. Referencing Trump's reported praise of Putin and North Korea's Kim Jong-un: 'I will leave it to the psychiatrists to explain his affection for tyrants', Hillary Clinton did not see anything odd in calling Putin a 'tyrant'; nor did most of the liberal US media, which praised the statesmanship of her speech. Subsequently, Russian intelligence was accused of having supplied Wikileaks with hacked Democratic National Convention emails in a bid to embarrass Clinton and help Trump. Hillary Clinton's election website boasted (in straight Michael McFaul language):

> Hillary has gone toe-to-toe with Putin before, and she'll do it again. She'll stand shoulder to shoulder with our European allies and push back on and deter Russian aggression in Europe and beyond, and increase the costs to Putin for his actions.

Leviathan (2014) is a beautiful and important allegorical film by a respected Russian filmmaker about the powerlessness of an ordinary decent man pitted against a ruthless greedy state bureaucracy and its powerful corporate friends and clients – a story set in Arctic Russia but of universal relevance. It was pushed hard in the West for months, in *Doctor Zhivago* style, as a case of a brave indirect criticism of Putin's government that had somehow got under the guard of Russian censorship. The film was actually funded by the Russian Ministry of Culture, but no matter. *Leviathan* ran in Canberra for well over a month – someone with deep pockets had booked it for a long run, ensuring maximum public exposure. When I went late in its run, urged by many friends to see it, I was by now curiously the only person in the cinema. I recognised here at first hand the cultural methods of the Cold War again playing out. With such heavy-handed Western championing of a Russian 'dissident' film, it quickly became impossible for Russians to debate usefully among themselves the issues of state corruption raised by *Leviathan*. It had been appropriated into the Western anti-Putin information war, and has been regularly trotted out ever since as the defining international trope for 'Putin's Russia'.

Which is really part of a more general pattern: each time Western liberal hawks condemn or mock Russia's present system of governance, they increase Putin's popularity at home, further marginalise Russia's small Westernising dissident minority, and deepen Russian people's growing alienation from and mistrust of the West. Anne Garrels put her finger on this dynamic in her book *Putin Country.*

People like Michael McFaul realise this – they are not stupid. One is forced to ask whether Western liberal hawks' real agenda might now be, not to encourage those Russians who would like to liberalise Russia from within, but rather simply to further isolate and exclude 'Putin's Russia' from the West, whatever the damage to Russian liberals' causes.

Western liberal hawks and their media voices are used to ignoring contradictions in their case. On the one hand, they allege that Putin wants to return to a revived Soviet Union, with communist-style authoritarian government and state control of the economy; on the other hand, that he and his inner circle are united by nothing but corruption and naked greed. Both things cannot be true, and probably neither is true. From time to time also, one sees stories alleging that Putin's circle of support in the Kremlin is shrinking, of alleged conflicts within a 'narrowing' circle of advisers. The problem is that, since Putin offers no definable fixed ideology to attack – except his Russian patriotism, which is unassailable – critics at different times try to hang different ideological labels on him.

In the end, the West's information war on Russia is all about slagging Putin, Putin, Putin. Do these neo-cold warriors ever stop to ask what worse alternatives there might be if he were not Russia's president? Do they want to see Russia – a nuclear-weapons state – go the way Ukraine has gone? With anti-Semitic ultra-nationalists of openly displayed fascist inclination and provenance running rampant, and scared minorities prudently keeping their heads down, hoping not to be noticed by the rampant mob?

I guess the critics hope that if anti-Putin stories are repeated often enough, they will become accepted as true. The authors don't seem to recognise – or perhaps just don't care – that patriotism, loyalty to the motherland, and a sense that Russians today in an increasingly hostile world might feel they need to hold onto a strong resolute leader like Putin, are potent unifying factors. Certainly this is what many Russians say when asked.

Russia commemorated its most solemn national anniversary in April 2015 – the 70th Anniversary of the 1945 Victory over Fascism in the Great Patriotic War. The gala Red Square military parade to which all world leaders had been invited was boycotted by almost every Western head of government or foreign minister, in a lockstep strategy orchestrated in the State Department in Washington, on grounds that it would send wrong signals to attend such a Russian anniversary parade while Russian aggression continued in Ukraine. Another opportunity for reconciliation was thus slapped down. With commendable sensitivity, Germany's Chancellor Angela Merkel – whose nation was locked into the boycott by allied pressure – paid a private visit to Moscow the next day as her quiet way of personally saying sorry to Putin and Russia for this pointed NATO and EU insult.

This Western boycott was a sharp kick in the face of every Russian family mourning its losses in World War II, and will not be forgotten or forgiven by Russians. Western media coverage of this profoundly significant Russian national anniversary – the last 'decade' anniversary in honour of the fast-dying surviving World War II veterans – was superficial, hostile, and focused on the claimed 'blow' to Putin's prestige of Western non-attendance. Actually, I would say, this insensitive boycott significantly increased ordinary Russians' support for Putin and their growing alienation from the West.

When a Russian civilian airliner was sabotaged and exploded over Sinai by Islamic State terrorists in November 2015, killing some 224 mostly Russian holiday-makers on their way home, including many women and children, the Australian Foreign Minister incredibly did not bother to send a condolence message to her Russian counterpart – something several NATO foreign ministers including US Secretary of State John Kerry to their credit promptly did, despite continuing poor East–West relations over Ukraine. No one in the Australian Government, opposition or media thought the Australian Foreign Minister's indifference to this major tragedy worth commenting on: a stark measure of how desensitised some governments in the Western alliance have become in recent years towards the need to observe normal international decencies towards Russia.

Syrian Government (pro-Assad) armed forces succeeded with Russian air support in expelling Islamic State and allied Islamist anti-Assad militants from the historic heritage city of Palmyra in

March 2016. A few weeks later, the Russian Government flew in from Saint Petersburg the famous Mariinsky Symphony Orchestra to give a celebration concert under its conductor Valery Gergiev, who was described in the BBC News report of the concert as 'a supporter of President Putin' who had 'backed him' over the annexation of Crimea from Ukraine. The concert was held in the ruins of an ancient classical temple vandalised by Islamic State militants during their ten-month occupation of Palmyra. I and many others saw it as an imaginative symbolic message of cultural inclusiveness and hope for Syria's multi-confessional communities fighting back with Russian support against Islamist fundamentalist attack.

British Foreign Secretary at the time, Philip Hammond had a different view. He was quick to condemn the concert as 'a tasteless attempt to distract attention from the continued suffering of millions of Syrians. It shows that there are no depths to which the [Assad] regime will not sink.'[6] The BBC helpfully reported by way of additional context that 'one of the soloists at the concert was cellist Sergei Roldugin, a friend of Putin's, who was recently named as the owner of offshore companies in the so-called Panama Papers. He denies all wrongdoing.' To make sure we did not miss this point, there was a captioned photograph of Mr Roldugin playing the cello in the concert. This episode would surely have to be one of the low points in the West's information war on Russia.

Even a scholar of the authority and eminence of Professor Stephen Kotkin of Princeton has allowed himself to be drawn into this unsavoury game. In a *Foreign Affairs* special issue titled *Putin's Russia: Down But Not Out*, published in May/June 2016, Kotkin contributed a commentary article titled *Russia's Perpetual Geopolitics: Putin Returns to the Historical Pattern*.[7] It was replete with sweeping, condescending assertions about Russian history and foreign policy like these:

For half a millennium, Russian foreign policy has been characterised by soaring ambitions that have exceeded the country's capabilities... high-water marks aside, Russia has almost always been a relatively weak great power...however much Russia might insist on being acknowledged as an equal to the United States, the European Union, or even China, it is not, and it has no near- or medium-term prospect of becoming one.

The real challenge today boils down to Moscow's desire for Western recognition of a Russian sphere of influence in the former Soviet space (with the exception of the Baltic States)...It remains a concession the West should never grant...Someday, Russia's leaders may come to terms with the glaring limits of standing up to the West and seeking to dominate Eurasia. Until then, Russia will remain not another necessary crusade to be won, but a problem to be managed.

No one needs to orchestrate such sustained Western media contempt for 'Putin's Russia'. It now almost writes itself, it is universal, and Russians are well aware of it. I am struck by the sheer volume and repetitiveness of this information warfare across so many dimensions of media, an echo-chamber effect that overpowers the senses, numbing people in the West who know no better into a sort of dull acceptance, on lines of Orwell's *Animal Farm*: 'Oh well, yes, two legs good four legs bad, if you say so.'

But it also seems, more dangerously, to have convinced the people who are writing it. The irony is that these Stalinist or Goebbelsian propaganda methods being applied by the West against Russia mirror the way the old Soviet press used to report the West, when every story published in *Pravda* or *Izvestiya* had to be contextualised to ram home an ideological message that Western capitalist governments are evil, and that people suffer in these countries as a result. Soviet journalists then had no need of official instruction or censorship in how to write such stuff with the right ideological spin: they knew it, and the more credulous of them even came to believe it. We are almost there now in reverse.

The *Guardian*'s Natalie Nougayrede sets a benchmark for such propagandised journalism.[8] In March 2016, Russian Foreign Minister Sergey Lavrov published a significant, elegantly written Russian foreign policy review article in the Moscow-based magazine *Russia in Global Affairs* (to which article I will return shortly).[9] Nougayrede, reporting the article, dismissed Lavrov as 'not a free thinker able to operate independently of his boss, Putin', but merely a 'technocrat' who 'plays the diplomatic instrument to a tune totally set by the president'. But then she reported, inconsistently, that 'Western officials say Lavrov was privately incensed in 2014 by Putin's sudden decision to annex Crimea'. She bagged Lavrov's article as 'a sweeping, paranoid version of history, in which "western" Europeans have, throughout the ages, conspired to victimise and humiliate Russia'. Few of her readers will have been tempted to search out the Lavrov article, to judge for themselves.

Elsewhere, I saw another Western commentary alleging this Lavrov article indicated differences between Putin's and Lavrov's judgements of the Stalin era and of Yeltsin's 1991 dissolution of the Soviet Union. I have seen no independent supporting evidence, and none of these stories have gone anywhere. They are, simply, disinformation – efforts at driving wedges in Putin's top team.

The constant Western pressure on 'Putin's Russia' today – military pressure, sanctions pressure, diplomatic insults, information warfare – brings to mind Nietzche's saying, 'That which does not break us makes us stronger'. This is what independent public opinion polling in Russia consistently shows up. In the well-respected Western-supported Levada NGO public opinion poll, which has run since 2000, between February and March 2014 – in the period of the Maidan uprising and Crimea referendum – Putin's approval rating leapt from 69 per cent to 78 per cent and his disapproval rating slumped from 30 per cent to 18 per cent. These sets of data have been pretty stable ever since then: in the latest poll (April 2016), they are 82 per cent and 17 per cent respectively.[10]

The gentlest Western liberal-hawk criticism of 'Putin's Russia' is that Russians are 'nice people but victims of a bad government'. Such critiques routinely refer to the distorting effects of state-controlled mass media, intimidation of opposition figures, vote rigging, and poorly informed voting in country areas. But even allowing generously for all those negative factors, the Levada data suggest the Western liberal-hawk critique of Putin badly needs a reality check. It seems that Russians have the government that most of them want. So what purpose is served by the constant sniping at Russia, except to feed and justify a new NATO Cold War?

Recently I found a worrying statistical measure of the effects on Russian public opinion of the deteriorating East–West relationship. According to a Levada poll published by the Russian official news site www.rt.com on 2 June 2016, 72 per cent of Russians identified the United States as the country that they believe is most hostile towards Russia, followed by Ukraine (48 per cent) and Turkey (29 per cent).[11] When asked about their own negative sentiments towards foreign nations, 70 per cent said that they disliked the United States the most, 62 per cent named the European Union, and 63 per cent Ukraine. So, as of now, more than two in every three Russians fear and dislike the United States more than any country in the world, with the European Union and Ukraine running a close second. Our governments' hostile policies towards Russia have reaped the antipathy they have sown.

Russia's official response to the West's information warfare has been patient, intelligent and well calibrated. Though audience reach is still small, the quality of Russian reporting and commentary is good. In news stories in the two top English-language official Russian news sites, www.rt.com (*Russia Today*, Russia's official international news voice) and www.rbth.com (*Russia Beyond the Headlines*, a lighter official news feature site), there is a cool and reader-friendly focus on reporting the facts and issues in world news as the Russian government sees them. The number of articles is limited, and the most important ones are kept up on the home pages for a long time. A variety of international columnists, commentators and interviewees are featured. On the complex war in Syria, I try to read the stories in *Russia Today* regularly, as a balance to Western media reporting.

In these Russian media sites, opinion commentaries are always clearly marked as such, and are well written. Russian extremists (and I have come across some nasties on some Russian websites) are not given a platform here. There are also professional interview shows or documentaries with politicians like Foreign Minister Sergei Lavrov or with Putin himself. The press spokespersons, Maria Zakharova of the Foreign Ministry, and Dmitry Peskov of the Kremlin, are professional in their regular televised and reproduced online media conferences.[12] Both respond calmly – often with drily ironic Russian humour – to provocations or challenges thrown up to them by international journalists.

In recent months, the Russian Government has rearticulated its general principles of relations with Europe and the United States and with the world as a whole. I suspect these settings will be long-lasting. They reflect the bitterness left by the past twenty-five years when Russia as the successor state to the Soviet Union – initially trusting in the good faith of the United States and European Union – was trying to build a close mutually respectful relationship with them, as a major fellow Euro-Atlantic nation, but then found itself successively penetrated, exploited, humiliated and finally cast aside. A lot of this disappointment is quietly implied in Lavrov's elegant March 2016 historical survey article, the criticisms of which by Natalie Nougayrede I noted above.[13] I quote here some of Lavrov's observations, which correspond interestingly to my own thoughts while writing this book:

> History doesn't confirm the widespread belief that Russia has always camped in Europe's backyard and has been Europe's political outsider... *Rus* was part of the European context. At the same time, Russian people possessed a cultural matrix of their own and an original type of spirituality and never merged with the West...*Rus* bent under but was not broken by the heavy Mongol yoke, and managed to emerge from this dire trial as a single state, which was later regarded by both the West and the East as the successor to the Byzantine Empire that ceased to exist in 1453...Already then [the Moscow state] was a powerful balancing factor in European political combinations, including the well-known Thirty Years' War that gave birth to the Westphalian system of international relations, whose principles, primarily respect for state sovereignty, are of importance even today...
>
> ...At this point we are approaching a dilemma that has been evident for several centuries. While the rapidly developing Moscow state naturally played an increasing role in European affairs, the European countries had apprehensions about the nascent giant in the East and tried to isolate it whenever possible and prevent it from taking part in Europe's most important affairs.

...Peter the Great managed to put Russia into the category of Europe's leading countries in a little over two decades. Since that time Russia's position could no longer be ignored...

...Not a single European issue can be resolved without Russia's opinion. During at least the past two centuries any attempts to unite Europe without Russia and against it have inevitably led to grim tragedies, the consequences of which were always overcome with the decisive participation of our country...We remember that Emperor Alexander I took an active role in the drafting of decisions of the 1815 Vienna Congress that ensured the development of Europe without serious armed clashes during the subsequent 40 years of peace.

In this connection, it is appropriate to recall yet another anniversary, which will be marked next year – the 100th anniversary of the Russian Revolution. Today we are faced with the need to develop a balanced and objective assessment of those events, especially in an environment where, particularly in the West, many are willing to use this date to mount even more information attacks on Russia, and to portray the 1917 Revolution as a barbaric coup that dragged down all of European history. Even worse, they want to equate the Soviet regime to Nazism, and partially blame it for starting World War II...

...In this context, the notion of the 'clash of two totalitarianisms' [Nazi and Soviet], which is now actively inculcated in European minds, including at schools, is groundless and immoral. The Soviet Union, for all its evils, never aimed to destroy entire nations.

...[In today's world] there are many development models – which rules out the monotony of existence within the uniform, Western frame of reference...Consequently, there has been a relative reduction in the influence of the so-called 'historical West' that was used to seeing itself as the master of the human race's destinies for almost five centuries.

Against this backdrop...We see how the United States and the US-led Western alliance are trying to preserve their dominant positions by any available method or, to use the American lexicon, ensure their 'global leadership'. Many diverse ways of exerting pressure, economic sanctions and even direct armed intervention are being used. Large-scale information wars are being waged. The technology of unconstitutional change of governments by launching 'colour' revolutions has been tried and tested...

...Today, international relations are too sophisticated a mechanism to be controlled from one centre. This is obvious given the results of US interference: There is virtually no state in Libya; Iraq is balancing on the brink of disintegration, and so on and so forth...A reliable solution to the problems of the modern world can only be achieved through serious and honest cooperation between the leading states and their associations in order to address common challenges.

Henry Kissinger visited Moscow on 4 February 2016 – while I was there. He was warmly received by Putin for one-on-one talks, and he also gave a major lecture in honour of his friend the former Russian security service chief, Foreign Minister and Prime Minister Yevgeny Primakov, who died in 2015. In his lecture, Kissinger set out his vision for US–Russian relations. His speech was published in the realist-conservative US foreign policy magazine *The National Interest*.[14] It was a far-reaching, philosophical speech. Kissinger said among other things:

> I do not need to tell you that our [US–Russian] relations today are much worse than they were a decade ago. Indeed, they are probably the worst they have been since before the end of the Cold War. Mutual trust has been dissipated on both sides. Confrontation has replaced cooperation...
>
> Russia should be perceived as an essential element of any new global equilibrium, not primarily as a threat to the United States...I am here to argue for the possibility of a dialogue that seeks to merge our futures rather than elaborate our conflicts. This requires respect by both sides of the vital values and interest of the other...We share such an approach. And we will continue to defend the principles of law and justice in international affairs...

Like Kissinger, Mikhail Gorbachev continues in old age to pursue peaceful and comprehensive US–Russia dialogue. Gorbachev, who was recently barred by the Kiev Government from visiting Ukraine, gave in Moscow on 3 June 2016 a speech that went unreported in the West. He was opening a conference dedicated to the 30th anniversary of the 1986 meeting in Reykjavik between himself as Soviet President and his US counterpart, President Reagan: a meeting now widely seen as marking the beginning of the end of the Cold War.[15] His speech expressed concern about the growing militarisation of international politics, calling this 'a departure from the...principles that allowed us to end the Cold War'. He said: 'There has been a collapse of trust in relations between the world's leading powers that, according to the UN Charter, bear primary responsibility for maintaining international peace and security'.

Gorbachev stressed that [East–West] dialogue is at the heart of the solution. He insisted that regional disputes [like Ukraine and Syria] should not dominate the agenda of world leaders and prevent comprehensive dialogue from taking place. He called on 'veteran politicians, civil society, scientists and all people who care, to urge their leaders' to return to peaceful, demilitarised East–West relations.

In conclusion, it seems to me that the Western alliance is now trapped inside its own falsely created alternative reality of 'Putin's Russia'. Except for a few lonely outliers like Cohen, Sakwa, Kissinger, the American Committee for East-West Accord, and wiser heads in the Wilson Centre and the affiliated Kennan Institute, the West's elite thinking about Russia is frozen in hostile prejudice. Russia, by contrast, has a cooler, more fact-based view of the world and its own role in it.

Western foreign policy blunders towards since 1991, and especially over the past nine years of increasingly open hostility, have had lasting consequences. Russia is now increasingly indifferent to US and NATO approval or disapproval of how it conducts its domestic affairs and foreign policies. And it retains an up-to-date nuclear weapons deterrent capability.

It seems unlikely in the short to medium term that Western governments will take heed of the advice from eminent realists like Kissinger or Gorbachev, and respond positively to this harder Russian position. We seem doomed at best to a worsening Cold War for years to come, with all the worries and risks to world peace that this entails.[16]

What can individuals of goodwill do in the apparently frozen present situation of widening East–West tension, mistrust and estrangement? Not a great deal immediately, but it seems to me possible to begin as I did: reading the work of credible scholars of integrity, who have done the hard yards of studying and thinking about recent Russian history, and have been prepared to lay their careers and reputations on the line in trying to share publicly what they have concluded about the heart-rending realities of this remarkable nation, which offers so much that the world can admire, and which has experienced so much unimaginable suffering in living memory. I have tried to reflect and reference in Endnotes some of the important recent work on Russia that guided this book.

Two Western scholars stand out today as leading defenders of rationality about Russia. First, Stephen Cohen, Emeritus Professor of Politics and Russian Studies at Princeton University 1968–98, and since 1998 Professor of Russian Studies and History at City University of New York. An outstanding historian of modern Russia, he has written many excellent books on Soviet and post-Soviet Russian history. He contributes regular articles on Russia to *The Nation* journal, and was a founding member in 2014 of the non-partisan American Committee for East–West Accord (www.eastwestaccord. com). Cohen is regularly reviled by anti-Russian ideological warriors as 'Putin's apologist' and worse. He is nothing of the kind.

The second stand-out scholar is Richard Sakwa, Professor of Russian and European Politics at the University of Kent, United Kingdom, who has written authoritative books on Putin's career and on the Ukraine crisis. Sakwa is also an Associate Fellow of the Russia and Eurasia Program of Chatham House.[17]

Somehow, people of goodwill in the West now need to remain mindful that in Russia today, ordinary people are going about their lives in happy, decent and dignified ways, sitting together in cafes, buses or trains, talking to friends on mobile phones or tablets, offering their seats to the old and frail, going on picnics, picking their children up after school, pushing babies in prams, offering to help lost strangers – all those myriad little exchanges and decencies of life in a good civil society. And we need to challenge the proposition that presiding over all these recognisably warm human realities of life sit power-hungry gangs of corrupt war-mongering kleptocrats out to challenge the peace and stability of the world, who must be resisted, contained and isolated, whatever the risks or costs to the world. We need to defy or ignore our rabid new cold warriors.

We need to call on our Western leaders to restore regular dialogue with Russia based on mutual respect for the other's sovereignty and national interests: not just on the issues on which we can agree, but particularly on the issues on which we disagree. We should demand that our governments end and eschew in future all forms of economic sanctions against Russia. We should demand of our leaders and major media not to be routinely rude or condescending to or about Russia, but to observe proper diplomatic protocols and courtesies in relations with this nation.

Under the false and demonising imagery of 'Putin's Russia' which has now taken hold in the United States and NATO world, the West is truly 'sleepwalking', as Kissinger, Gorbachev, Sakwa, Cohen and others have urgently warned, into a potential nuclear war with Russia.[18] It is the Cuban missile crisis all over again, but actually worse now, because there are so many irresponsible minor European actors crowding onto the policy stage, and because American policy under recent US presidents has been so lacking in statesmanship, consistency or historical perspective where Russia is concerned.

Some might say that I am picturing here conflicts of views in a policy-wonk world of international security rivalry which has little relevance to real life. But it does. The attempts since the early 2000s to push Russia away from normal human and commercial exchanges with the rest of Europe are real, vicious in their intent, and have already been far-reaching in their strategic and human consequences. The mass military destruction since 2014 of cities, homes and lives in Eastern Ukraine, as carried out by the West's reckless and irresponsible protégés in Kiev, is a real war. The still unsolved tragedy of MH17 was a real criminal shoot-down of innocent international passengers. The burnings to death by Ukrainian Nazis of peaceful protesters deliberately trapped in an Odessa trade union building, as Ukrainian police looked on doing nothing, were real. These are all crimes against humanity. There are grave dangers of more of the same if East–West relations continue to worsen.

The Ukraine crisis remains the ugly cockpit of present danger. And those Russian opinion polls send their own warnings of where Russia might go if she is pushed too far.

I would conclude to people of goodwill in the West who read this book: try to keep an open mind. Read and learn about Russian culture and history – all of it, Tsarist, Soviet and post-Soviet. Read critically, taking into account authors' historical and cultural biases. Consider learning Russian – a beautiful language with a wonderful literature, and an excellent way to keep ageing brains supple. Listen to Russian music. Visit Russia if you can, with friends or alone. Do not accept the untrue pictures of Russia and its leaders, offered to us by purveyors of false realities.

If enough people do these things, truth will hopefully over time break through falsehood and disinformation. Russia – one of the world's great civilisations, which has one of the best-educated and most cultured populations in the world today – has so much to contribute to the evolution of a stable and environmentally responsible world order. The world needs Russia as a policymaking and scientific cooperation partner, not as a perpetual ideological adversary and bogeyman.

And if any Russians read this book, in English or in translation – thank you for your hospitality and friendship towards me in your country. I have tried in this book to represent to English-language readers a little of its warm reality.

Postscript – US President-elect Donald Trump

As this book was going to press, news came through of Donald Trump's surprise election win. President Putin was quick to congratulate President-elect Trump by phone and to suggest an early summit meeting. Stephen Cohen welcomed the news[19] but warned that if Trump moves towards a detente with Russia, 'he will be opposed by a fierce and powerful pro–Cold War coalition, Democratic and Republican, and including the media, here in the US'. Trump will have to fight very hard, if he wants to establish any kind of detente or strategic partnership with the Kremlin.

I don't know if Trump could sustain this aim. To his credit, he starts with a vague intuitive insight that there is no real reason for US–Russian relations to have gotten so bad: that the real adversary of both nations is Islamic fundamentalist violent extremism. He would like to get things right with Putin. Putin will do his best to encourage Trump in this. But Putin knows there is a high chance Trump will buckle under pressure from the Washington establishment. As in many ways Obama buckled during his presidency 2008–16, in allowing reckless regime-change goals for Libya, Ukraine and Syria to become dominant in US foreign policy. Putin will keep trying for detente with Trump, but will continue prudently to plan for worst-case scenarios in US–Russian relations.

Acknowledgements

First and foremost, heartfelt thanks to my children at home in Canberra –
Vanny, Raingsey and Julius Kevin – for your steadfast support and
encouragement, and for giving me the time and space I needed to tackle this
labour of love. To my wider family: Charles, Naomi and Patrick, and to my
dear cousin Diane Schick who passed away, sadly far too soon, in August
2015. Diane had wanted so much to be able to read this book, which we
often talked about as a project in her last months.

To my always cheerful, interested and lively travelling companions,
Grahame Bates and Julian Oliver. You brightened my journey and you
sharpened my thoughts.

To the many friends and colleagues who took an interest and offered
helpful suggestions at various stages in this project – both before I went
into Russia, and after I came home and completed this book. I cannot
name everybody, but in particular, Sharon Blane, Chris and Jenelle
Brangwin, Alison and Richard Broinowski, Alex Brooking, Joanna
Buckingham, Jean Garon, David Golovsky, Justin Glyn S.J., Leigh Hobba,
Wio Joustra, Penny Lockwood, John McCarthy, John Menadue, Tony
Milner, Robert Newton, Julian Oliver, Colin Penter, Peter Reid, Cisca
Spencer, Dierk and Margaret Swieringa, Tom Switzer, Ramesh Thakur,
John Tilemann, Irina Vasilieva, Pera Wells, Virginia Wilton and Peter
Zoller. To the patient and highly professional team at UWA Publishing –
Director Terri-ann White, and Charlotte Guest, Alexandra Nahlous and
Kate Pickard – my sincere thanks.

To Peter Varghese, former Secretary in DFAT Canberra, and to
Ambassador Peter Tesch and his Chargé d'Affaires Melissa O'Rourke of

the Australian Embassy in Moscow, for your support and hospitality during my visit.

Particular thanks to authors Anne Garrels, Conor O'Clery and Andrei P. Tsygankov, whose insightful books greatly assisted me towards a deeper understanding of Russia (see my Note on Sources).

Finally, to various Russian and resident expatriate interlocutors whom I met during my journey into Russia, whom I will not name out of respect for your privacy: thank you for your time, good fellowship, expertise and candour. I learned much from you all.

All judgements and opinions in this book are needless to say mine alone.

Appendix: The American Committee for East–West Accord

The American Committee for East–West Accord (ACEWA) was re-founded in 2015. It is an update on a similarly titled organisation which was established in 1974 and functioned until the end of the Cold War in 1992. See 'Reviving Detente', John Richard Cookson, Assistant Managing Editor, *The National Interest*, 5 November 2015, http://nationalinterest.org/blog/the-buzz/reviving-d%C3%A9tente-14263.

ACEWA Mission Statement (http://eastwestaccord.com/mission-statement/)
The Committee for East–West Accord is a nonpartisan, tax-exempt educational organisation of American citizens from different professions – business, academia, government service, science, law and others – who are deeply concerned about the possibility of a new (potentially even more dangerous) cold war between the United States/Europe and Russia. Our fundamental premise is that no real or lasting American, European, or international security generally is possible without essential kinds of stable cooperation with Russia.

Since early 2014, we have therefore watched with growing dismay as East–West cooperation created over decades – in diplomacy, arms control, economics, energy, education, science, space, culture, even in preventing nuclear proliferation, terrorism, and environmental threats – have been heedlessly discarded or gravely endangered. While experts warn of an unfolding new nuclear arms race, and with it the risk those weapons may actually be used, there may already be less East–West cooperation than existed during the latter decades of the preceding cold war.

And yet, these looming dangers, whose immediate cause was the US/EU–Russian confrontation over the future of Ukraine but whose origins lie in policy decisions taken and not taken on both sides since the end of the Soviet Union in 1991, have developed virtually without any significant public debate in the United States – in Congress, the mainstream media, academia, think tanks, or anywhere else that might influence the course of events. There may be no precedent for such an absence of American democratic discourse at such a fateful moment.

The primary mission of the Committee is to promote such discussion about East–West relations and thus to create broad public awareness of the new dangers and of ways to end them. The Committee encourages open, civilised, informed debate of all the related issues, current and past, among Americans with different, even opposing, positions, perspectives, and proposals. And the Committee seeks to do this in as many ways as possible, including an informational website for engaging individuals and other groups; sponsoring or cosponsoring public events in Washington, at universities, and across the country; and in the national media, including social media.

The Committee is new but not without a distinguished predecessor. Its name derives from The American Committee on East–West Accord, a pro-détente organisation founded in 1974 by illustrious Americans – among them, CEOs of multinational corporations, political figures, educational leaders, and policy thinkers such as George F. Kennan. That Committee, believing the Cold War had ended, closed its doors in 1992, though not before being credited with having contributed to the historic agreements reached by Presidents Ronald Reagan, George H. Bush, and Mikhail Gorbachev in 1985–1991.

Today's need for something akin to a new détente is no less imperative. And the new Committee for East–West Accord, which expects to be joined soon by an affiliated European branch in Brussels, strives for even more: A conclusive end to cold war and its attendant dangers.

ACEWA Current Board (2016):

Bill Bradley, US Senator 1979-97.

Stephen F. Cohen, Professor Emeritus of Russian Studies, History and Politics at New York University and Princeton University.

Gilbert Doctorow, writer, PhD in Russian History, Columbia University 1975.

Chuck Hagel, US Senator 1997–2009 and US Secretary of Defence 2013–15.

Jack F. Matlock Jr, writer and retired diplomat, was the last US Ambassador to the Soviet Union 1987–1991. Prior to that was Senior Director for European and Soviet Affairs on President Reagan's National Security Council staff.

Donald F. McHenry, Ambassador and United States Permanent Representative to the United Nations 1979-81.

Ellen Mickiewicz is James R. Shepley Emeritus Professor of Public Policy and Political Science at Duke University.

John Pepper is the former Chairman and CEO of The Procter & Gamble Company. He also served as Chairman of The Walt Disney Company and of the Yale Corporation.

Anna Eleanor Roosevelt is the President and CEO of Goodwill Industries of Northern New England and chairs The Roosevelt Institute in New York.

David C. Speedie is a Senior Fellow and the director for US Global Engagement at the Carnegie Council for Ethics in International Affairs in New York.

Sharon Tennison has worked for thirty years in Russia and the countries of the former Soviet Union, creating numerous multi-year programs to provide training for Soviet and Russian citizens to gain independence and skills designed for self-governance.

William J. vanden Heuvel served as the American Ambassador to the United Nations by appointment of President Carter and is currently Senior Advisor to the investment banking firm of Allen & Company. Ambassador vanden Heuvel is the Founder and Chair Emeritus of the Franklin and Eleanor Roosevelt Institute.

Contact details:

American Committee for East–West Accord, PO Box 2134 New York, NY 10025, Email: editor@eastwestaccord.com.

Website content: See especially articles in the section, http://eastwestaccord.com/category/analysis/.

Endnotes

Notes to the Prologue

1 *Moscow, December 25, 1991: The Last Day of the Soviet Union*, Conor O'Clery, Public Affairs Press, New York 2011. This is a highly readable, excellent account of the bitter four-year-long feud between two larger-than-life Russian leaders, Mikhail Gorbachev and Boris Yeltsin, and how it destroyed the Soviet Union.

2 The Tsarist tricolour was first flown by Tsar Peter the Great in 1695. It was the battle flag of the White armies in the Russian Civil War, and Russian émigré communities continued to fly it throughout the Soviet period. It is deeply significant that Boris Yeltsin reinstated it as the flag of the new Russian Federation in 1991, following a referendum. It was the popular choice to replace the Red flag. See *Flag of Russia* www.en.m.wikipedia.org.
   For my general practice in citing Wikipedia subject files in this book, see my Note on Sources.

3 Most historians agree that the Cold War started in 1946–47, though some argue it really started with the 1917 October Revolution when the communists seized power. Defining documents were US diplomat George Kennan's famous 'Long Telegram' sent from Moscow in February 1946 and published in 1947, advocating a firm long-term US containment policy to counter Stalin's ambitions; and, less well known in the West, the responding 'Novikov Telegram', sent home by the Soviet Ambassador in Washington in September 1946, but thought to have been co-authored by Soviet Foreign Minister Molotov, warning that the US was under the control of monopoly capitalists who were building up military power 'to prepare the conditions for winning world supremacy in a new war'. See *Cold War* www.en.m.wikipedia.org.

4 The Conference on Security and Co-operation in Europe (CSCE) was negotiated in Helsinki and Geneva over two years, 1973–75. Its Final Act was signed in Helsinki in 1975. It set up a permanent Organisation for Security and Co-operation in Europe (OSCE), which continues to operate today, e.g., in monitoring ceasefire violations and human rights abuses in the currently frozen armed conflict in Ukraine. See *Organisation for Security and Co-operation in Europe*, www.en.m.wikipedia.org.

5 A Soviet Foreign Ministry spokesman coined the phrase in late 1989: 'We now have the Frank Sinatra doctrine. He has a song *I Did It My Way*. So every

country decides on its own which road to take'. It was recognition of the reality: Poland had already elected its first non-communist government, and Hungary had opened its borders to East Germans fleeing to the West. See *Sinatra Doctrine*, www.en.m.wikipedia.org.

6   *The Man Who Saved the World – Secrets of the Dead*, PBS, USA videofilm, 23 October 2012, https://www.youtube.com/watch?v=453PEldRoIE. And see Edward Wilson, *Thank you Vasili Arkhipov, the man who stopped nuclear war, Guardian*, 27 October 2012, http://www.theguardian.com/commentisfree/2012/oct/27/vasili-arkhipov-stopped-nuclear-war.

7   See endnote 4.

8   Op. cit., O'Clery; and see Stephen Kotkin's *Armageddon Averted: The Soviet Collapse 1970–2000* (Oxford University Press, 2002).

9   Ryszard Kapucinski, *Imperium* (first published in Polish 1993, in English by Knopf in 1994) offers unforgettable word pictures of the Soviet Union as it was disintegrating.

10   According to the last Soviet Census in 1989.

11   For these and more details, see *1954 Transfer of Crimea*, https://en.wikipedia.org/wiki/1954_transfer_of_Crimea.

12   In a major speech to the Russian Federal Assembly on 25 April 2005, Putin said, 'Above all, we should acknowledge that the collapse of the Soviet Union was the major geopolitical disaster of the [twentieth] century.'
On Putin's view of Soviet communism, according to Masha Lipman, Putin in 2014 speaking to young people at a national youth camp at Camp Seliger recalled the events of 1917 as a time when 'some were shaking Russia from within, and shook it to the point that Russia as a state collapsed and declared itself defeated'. He also criticised the Bolsheviks' 'betrayal of Russian national interests'. It was, he said, the Bolsheviks, after all, who 'wished to see their fatherland defeated while Russian heroic soldiers and officers shed blood on the fronts of the First World War'. (*Putin disses Lenin*, Masha Lipman, *New Yorker*, 3 September 2014). Contemporary Russian cinema reflects such views of the events of 1917, e.g., *Solnechny Udar* (1915) and 'Geroi' (2016).

13   Vladimir Putin, *Interview with Andrei Kolesnikov in Kommersant*, 30 August 2010. Cited in Stephen Cohen, *Soviet Fates and Lost Alternatives*, Columbia University Press, 2011, pp. 212, 325.

14   See a detailed account in *Annexation of Crimea by the Russian Federation*, https://en.wikipedia.org/wiki/Annexation_of_Crimea_by_the_Russian_Federation.

15   I take away such a broad-brush picture of various perceptions of Putin from British scholar Richard Sakwa's latest rewrite of his successive editions of political biographies of Putin, *Putin Redux: Power and Contradiction in Contemporary Russia* (Routledge, 2014). A harsher view of Putin is offered in most Western books on the subject, both scholarly and generalist. See, for example, a highly praised new narrative biography by Steven Lee Myers, *The New Tsar: The Rise and Reign of Vladimir Putin*, Random House, New York, 2016. Myers was *New York Times* Bureau Chief in Moscow during Putin's early years as President of Russia.

16   Arthur Koestler and five other authors, in *The God That Failed*, Harper, 1949. Six essays by famous ex-communists, edited by Richard Crossman. The title has become proverbial.

17   L. P. Hartley, *The Go-Between*, Hamish Hamilton, 1953.

18   In the excellent recent Russian film *Sunstroke* (*Solnechny Udar*), by director Nikita Michalkov, based on classic stories by Russian émigré author Ivan Bunin (the first

Russian writer to win the Nobel Prize for Literature, in 1933), which I saw at the 2015 Russian Film Festival in Canberra, the main (fictional) protagonist – a lieutenant in a captured rearguard of General Wrangel's defeated White Army in 1920, interned in Crimea by the victorious communists and awaiting his fate of death or exile – at several points asks himself such existential questions about Russia's recent history. They are part of the continuing Russian political conversation.

Notes to Chapter 1: Going In

1   *The Strong State in Russia: Development and Crisis*, Andrei P. Tsygankov, Oxford University Press, New York, 2014.
2   Willy Bach to author, in private correspondence.
3   A recent excellent Steven Spielberg movie, *Bridge of Spies*, (2015) well evokes the harsh and fearful mood of the early years of the Cold War in the mid-sixties, just a few years before my posting to Moscow. Le Carré's novel *The Russia House* (1989),which was made into an excellent film, offers perceptive and moving insights into the turbulent and uncertain late Soviet perestroika period.
4   See *Moura Budberg*, an unflattering Wikipedia file, https://en.wikipedia.org/wiki/Moura_Budberg. I prefer to imagine Moura through Lockhart's eyes as he recalls when Moura first came to live with him in Moscow in April 1918 (*Memoirs of a Russian Agent*, Folio edition, p. 196).
5   Andrei P. Tsygankov, a Russian who is Professor of International Relations and Political Science at San Francisco State University, writes clearly, and with a profound Russian sensibility, on this history. See my Note on Sources.

Notes to Chapter 2: Moscow 1968–71

1   See entry on my ambassador, Frederick Joseph Blakeney (1913–90), in *Australian Dictionary of Biography*, MUP, 2007, http://adb.anu.edu.au/biography/blakeney-frederick-joseph-12220.
2   This classified national heritage property is still, fortunately, the Australian Ambassador's Residence, on an indefinitely long UpDK lease. See online updk.ru/en/about/cultural/?id_4=6.
3   Stalin's death in 1953 was followed by a decade of relaxation under Nikita Khrushchev, who held the most senior party and government positions between 1953 and 1964.
4   Whenever counter-intelligence agencies in London or Washington exposed spies operating out of Soviet embassies and declared them persona non grata, demanding their immediate expulsion, the Soviet side retaliated with reciprocal expulsions of equal or greater numbers of Western diplomats in Moscow. These were, and were meant to be, disruptively punitive responses. In our case, operating on minimal staff, any expulsions would have made our work impossible.

Notes to Chapter 3: Laurie

1   *The Ivanov Trail*, David Marr, Nelson, 1984.
2   Marr, op. cit., photo insert at p. 167.
3   Marr, op. cit., pp. 84–6 in particular.
4   Marr, op. cit., pp. 85–6 and chapter endnote 33.
5   Marr, op. cit. This final chapter, pp. 336–41, sums up the findings of the Commission.

6   Much of the following factual information is sourced from Boris Schedvin, *Emissaries of Trade; a History of the Australian Trade Commissioner Service* (the official history published by DFAT and Austrade, 2008), https://dfat.gov.au/about-us/publications/historical-documents/Documents/history-of-trade-commissioner-service.pdf.

7   Schedvin, op. cit., p. 152.

8   Schedvin, op. cit., p. 249.

9   Marr, op. cit., pp. 70–86. Chapter 4, *To See the World,* is the most detailed source I have found for factual information on Laurie's life. Marr drew it from Hope Commission testimony.

10   *The Australian Security Intelligence Organisation: An Unofficial History,* Frank Cain, Routledge, 2012. For completeness I include this unreferenced biographical account of Laurie's early life. Cain writes (p. 228):
    'The Third Man – Lawrence Matheson: Matheson was born on 25 April 1930 as Lawrence Phelan. He changed his name in June 1948 after he joined the Australian Navy in 1947 as a seaman. He was taught Russian for a year at the Australian Air Force language school at Point Cook and was commissioned an officer in approximately 1959. He left the Navy in 1968 to join the Department of Trade and later was posted to Vienna and Moscow to assist in the development of Australian–Soviet trade... his relationship with ASIO has been surrounded with mystery.'

11   *Memoirs of a British Agent,* Robert Bruce Lockhart, London, 1932, Folio edition, 2003.

Notes to Chapter 4: Quiet Days in Moscow

1   *Children of the Arbat* (1987) by Anatoly Rybakov is the first in a four-part series of semi-autobiographical novels portraying the lives of a group of young Moscow intellectuals under communism, especially under Stalin. It was written between 1966 and 1983 but was suppressed, only being published in 1987 under Gorbachev, when it became a great sensation. It has been translated and published in English.

2   *The New Penguin Russian Course: A Complete Course for Beginners,* Nicholas J. Brown, Penguin Books, 1996.

Notes to Chapter 5: Peredelkino and Boris Pasternak

1   See article and photographs in *The real Varykino: Boris Pasternak's summer dacha,* Ian Mitchell, www.passportmagazine.ru/article/1182/.

2   Introduction specially written in 1997 in New York by Russian poet Yevgeny Yevtushenko, for the 1997 Folio Society new edition of *Doctor Zhivago,* using the translation by Max Hayward and Manya Harari first published by William Collins in 1958.

3   I relied especially on these sources:
    Boris Pasternak, http://en.wikipedia.org/wiki/Boris_Pasternak.
    Jewish Virtual Library article on Pasternak, https://www.jewishvirtuallibrary.org/jsource/biography/Pasternak.html.
    Boris Leonidovich Pasternak, Karen Rae Keck, The Saint Pachomius Library, http://www.voskrese.info/spl/Xpasternak.html.
    Boris Pasternak (1890–1960), Rich Geib http://www.rjgeib.com/heroes/pasternak/paster.html.
    Boris Pasternak, http://en.wikipedia.org/wiki/Boris_Pasternak.

4   *Buddenbrooks* by Thomas Mann tells the story of three generations of a German nineteenth-century wealthy industrialist's family. The first generation makes the

money; the second generation uses the money productively to support culture and art; the third generation loses the money.

5   Op. cit., endnote 3, Keck.

6   *Doctor Zhivago*, Part 1, Chapter 4, Section 12.

7   The first of the *Doctor Zhivago* poems, *Hamlet*, ends with the old Russian proverb – *'zhizn prozhit – nye polye pereiti'* ('Life must be lived – it is not a walk across a field'). This may be the origin of Australian Prime Minister Malcolm Fraser's memorable quote, 'Life wasn't meant to be easy'.

8   https://slavica.indiana.edu/sites/default/files/bookContent_pdf/Hunt_Kobets_Intro_o.pdf.

9   *Doctor Zhivago*, Part 2, Chapter 16, Section 2.

10   *Doctor Zhivago*, Part 2, Chapter 15, Section 17.

11   *Doctor Zhivago*, Part 2, Chapter 16, Section 5.

12   See endnote 40. In 1997 Folio Society edition, new Yevtushenko introduction.

13   'Nobel Prize', samizdat poem translated by Rich Geib in http://www.rjgeib.com/heroes/pasternak/paster.html.

Notes to Chapter 6: Suzdal and Russian Identity

1   Any good general history of Russia covers these early phases in the formation of a distinctive Russian identity. And see Wikipedia entries for *Varangians*, *Kievan Rus'*, and *The Christianisation of Kievan Rus'*.

2   *Dmitry Pozharsky*, https://en.wikipedia.org/wiki/Dmitry_Pozharsky offers a good summary of the history of this troubled period.

3   Ronald Hingley (1920–2010) was an English scholar, translator and historian of Russia, specialising in Russian history and literature. His *Russian Writers and Society in the Nineteenth Century (1977)*, an excellent book now out of print, briefly addresses the 'Slavophiles versus Westernisers' issue in Russian nineteenth-century politics and literature. See also his *Concise History of Russia* (London, 1972).

4   The Tretyakov Gallery in Moscow contains many wonderful examples of great Russian representational art of this period. A day spent there, especially with the help of a knowledgeable guide as we had, is a lesson in Russian history and historical myths.

5   Operas like Borodin's *Prince Igor*, and Mussorgsky's *Boris Godunov* and *Khovanschina*. Stravinsky's ballets. Tchaikovsky's *Evgeny Onegin* contains Slav musical echoes. They are present in all Russian classical music, once one's ear knows what to listen for.

6   *Red Cavalry*, a powerful collection of stories first published in the 1920s by the Russian Jewish writer Isaac Babel, and based on his war diary as a Soviet journalist assigned to Red Cossacks fighting against White Army and Polish forces in the Civil War.

7   *The Scythians*, Alexander Blok, 1918. Translated by Alex Miller©, provided by owner to internet at no charge for educational purposes, http://allpoetry.com/The-Scythians.

> You are but millions. Our unnumbered nations
> Are as the sands upon the sounding shore.
> We are the Scythians! We are the slit-eyed Asians!
> Try to wage war with us – you'll try no more!
> You've had whole centuries. We – a single hour.
> Like serfs obedient to their feudal lord,

We've held the shield between two hostile powers –
Old Europe and the barbarous Mongol horde.
Your ancient forge has hammered down the ages,
Drowning the distant avalanche's roar.
Messina, Lisbon – these, you thought, were pages
In some strange book of legendary lore.
Full centuries long you've watched our Eastern lands,
Fished for our pearls and bartered them for grain;
Made mockery of us, while you laid your plans
And oiled your cannon for the great campaign.
The hour has come. Doom wheels on beating wing.
Each day augments the old outrageous score.
Soon not a trace of dead nor living thing
Shall stand where once your Paestums flowered before.
O Ancient World, before your culture dies,
Whilst failing life within you breathes and sinks,
Pause and be wise, as Oedipus was wise,
And solve the age-old riddle of the Sphinx.
That Sphinx is Russia. Grieving and exulting,
And weeping black and bloody tears enough,
She stares at you, adoring and insulting,
With love that turns to hate, and hate – to love.
Yes, love! For you of Western lands and birth
No longer know the love our blood enjoys.
You have forgotten there's a love on Earth
That burns like fire and, like all fire, destroys.
We love cold Science passionately pursued;
The visionary fire of inspiration;
The salt of Gallic wit, so subtly shrewd,
And the grim genius of the German nation.
We know the hell of a Parisian street,
And Venice, cool in water and in stone;
The scent of lemons in the southern heat;
The fuming piles of soot-begrimed Cologne.
We love raw flesh, its colour and its stench.
We love to taste it in our hungry maws.
Are we to blame then, if your ribs should crunch,
Fragile between our massive, gentle paws?
We know just how to play the cruel game
Of breaking in the most rebellious steeds;
And stubborn captive maids we also tame
And subjugate, to gratify our needs.
Come join us, then! Leave war and war's alarms,
And grasp the hand of peace and amity.
While still there's time, Comrades, lay down your arms!
Let us unite in true fraternity!
But if you spurn us, then we shall not mourn.
We too can reckon perfidy no crime,
And countless generations yet unborn
Shall curse your memory till the end of time.

We shall abandon Europe and her charm.
We shall resort to Scythian craft and guile.
Swift to the woods and forests we shall swarm,
And then look back, and smile our slit-eyed smile.
Away to the Urals, all! Quick, leave the land,
And clear the field for trial by blood and sword,
Where steel machines that have no soul must stand
And face the fury of the Mongol horde.
But we ourselves, henceforth, we shall not serve
As henchmen holding up the trusty shield.
We'll keep our distance and, slit-eyed, observe
The deadly conflict raging on the field.
We shall not stir, even though the frenzied Huns
Plunder the corpses of the slain in battle, drive
Their cattle into shrines, burn cities down,
And roast their white-skinned fellow men alive.
O ancient World, arise! For the last time
We call you to the ritual feast and fire
Of peace and brotherhood! For the last time
O hear the summons of the barbarian lyre!

8   For a sophisticated discussion of this question by a contemporary Russian scholar, see Andrei P. Tsygankov, *The Strong State in Russia*, OUP, New York, 2014, Chapter 13, 'Ethno-nationalism'.

9   *Russia's Patriarch Kirill: Some Human Rights are 'Heresy'*, Moscow Times, 21 March 2016, http://www.themoscowtimes.com/news/article/russias-patriarch-kirill-some-human-rights-are-heresy/563065.html?utm_source=fark&utm_medium=referral&utm_campaign=im.

Notes to Chapter 7: Nizhny Novgorod and Andrei Sakharov

1   The full English translation of Sakharov's essay, first published in the *New York Times* on 22 July 1968, and available online as a *NYT* original page reprint, can be more easily read at http://www.sakharov-center.ru/asfconf2009/english/node/20.

2   http://www.nobelprize.org/nobel_prizes/peace/laureates/1975/sakharov-lecture.html.

3   *Andrei Sakharov from Exile: Texts provided by the International League for Human Rights*, New York, October 1983, https://www.aip.org/history/exhibits/sakharov/essay2.htm#Banishment.

4   *Moscow, December 25, 1991*, Conor O'Clery, Public Affairs, New York, 2011.

5   O'Clery, op. cit., pp. 66–7.

6   O'Clery, op. cit., pp. 80–1.

Notes to Chapter 8: Yekaterinburg and Boris Yeltsin

1   I read these five interesting journalists' reports on the opening of this new museum:
Boris Yeltsin museum opens in Russia – complete with 'nuclear button', Agence France-Presse, Moscow, 26 November 2015, http://www.theguardian.com/world/2015/nov/25/boris-yeltsin-museum-opens-in-yekaterinburg.
Yeltsin memorial centre opens in Ekaterinburg, 26 Nov 2015, https://www.rt.com/politics/323545-yeltsin-memorial-center-opens-in/.
Museum to Russia's first president Boris Yeltsin opens to public, Martina Obrazkova,

Russia Beyond the Headlines, 27 November 2015, https://rbth.com/politics_and_society/2015/11/27/museum-to-rusias-first-president-boris-yeltsin-opens-to-public_545139.

Boris Yeltsin quietly challenges Putin, Masha Gessen, *New Yorker*, 9 December 2015, http://www.newyorker.com/news/news-desk/boris-yeltsin-quietly-challenges-putin.

Putin's homage to Yeltsin, and the ghost of freedom past, Anna Nemtsova, 26 December 2015, http://www.thedailybeast.com/articles/2015/12/26/putin-s-homage-to-yeltsin-and-the-ghost-of-freedom-past.html.

2   O'Clery, op. cit., p. 82.

3   O'Clery, op. cit., pp. 87–8.

4   O'Clery, op. cit., p. 117.

5   'Yeltsin sworn in as Russia's Leader', Serge Schemann, *New York Times*, 11 July 1991, http://www.nytimes.com/1991/07/11/world/yeltsin-sworn-in-as-russia-s-leader.html.

6   O'Clery op. cit. p. 144.

7   O'Clery, op. cit., p. 285.

8   *1993 Russian constitutional crisis*, https://en.m.wikipedia.org/wiki/1993_Russian_constitutional_crisis.

9   O'Clery, op. cit., p. 281.

10   *Gennady Zyuganov*, https://en.wikipedia.org/wiki/Gennady_Zyuganov.

11   O'Clery, op. cit., p. 281.

12   Gennady Zyuganov, Wikipedia, https://en.m.wikipedia.org/wiki/Gennady_Zyuganov, 'Post-2008'.

13   Full text at http://news.bbc.co.uk/2/hi/world/monitoring/584845.stm.

14   See endnote 4 of Chapter 7.

Notes to Chapter 9: Yasnaya Polyana and Leo Tolstoy

1   *The Mystery of Krasnodar Tea*, https://rbth.com/arts/2014/02/19/the_mystery_of_krasnodar_tea_34349.html.

2   *Teile – its history*, in *Samovar Masters* (Russian script), http://www.kiev-samovar.com/tejle-ego-istoriya/.

3   http://www.kiev-samovar.com/samovar-dulya-fabrika-b-g-tejle-tula-nach-hh-v-latun-nikelirovka-396/.

4   *History of Tula samovars – the samovar and Tula are inseparable* http://www.shopsamovar.com/hystory.html.

5   Twelve cities including Tula were awarded the title 'Hero-City of the Soviet Union' for their outstanding heroism during the Great Patriotic War. Russia upheld the award 'Hero-City' after 1991, and the twelve cities are monumentalised with plaques in Manege Square near the equestrian statue to Marshal Zhukov. See https://en.m.wikipedia.org/wiki/Hero_City for brief historical details. The cities are, in alphabetical order: Kiev, Kerch, Minsk, Moscow, Murmansk, Novorossiysk, Odessa, Saint Petersburg (Leningrad), Sevastopol, Smolensk, Tula, and Volgograd (Stalingrad). See also for more detail the 'Hero Towns' section, http://victory.sokolniki.com/eng/Memory/HeroTowns.aspx.

6   https://en.m.wikipedia.org/wiki/Leo_Tolstoy.

7   www.voinaimir.com, streamed from live sixty-hour broadcast 8–11 December 2015. See also https://m.youtube.com/watch?v=oskt5iNtVYw for further links and background.

8 An unusual but insightful perceptive into Tolstoy and his world is this 1917 article by an American scholar: *Tolstoy and the Russian Sphinx*, Wilbur M. Urban, *International Journal of Ethics*, Vol. 28, No. 2, January 1918, pp. 220–39, University of Chicago Press Stable, http://www.jstor.org/stable/2377538.

9 https://en.m.wikipedia.org/wiki/Crimean_War.

10 *How the Horrors of Crimea Shaped Tolstoy – how a war made the great Russian novelist*, Charles King, *New Republic*, 24 March 2014, https://newrepublic.com/article/117102/tolstoy-crimea.

11 *Russian Writers and Society in the Nineteenth Century*, Ronald Hingley (McGraw-Hill paperback 1967, Weidenfeld and Nicholson hardcover 1977).

12 *Tolstoy v Tolstaya: the Life of Countess Sophia Tolstaya*, posted 12 April 2012, 'Ab Aeternite', https://thealphabetician.wordpress.com/2012/04/12/tolstoy-v-tolstaya-the-life-of-countess-sophia-tolstaya/.

13 *Siege of Sevastopol*, https://en.m.wikipedia.org/wiki/Siege_of_Sevastopol_(1854%E2%80%9355).

14 *Russian Industrialisation*, from the *Alpha History of the Russian Revolution* http://alphahistory.com/russianrevolution/russian-industrialisation/.

15 These statistics from *Russia's Perpetual Geopolitics*, Stephen Kotkin, *Foreign Affairs*, May–June 2016 https://www.foreignaffairs.com/articles/ukraine/2016-04-18/russias-perpetual-geopolitics.

16 *Alexandra Tolstaya*, https://en.m.wikipedia.org/wiki/Alexandra_Tolstaya.

Notes to Chapter 10: The Gulag Museum

1 Wikipedia, https://en.wikipedia.org/wiki/Vergangenheitsbew%C3%A4ltigung.

2 *The Sixties*, Jenny Diski, Picador Books, 2009, Introduction, p. 1. Quote on https://www.amazon.co.uk/Sixties-Big-Ideas-Jenny-Diski/dp/1846680042#reader_1846680042.

3 *Darkness at Noon*, Arthur Koestler, 1940, in German, https://en.wikipedia.org/wiki/Darkness_at_Noon. And see *A Different 'Darkness at Noon'*, Michael Scammell, *The New York Review of Books*, 7 April 2016. http://www.nybooks.com/articles/2016/04/07/a-different-darkness-at-noon/.

4 *The Noise of Time review – Julian Barnes' masterpiece*, Alex Preston, *Guardian*, 17 January 2016, https://www.theguardian.com/books/2016/jan/17/the-noise-of-time-julian-barnes-review-dmitri-shostakovich.

5 *Lonely Planet Russia Guide*, March 2015 edition, p. 73, still lists the old Petrovka address. The new, much enlarged and re-designed museum opened in Dostoyevsky district in November 2015. Full details on new official Moscow Gulag Museum website (in two language options – Russian and English) – at www.gmig.ru.

6 *One Day in the Life of Ivan Denisovich*, https://en.m.wikipedia.org/wiki/One_Day_in_the_Life_of_Ivan_Denisovich was published in the Soviet Union in 1963 in the years of the *Khrushchev Thaw* (1953–64), https://en.m.wikipedia.org/wiki/Khrushchev_Thaw.
Solzhenitsyn was sentenced to the Gulag for ten years in 1945 for criticising Stalin's conduct of the War. He was released under Khrushchev's amnesty in 1953. No one has ever bettered his descriptions in this novel – of course it is based on his own experiences – of daily life for prisoners in the Gulag.

7 *Children of the Arbat*, followed by *1935 and Other Years, Fear*, and *Dust and Ashes*, https://en.m.wikipedia.org/wiki/Children_of_the_Arbat.

8   *Gulag: An Introduction*, Anne Applebaum, in *Gulag – Museum on Communism*,
http://www.thegulag.org/print/164.
Applebaum is the highly regarded author of the Pulitzer Prize-winning English-
language *Gulag: A History*, Doubleday, 2003. An American citizen by birth, and
a former senior Western newspaper correspondent in post-communist Eastern
Europe, she lives in Poland. She became a Polish citizen in 2013.

9   *Comparison of United States incarceration rate with other countries,* https://
en.wikipedia.org/wiki/Comparison_of_United_States_incarceration_rate_with_
other_countries.

10   *Article 58, RSFSR Penal Code*, https://en.wikipedia.org/wiki/Article_58_
(RSFSR_Penal_Code)

11   *Anti-Soviet agitation*, https://en.wikipedia.org/wiki/Anti-Soviet_agitation.

12   *The Gulag Museum on Communism*, www.thegulag.org.

13   *New Museum Stakes Claim to Russia's Gulag Legacy*, Howard Amos, *Moscow Times*,
5 November 2015.
http://www.themoscowtimes.com/arts_n_ideas/article/new-museum-stakes-
claim-to-russias-gulag-legacy/542211.html.

14   Op. cit. Amos, endnote 105.

15   See Amos. endnote 105.

Notes to Chapter 11: The Jewish Museum

1   I prepared this review of Russian usage of words for 'tolerance' from a variety of
internet sources, too many to list here.

2   *History of the Jews in Russia,* https://en.m.wikipedia.org/wiki/History_of_the_
Jews_in_Russia.

3   Sholem Aleichem (1859–1916), born in what is now Ukraine and died in New
York, was a leading Yiddish-language author and playwright. *Fiddler on the Roof*,
the musical, is based on his sequence of stories about *Tevye the Dairyman*.

4   *Red Cavalry*, Isaac Babel (1926), a brilliant collection of stories which gives the
flavour of this period. Babel (1894–1940), a pro-communist Jewish writer and
intellectual, born in Odessa, served with Red Cossack cavalry in the Polish–
Soviet War fought in the Pale region. His stories are harsh and powerful. He was
later executed in Stalin's Great Purge in the late 1930s.

5   *Russia's Jewish population fading away?*, Chana Ya'ar, 25 October 2010, www.
israelnationalnews.com.

6   *Babii Yar – Poetry for Students*. A good English translation and notes.
http://www.encyclopedia.com/article-1G2-3232100014/babii-yar.html.

7   See *Ilya Ehrenburg*, https://en.wikipedia.org. And also for comparison *Ilya
Ehrenburg – Russiapedia LIterature Prominent Russians*, http://russiapedia.rt.com/
prominent-russians/literature/ilya-ehrenburg/.

8   *Life and Fate,* by Vasily Grossman, see https://en.m.wikipedia.org/wiki/Life_and_
Fate.

9   *Refusenik*, see https://en.m.wikpedia.org/wiki/Refusenik.

10   *1990s Post-Soviet aliyah*, https://en.m.wikipedia.org/wiki/1990s_Post-Soviet_aliyah.
An open-access information source on facts and statistics of emigration of Russian
Jews in the late Soviet period 1970–88 and in the post-perestroika period 1989–
2006. For more detail, see Cohen, Yinon, Haberfeld, Yitchak and Kogan, Irena
(2011), *Who went where? Jewish immigration from the Former Soviet Union to Israel, the
USA and Germany, 1990–2000, Israel Affairs*, 17: 1, 7–20 (behind paywall),
http://dx.doi.org/10.1080/13537121.2011.522067.

Notes to Chapter 12:City of the Tsars

1   *The Bronze Horseman* (poem), Wikipedia subject file, https://en.m.wikipedia.org/wiki/The_Bronze_Horseman_(poem).

2   See an interesting post on difficulties of translating Pushkin, *Lost in Translation*, Richard Fenwick (2012),
    http://ruiningsterner.com/lost-in-translation/.

3   *Pushkin Threefold: Narrative, Lyric, Polemic and Ribald Verse,* translated by Walter Arndt (Allen and Unwin, London. 1972), pp. 131, 400, 401. This wonderful book contains Russian originals, Arndt's literal English translations and his English verse renditions, of many of Pushkin's most famous poems.

4   *Eugene Onegin,* Wikipedia file, https://en.m.wikipedia.org/wiki/Eugene_Onegin.

5   *Pushkin Threefold,* Walter Arndt, Allen and Unwin, London, 1972, pp. 37, 232, 233.

6   I found a good dual-language text here, also by Walter Arndt, http://sageshome.net/blog/index.php/sage/2008/08/13/to_the_slanderers_of_russia_pushkin (also in his *Pushkin Threefold,* pp. 44, 248, 249).

Notes to Chapter 13: An Alternative Reality

1   *L'Usage du monde,* Nicholas Bouvier (1929–98), Swiss travel writer, 1963. Published in English translation as *The Way of the World,* https://en.m.wikipedia.org/wiki/Nicolas_Bouvier.

2   Here are two recent representative examples of both versions of Russian reality: 'Russia's Very Different Reality', *Consortium News,* Natylie Baldwin, 24 October 2016, https://consortiumnews.com/2016/10/24/russias-very-different-reality/. 'The Threat from Russia – How to contain Vladimir Putin's deadly, dysfunctional empire', *The Economist Special Issue* on 'Putinism', 22 October 2016, http://www.economist.com/news/leaders/21709028-how-contain-vladimir-putins-deadly-dysfunctional-empire-threat-russia.

3   *Mordor* and *Sauron,* familiar Tolkien *Lord of the Rings* terms, are often used in anti-Russian Ukrainian nationalist polemic, to refer to Russia and Vladimir Putin respectively.

4   *The Wars of Vladimir Putin,* Timothy Snyder, *New York Review of Books,* 9 June 2016, http://www.nybooks.com/articles/2016/06/09/the-wars-of-vladimir-putin/.

5   *Faith, Certainty and the Presidency of George W. Bush,* Ron Suskind, *New York Times Magazine,* 17 October 2004, http://www.nytimes.com/2004/10/17/magazine/faith-certainty-and-the-presidency-of-george-w-bush.html?_r=0.

6   *Pure Vibe,* quoted in Christopher Tayler's review of *Zero K* by Don DeLillo, *London Review of Books,* 5 May 2016, pp. 15–16.

7   *More of Kremlin's opponents are ending up dead,* Andrew E. Kramer, *New York Times,* 20 August 2016, http://www.nytimes.com/2016/08/21/world/europe/moscow-kremlin-silence-critics-poison.html?_r=0.

8   '*Powerful people in the West and in Kiev do not want a Ukrainian settlement',* Professor Stephen Cohen, interview with rt.com, 19 June 2015, https://www.rt.com/op-edge/268372-us-foreign-policy-russia-ukraine/.

9   *The World According to Putin, Putin According to the World,* Lennart Meri Conference, held in Riga, Latvia, 25 April 2015, posted on www.youtube.com 14 May 2015.

10 *Russia is greatest threat to the US, says Joint Chiefs chairman nominee Gen. Joseph Dunsford,* Dan Lamothe, *Washington Post,* 9 July 2015, www.washingtonpost.com.

11 *NATO Commander: Russia Poses 'Existential Threat' to West,* on RadioFreeEuropeRadioLiberty, 25 February 2016, www.rferl.mobi.

12 *NATO Risks Nuclear War with Russia, Retired General Warns*, 18 May 2016, *Moscow Times*, http://www.themoscowtimes.com/news/article/nato-risks-nuclear-war-with-russia-retired-general-warns/569816.html.

13 *Changing of the Guard: NATO Brings In Army General to Deter Russia*, Matthew Bodner, *Moscow Times*, 12 May 2016, http://www.themoscowtimes.com/opinion/article/how-putin-changed-the-balance-of-power-among-russias-elite-op-ed/news/article/changing-of-the-guard-nato-brings-in-army-general-to-deter-russia/569142.html.

14 *Moscow calls NATO buildup in E. Europe 'unjustified' as largest drills since Cold War kick off*, 6 June 2016, News, https://www.rt.com/news/345615-us-nato-drills-poland/.

15 I could find no original citation for this saying which has entered the folklore: that in 1999, Putin as a contender for the post-Yeltsin presidency is said to have pledged to 'get Russia up off its knees'. It was a phrase used by Yeltsin.

16 See website osce.org for Organisation for Security and Cooperation in Europe (OSCE) Special Monitoring Mission to Ukraine.

17 A well-made Russian documentary film on YouTube, *Crimea: the Way Home*, (*Krim: Put na Rodiny*) by Andrey Kondrashev (there are Russian and English versions), posted on YouTube 15 March 2015. It sets out in depth the Russian version of the February–March 2014 events in Ukraine and Crimea. It contains extensive real-time newsreel footage and retrospective interview footage with Putin. It diverges greatly from the story with which we are familiar in the West, and makes for interesting comparative viewing.

18 *The Geographical Pivot of History*, https://en.m.wikipedia.org/wiki/The_Geographical_Pivot_of_History.

19 *Anti-Russian sentiment*, https://en.m.wikipedia.org/wiki/Anti-Russian_sentiment.

20 *The Russophobia Card*, Andrei P Tsygankov, 19 May 2008, http://www.atlantic-community.org/index.php/Open_Think_Tank_Article/The_Russophobia_Card.

Notes to Chapter 14: The West's Information War on Russia

1 *Plea for Caution from Russia*, Vladimir Putin, *New York Times*, 12 September 2013, http://www.nytimes.com/2013/09/12/opinion/putin-plea-for-caution-from-russia-on-syria.html?_r=0.

2 *Vladimir Putin, Interview to the Italian newspaper Il Corriere della Sera*, Luciano Fontana, English text, 8 June 2015, http://www.corriere.it/english/15_giugno_07/vladimir-putin-interview-to-the-italian-newspaper-corriere-sera-44c5a66c-0d12-11e5-8612-1eda5b996824.shtml.

3 *Corriere della Putin: Interview raises questions*, Andrew Rettman, 10 June 2015, https://euobserver.com/foreign/129056.

4 *Panama Papers Show How Rich US Clients Hid Millions Abroad*, 6 June 2016, *New York Times*, http://www.nytimes.com/2016/06/06/us/panama-papers.html?emc=edit_na_20160606&nlid=69467329&ref=cta.

5 *Hillary Clinton: Trump 'not someone who should ever have the nuclear codes'*, Taylor Wofford, *Newsweek*, 2 June 2016, http://www.newsweek.com/hillary-clinton-foreign-policy-speech-donald-trump-465962.

6 *Russia's Valery Gergiev conducts concert in Palmyra ruins*, 5 May 2016, *BBC News*, www.bbc.com/news/world-middle-east-36211449.

7 *Russia's Perpetual Geopolitics: Putin Returns to the Historical Pattern*, Stephen Kotkin, Foreign Affairs May–June 2016. As Professor in History and International Affairs at Princeton University and a fellow at Stanford University's

Hoover Institution, Kotkin's influence on US policy towards Russia would now be high. https://www.foreignaffairs.com/articles/ukraine/2016-04-18/russias-perpetual-geopolitics.

8   *Putin's long game has been revealed, and the omens are bad for Europe*, Natalie Nougayrede, *Guardian*, 19 March 2016, http://www.theguardian.com/commentisfree/2016/mar/18/putin-long-game-omens-europe-russia.

9   *Russia's Foreign Policy: Historical Background*, Sergey Lavrov, *Russia in Global Affairs*, 3 March 2016, http://www.mid.ru/en/foreign_policy/news/-/asset_publisher/cKNonkJE02Bw/content/id/2124391 (Russian Ministry of Foreign Affairs website).

10 Levada Center, Moscow, nationwide results (since 1999), based on a representative sample of 1600 over-18s from 130 sampling points across 45 regions of the Russian Federation, http://www.levada.ru/eng/indexes-0.

11 *Russians list US, Ukraine & Turkey as country's main enemies in latest poll*, 2 June 2016, News, Russian Politics, https://www.rt.com/politics/345164-russians-name-usa-ukraine-and/.

12 Maria Zakharova also danced a neat *Kalinka* at the recent ASEAN Summit in Sochi (under the ASEAN tradition that every participant must offer a national song or dance) – see *Zakharova Rocks the Dancefloor with Kalinka* – YouTube, 19 May 2016. I fear I will risk being accused of sexism for commending her dance, as Dmitry Peskov has not been seen dancing yet.

13 *Putin's long game has been revealed, and the omens are bad for Europe*, Natalie Nougayrede, *Guardian*, 19 March 2016, http://www.theguardian.com/commentisfree/2016/mar/18/putin-long-game-omens-europe-russia.

14 *Kissinger's vision for U.S.-Russia Relations*, 4 February 2016, *The National Interest*. http://nationalinterest.org/feature/kissingers-vision-us-russia-relations-15111.

15 *Gorbachev warns world of 'cult of force,' says all recent conflicts could have had peaceful solution*, RT News, 3 June 2016, https://www.rt.com/news/345374-gorbachev-world-leaders-biggest-mistake/.

16 See 'Cold War 2.0: how Russia and the west reheated a historic struggle', Patrick Wintour, Luke Harding, Julian Borger, *Guardian*, 24 October 2016, https://www.theguardian.com/world/2016/oct/24/cold-war-20-how-russia-and-the-west-reheated-a-historic-struggle.

17 *Putin Redux: Power and Contradiction in Contemporary Russia*, Richard Sakwa (2014).
     Frontline Ukraine: Crisis in the Borderlands, Richard Sakwa (Tauris, 2014).
     Frontline Ukraine: Crisis in the Borderlands by Richard Sakwa, book review by Jonathan Steele, *Guardian*, 19 February 2015, https://www.theguardian.com/books/2015/feb/19/frontline-ukraine-crisis-in-borderlands-richard-sakwa-review-account.

18 *The Slide Toward War with Russia*, editorial in *The Nation*, *19 October 2016* https://www.thenation.com/article/the-slide-toward-war=with-russia/. *West could sleepwalk into a Doomsday war with Russia – it's time to wake up*, Richard Sakwa, *The Conversation* (UK), 26 May 2016, https://theconversation.com/west-could-sleepwalk-into-a-doomsday-war-with-russia-its-time-to-wake-up-59936.

19 If Trump moves to heal ties with Russia, establishment will oppose him fiercely - Stephen Cohen, *Sophie Shevardnadze interview with Stephen Cohen*, rt.com, 11 November 2016. https://www.rt.com/shows/sophieco/366442-trump-promises-foreign-policy/.

Note on Sources

This book, as the personal story of my Russian journey and what came before and after it, can be read straight through as text without referring to the Endnotes. For those curious to explore further the sources on which I have based some of my statements and references, the Endnotes offer ideas for detailed further reading, with URL references where possible.

These are not academic citations, and I have made some use of Wikipedia. Wikipedia files usefully reference further possible reading. Used selectively, they are a help to the general reader. These files are sometimes convenient pathways into complex and controversial historical subjects like 'History of the Jews in Russia' or 'Gulag', because the unending collective editorial process in Wikipedia usually results in non-contentious summations of material, which has been argued down by contributing editors to something approaching objectivity. But not always – some Wikipedia files can be quite one-sided, e.g., on the 'Russian mafia', a contentious file awaiting important citations and clarifications, or on Moura Budberg, an uncharitable dismissal of Bruce Lockhart's Russian lover as 'an adventuress and double agent of OGPU and British Intelligence Service'. I prefer to think of Moura as Lockhart saw her – see his *Memoirs of a British Agent*, Folio Society edition, 2003, p. 196.

My bookshelf of favourite Russia books – most already noted in text and/
or notes – includes:

Walter Arndt, (translated), *Pushkin Threefold: Narrative, Lyric, Polemic and Ribald Verse*, Allen and Unwin, London, 1972.

R. H. Bruce Lockhart, *Memoirs of a British Agent*, first published by Putnam, London, 1932. I recommend the Folio Society edition of 2003, with its marvellous photographs.

Stephen Cohen – any of his books on Russia, his most recent being *Soviet Fates and Lost Alternatives: from Stalinism to the new Cold War*, Columbia Press, New York, 2009, 2011, with new epilogue. His regular articles in *The Nation*, and his regular interviews in *Salon* and on the John Batchelor radio show (on YouTube).

Robert Dessaix, *Twilight of Love: Travels with Turgenev*, Scribner, New York, 2005, 2006.

Anne Garrels, *Putin Country: A Journey into the Real Russia*, Farrer Strauss and Giroux, New York, 2016.

Ronald Hingley, *Russian Writers and Society in the Nineteenth Century* Weidenfeld and Nicolson, London, 1967, 1977.

Ryszard Kapuscinski, *Imperium*, published in Polish in 1993, first English publication by Knopf, New York, 1994.

Stephen Kotkin, *Armageddon Averted: The Soviet Collapse 1970–2000*, Oxford University Press, New York, 2001, updated edition 2008.

John Le Carré, *The Russia House*, Hodder and Stoughton, Sydney, 1989.

Conor O'Clery, *Moscow, December 25, 1991: the last day of the Soviet Union*, Public Affairs, Perseus Books Group, New York, 2011.

Boris Pasternak, *Doctor Zhivago*, 1958; I recommend the Folio edition of 1997 with introduction by Yevgeny Yevtushenko.

Richard Sakwa, *Putin Redux: Power and Contradiction in Contemporary Russia*, Routledge, Abingdon, UK, 2014 and New York, 2014.

Richard Sakwa, *Frontline Ukraine: Crisis in the Borderlands*, I. B. Tauris & Co, London, 2015.

Andrei P. Tsygankov, *Russia's Foreign Policy – Change and Continuity in National identity*, Rowman and Littlefield, Maryland US, second edition, 2010.

Andrei P. Tsygankov, *The Strong State in Russia – Development and Crisis*, Oxford University Press, New York, 2014.

In terms of further news reading and keeping up with what is happening in Russia and East–West relations today: Jonathan Steele, Shaun Walker and Luke Harding in *The Guardian*, Anna Nemtsova of *Newsweek* and *The Daily Beast*, Masha Gessen (freelance – various publications), Mark Galeotti (various publications), Maxim Trudolyubov (Kennan Institute website), Seymour Hersh on anything touching on Russian policies in the Middle East.

Journals – *Huffington Post, Salon, Slate, Nation, The New Yorker, The New York Review of Books* and *The London Review of Books* frequently cover Russian topics from various points of view.

Selected US websites:

The American Committee for East–West Accord carries a good range of current articles, www.eastwestaccord.com.

Johnson's Russia List, www.russialist.org.

Wilson Center website www.wilsoncenter.org.

Kennan Institute website www.kennan-russiafile.org.

Moscow-based English-language websites – the two official government-supported sites www.rt.com and www.rbth.com, and the independent online journal www.themoscowtimes.com.

Russian Foreign Ministry Media Center official English – language website (includes Foreign Minister and Spokesperson media briefings) http://www.mid.ru/en/main_en.

www.russia-insider.com, a quirky independent site run by pro-Russian Western expatriates living in Russia. A venue for Russian second-track diplomacy and floating trial balloons.

Index